Jt's Conversations
on
True BASIC

Becoming Acquainted with Basic on the Macintosh

Jt

KENDALL/HUNT PUBLISHING COMPANY
4050 Westmark Drive   Dubuque, Iowa 52002

Information For Rutgers Students

PLEASE READ AND REACT

Being a student at Rutgers, you have probably seen many courses that could have used some type of modification. However, you probably find that there is little you can do to really help improve a course. The instructors pretty much seem to do what they want. However, long being a student myself, I am very aware of this and therefore I really try to listen to suggestions that students make regarding the course I teach.

"Jt's Conversations on True BASIC" was not originally designed to be the textbook for this course. In fact, its previous name, "Jt's Lecture Notes", gave a better indication of the purpose of this material — it was used by students who wanted a detailed written account of what was discussed during lecture. For several years these notes were optionally available at a local copying center. Due to the fact that students seem to rate these lecture notes highly, while criticizing almost all of the other books we have used, this is now the official book. Still we realize that there are some problems with this material. We try to improve it as often as possible.

We are asking you to help us so that we can make the text better. Please fill out the form on the next page while you are using the book, or when you are completely finished with it. Then rip it out, fold it up and mail it to me. The address is already on the back. Rutgers students need not place a stamp on it since they can send it through campus mail. Yes, I do read these things and try to determine what can be done to improve the text. I am looking for specific comments; as you can see on the enclosed comment page, the remarks made by students on course evaluations at the end of the semester generally do not have any really helpful advice in them.

So if you think up something you want to say about the book please write it down and mail it to me. Try to discuss both the good points and the bad points of this material. If fifteen people say "the book insulted my intelligence", and no one says "the book made the material easy to understand", then we'll conclude that we should exclude some of the elementary trivial details.

This is your chance to actually do something to improve a course at Rutgers. Thank you.

Have fun,

-Jt

- Who is your lecturer? ⎯⎯⎯⎯⎯⎯⎯⎯⎯⎯⎯⎯⎯

- **What was bad about the book? What should be excluded or modified? What sections were too confusing?**

- **What is good about the book? What sections were helpful to you? What did you like?**

- **Point out any typographical, spelling, grammatical or factual errors that you think need to be corrected. List page number, and quote the actual line. (Use the space here and on the top of the back of this page for this purpose. Attach another sheet if necessary.)**

——— Fold Here ——————————————— Fold Here ———
Front outside flap

Jt
Loree Computer Center - Room 009
LOREE ANNEX
Cook Campus
Rutgers University
New Brunswick, NJ, 08903

Front outside flap
——— Fold Here ——————————————— Fold Here ———
Back outside flap

Back outside flap

What Previous Students Have Said About These Notes

The following are comments lifted verbatim off of previous course evaluation forms and book reviews from both my students and students who had other instructors. My book previously had the name "Jt's Lecture Notes" and was available at Kinko's. Prior to this these notes were printable off of a minicomputer — thus the phrase "on-computer" lecture notes. We have used other books on True Basic in the past — including one written by John Avitabile, a former course coordinator here at Rutgers. You can see how students feel about my material compared to these previous books.

-Jt

- The note by Jt at the end of his Lecture Notes [was the best thing about the course] ! **Spring 88: Best Thing**

- The only thing Jt could have done to make his book easier would be to do it in coloring book form. It was a great help and it got me thru his course as it made lectures so simple. **Fall 88: The Book**

- Jt's Lecture Notes are the greatest things since shoelaces (no offense Jt). They were great for additional information, review or if you accidently slept though a class. **Spring 88: The Book**

- Jt's Lecture Notes are awesome. They're funny and great. I laughed and cried. I was born and died. (well, maybe not.) But anyway they helped me tremendously and I loved the funny programs. Kool beans they are. **Spring 89: The Book**

- Jt's Notes were my computer Bible. **Spring 91: The Book**

- The Lecture Notes were great. They made it very easy to understand. Finally a book that doesn't talk down to you. I must admit I never liked computers, and I still don't, but at least now I understand them. **Spring 91: The Book**

- Jt you know your shit. Lecture Notes were excellent. **Fall 87: Other**

- The fact that Jt was willing to put the book together and teach the course according to it. Most lecturers, etc., don't care. They put their hours in and that's it. He also didn't try to impress us in the book with technical jargon etc. It was very easy to understand and he broke the programs, etc, into logical components to help even more. **Fall 88: Best Thing**

- The Lecture Notes helped a lot. It may seem simplistic to some, but I found it Easy to understand which really helps when you are anti-computer to begin with! It was nice when the Notes explained precisely what functions were on the Mac and how to use them. Don't change a thing. **Fall 88: Goelz Student**

- The Notes were basically good and easy to understand and it was only difficult in understanding how some of the Mac functions were activated or worked. Visual pictures off of the screen and into the book aren't absolutely needed but would be a big help. : Lecture notes do not sound like a computer. They sound like a real person talking instead of some goof in a shirt and tie. **Fall 88: Golez Student**

- Information made simple and palatable. **Fall 88: Koenemann Student**

- Nothing was terribly confusing. Some sections had to be read over, because I was totally unfamiliar with the material, not because it was too hard. I also don't think the Notes are too easy. : The book does make the material easy to understand, but I don't think you should exclude the elementary details. Those elementary details are what keeps me from begin totally lost. I like your little corny jokes. **Fall 88: Marathe Student**

- The book (Jt's) was very useful. But the Basic book is impossible. **Fall 88: Byerly Student**

- Jt's books were great! (As compared to the books that they used to use!!) **Fall 88: Byerly Student**

- On-computer Lecture Notes were a BIG help! I went to lectures but the Notes added a lot more. **Spring 87: Best Thing**

- I really enjoyed the luxury of being to print up on-computer Lecture Notes. I could listen and follow in class with the lecture notes at my side. I used these lecture notes like a book. **Spring 87: Other**

- Jt's Lecture Notes should be the book. They were the most informative and easiest to understand. **Spring 87: Suggestions**

- I think Jt should publish a book for the course. **Spring 87: Suggestions**

- A different book would be nice. Better yet, just publish Jt's Lecture Notes so he doesn't have to deal with rude and assinine people stealing them! They are much much better than the book anyway. **Fall 87: Suggestions**

- The Lecture Notes should be a book for the class. **Fall 87: Other**

- Just use Jt's Lecture Notes. It is really sufficient. **Spring 88: Suggestions**

- Just have the students buy both of Jt's books. And give photocopies of the assignments in Avitabile's book because it is not worth it to buy all three books. **Fall 88: Suggestions**

- I found Jt's Lecture Notes to be the key to the course. **Spring 88: The Book**

- Jt's book was very good – easy to understand and funny. **Spring 88: The Book**

- Just as if Jt was speaking in real life! helped a great deal. **Spring 88: The Book**

- Easy to understand and useful. I liked the informal approach in Jt's Lecture Notes. Taught without boring me to death. **Fall 88: The Book**

- Jt Lecture Notes helped tremendously and were very interesting and informative. **Spring 88: The Book**

- Jt's Notes are the best! **Spring 88: The Book**

- Jt's Lecture Notes were fantastic. **Fall 88: The Book**

- Jt is a very good instructor and his Lecture Notes were also excellent. **Spring 88: Best Thing**

- The book, Jt's Lecture Notes, was much better than other books I've seen. **Fall 88: The Book**

- Both parts of Jt's Lecture Notes were excellent, as was the True Basic book. **Fall 88: The Book**

- Jt's Lecture Notes were super. Avitabile's book ok but somewhat confusing. **Fall 88: The Book**

- Jt's book was great. The True Basic book wasn't. **Fall 88: The Book**

- Jt's book is too cute, condensending, and yet at the same time trying so hard to make it look like he's a layed-back, experienced academic whiz. Don't talk to me like you know me or give me advice about life, I'm probably the same age as him and have done and seen more in my life than he ever will. **Fall 88: The Book**

INTRODUCTION

This information is provided for students in the course 198:110 at Rutgers University. It gives background on the development of this book and some hints on what to expect in this course. It draws upon observations I have made during my many years of teaching this course.

Following is some general information about myself, this book and the course. You can probably survive without reading this information. On the other hand, I suspect that many of you will find this information helpful. Though I have tried to be careful about what I have placed here, if you have a lecturer other than myself, some of this information might not be exact. Your lecturer will give you the real info during his/her first lecture.

What Course?

Hi. Welcome to Introduction to Computers and Applications. Commonly known as 110. From now on, until you manage to finish this course, you will affectionately be called a 110er.

Who Am I?

I'm Jt. You might have heard of me; if not then I am sure you will know me pretty well by the end of the semester. First, before explaining more about the course, I reckon I should say a little bit about myself. Some of you may be curious how it is that I get to write books like this and parade around in lecture halls with my bare feet and bandanas, pretending to be a lecturer.

I graduated from Rutgers a couple[1] of years back with a degree in Computer Science. Since then I have been running the Loree Computer Center on the Cook/Douglass campus. Along with that, I have been doing various projects on the side, such as teaching various courses, doing some program consulting and attending graduate school earning a Masters degree.

I have been associated with 110 in a number of ways ever since this course was created many years back. When I was going to classes here, I worked in the various computer centers around Rutgers about 20 hours per week acting as a student consultant. This meant that all day long I was pestered by 110ers in various stages of confusion asking me to do numerous mundane tasks. Because I worked so many hours a week and spent so much of that time answering 110 questions, I became very good at understanding and explaining the material of the course. It got to the point where a lot of students were asking me why I wasn't a TA for the course. Seems that a lot of them were having trouble learning anything in recitation. The problem was intensified since many had non-native-English-speaking TAs. After seeing how confused these students seemed, I eventually started asking myself the same question — "Why wasn't I a 110 TA?" Well, after a bit of maneuvering, I was allowed to become a 110 TA even though most TAs are grad. students and I wasn't one at that time.

I was a TA several years ago. I really enjoyed being a TA because the students seemed to be really pleased with my teaching abilities, and I kinda felt as if I was accomplishing something. At the end of each semester I got very good evaluations from the students. However, because of this, it was decided that I should no longer be a TA, but rather the lecturer — instructor — professor — whatever you choose to call it. Some time during the 1980's was my first year as a lecturer and it took me a while to get used to it. I don't know if you realize what it is like lecturing in front of 250 students, but at times it isn't fun. After all, face it, some students out there don't really care if they learn anything from this course or not. They just wanna get outta Rutgers with a degree in something. It can be pretty amazing up there on stage when I am teaching some stuff and some people are going to sleep due

---

[1] Read this as "between one and fifty"

to boredom while others are getting confused because the material seems so difficult to them. At first I did not like lecturing as much as TAing. As a TA, my function was to clear up confusion caused by the lecturer, and thus I was looked on as a hero of sorts. I also felt as if I taught much better as a TA and was a lot closer and more comfortable with the students. For these reasons, I was beginning to think as the semester progressed that I wasn't doing a job any better than that which previous lecturers had done before me and that bothered me. Turns out, that when the course evaluations came in at the end of the course, the students seemed to feel that I did a pretty good job. Since I have been lecturing for several years now, I feel much more comfortable. I am getting slightly better at it and I feel that I can accomplish a lot as a lecturer, as I did as a TA.

The Origin Of These Notes

When I first began lecturing this course, I did much preparation prior to each lecture. Partly because I am used to doing all work in front of a computer and partly because I realized that I could cut down on how much preparation I had to do in future semesters, I started entering all my "notes" into the computer. Furthermore, I decided that rather than just building an outline, I would expound upon the subject matter more fully in writing to better prepare myself for what I would say in front of the class. As you may gather from what I mentioned above, I was hardly trained to speak in front of so many people, and this helped me organize my thoughts and become a better lecturer.

Being that all the notes were already entered into a computer, and since 110 was taught on a minicomputer at that time, it soon became evident that I should just make copies of my notes available through the computer for the students in the class. Unfortunately, things soon got out of hand. 110 has upwards of 1200 students per semester and I had some twenty different 10-20 page lectures available on the computer. Within a short time, the printers at the Loree Computer Center were being swamped all day with copies of my lecture notes being printed out. When 110 was moved over to the Macintoshes, students no longer had access to the notes. But through word of mouth, they knew such notes were around and asked for me to make them accessible. So copies were made available at Loree for borrowing. This too soon became too troublesome. Thus it was time to make the notes available in a more formal way. So I spent many months putting these notes into the format in which you now see them so they could be mass-copied at Kinko's. Now, the book is being published by Kendall-Hunt. Unfortunately, this means they are no longer free — you now have to pay money for them.

These notes really come in two parts. The first part is on the non-BASIC material. The second part deals with the TRUE BASIC programming language. You are now looking at the portion that deals with BASIC — it now goes by the name "Jt's Conversations on True BASIC".

Over the last several years various parts of these notes have switched back and forth from being official reading, to being optional. This semester the part on BASIC is official reading while the first part is not. However, many people will still buy and use the first part since it is very helpful. I do not make the decision as to which part of these notes will be required reading. That is a decision that all the instructors make together. It is desireable to include only the official reading in one package — we don't want to make students buy what they don't need. Even though many students buy both parts, some students do not see a need for the first part and should not have to be forced to pay for it.

Part I of these Notes will be made available through a local copy center. Should you buy Part I? Let's put it this way, they were not required in previous semesters and yet by the end of the semester most of my students had purchased them along with many students in other lectures. Comments on the course evaluations have clearly shown that my students find these lecture notes to be much more interesting and useful than the textbook. I suspect that both parts of these notes will turn out to be quite understandable and helpful to any students who choose to buy them.

Some of the chapters in the material available in Part I have a special format. These chapters will contain generalizations about various computer software which will be given interspersed with specifics on how to use the particular software we are using (ClarisWorks). This makes it somewhat easier for you to use the notes as a reference manual when you are actually sitting at a computer and need to use a particular command.

[Jt Students: These notes are also advantageous since they save you a lot of note-taking during lecture. This is especially true with Conversations on True BASIC which contains a lot of programs that are written on the board. By having these notes, you will not have to copy the examples off the board.]

Material Covered

The material presented in this book is very specific to this course. It ties in very closely with how most of the Rutgers 110 lecturers teach this course currently. Because its original purpose was just to be a back up for what was taught in lecture, I rarely approach subjects that are not fully covered in lecture. Occasionally I do touch upon a subject that is no longer taught or is not covered by the other lecturers. Still, you will find little material in these notes that will not also be explained in lecture. In some ways this is good. The notes help in pre-lecture or post-lecture understanding of the material and you can read them at your own pace until you grasp what is being taught. They are obviously much more extensive than any notes you can take while sitting through lecture. Furthermore, they don't attack you with tons of new ideas thus obscuring the particular topics that this course concentrates on. In short, these notes prepare you for the hw and exams.

On the other hand, a real crime is being committed here. A more extensive textbook would be loaded with lots of interesting and informative material that you can use even after this course is over to broaden your knowledge on computer topics. The subject of computers is very large and more extensive than one could possibly expect to learn in one course. And as you should realize by now, education is more than just sitting through classes in some school some place. You should think of education as a life-long entertaining process. So while I have decided to just give you a small amount of written material now to help you get through the course, I hope that enough of you will be interested and that after the course is over, you will seek more reading material and other experiences to further enhance your knowledge of computers.

"Preachings on the merits of a good education" now off.

Lies, Errors and Style

Ok. Look I admit there are some spelling, grammatical and typographical errors contained within. Please forgive me. I try to fix them as I notice them but it is a never-ending job. I spend a week prior to every semester just editing and updating this text. I especially try to fix errors and problems pointed out by students (see the enclosed form at the beginning of this text). Keep in mind that I am the sole person responsible for these notes; I don't have editors and proofreaders helping me out. So I'd appreciate it if you help me out with these jobs.

Oh and another thing. I lie. I occasionally simplify a topic so much that it no longer has any basis in reality. But it generally gets the point across. Your lecturer, if not me, is the ultimate authority and will correct any errors I make. You are expected to be accountable for the subject as he/she teaches it.

You will notice that this text is much more informal than most of your other textbooks. Fortunately, most students seem to enjoy my writing style. Some of the lecturers don't find this text to be scholarly enough. But this book was written for use by the students, not the lecturers, and thus I fight hard to keep it in its current informal tone. I try to make it enjoyable and easy for you to read. I hope I have succeeded. If you are an English teacher, you will not like my style at all. The rest of you normal people will probably enjoy it very much.

A Course That Is Constantly Changing:

Which brings me to another topic ... the "evolution" of 110. Seems that every semester 110 has some changes from the previous semester. This is partly because the lecturers and TAs get bored with teaching the same thing, and partly because we learn from our mistakes and thus modify the course accordingly. Books change, test formats change, TAs get promoted, and HW is modified. This semester things should be better than last semester but then again we always say that. We seem to have many computers available and most of them are in good shape. (By the way, you will be using the Macintosh. It is a microcomputer that is very user friendly and easy to use.) Things worked out fairly well last semester and so we will probably not make too many changes.

What Is The Course About?

And what topics will be covered? Well this course is a interesting mixture of numerous topics related to computers. A good portion of the course will be spent on the fundamentals of computer programming. If you don't already know how, you will soon be able to write programs on a computer in the BASIC programming language. The other portion of this course will cover what is known as computer applications. These are different "software packages" that are commonly used on a computer. You will be learning and possibly using a number of these including word processors, spreadsheets, graphical editors and databases. Before we learn about programming and applications, we will first learn a bit about the makeup of a typical computer, including topics such as *hardware* and *system software*.

You should be receiving a syllabus that will fill you in on the actual details.

Survival in 110

It is a good idea for me to tell you some information about the course and give you some hints on how to survive in this course and get a good grade. Any "hints" recommended here are my own personal opinion. While I have had enough experience with this course to feel a student is well-advised to follow these hints, some of the suggestions here, or the wording, may make some of the other lecturers cringe.

Attending Recitation

Realize that you will have two 55 minute lectures per week with your lecturer and one 55 minute recitation with your TA. Some recitations may be held in the computer room. In the past there has been no recitation the first week of classes. **If this is true this semester, we will announce it in the first lecture.** Please show up for your first recitation. You will meet your TA then. This will be your official TA all semester. You must hand in your homework to him/her. It would be wise to attend recitation frequently since the more the TA sees of you, the more likely that TA will associate the good work you are doing with your name and face.

It is especially important to attend the lectures during which we learn about BASIC. There is a high correlation between students who attend these lectures and students who earn good grades. For some reason some students choose to ignore this advice. But I am not just saying it — if you want a good grade you would be very wise to attend all the lectures on BASIC! There is not enough time in lecture to cover the topics completely. In recitation you will go over exercises, see new examples, get hints for writing programs and help with interacting with the computer. You will not get much of this in lecture.

Books:

You will have to buy at least two books and a computer diskette. There may be other material that you can also purchase to help you in this course.

There have been some students in the past who took this course without acquiring the books and still got decent grades but I do not encourage this practice. If a lecturer is doing his/her job correctly, all the testable information will be covered in lecture, making the book unnecessary. (Note, I said "IF" and "SHOULD" ...if you don't get the book then you are trusting me ... this has been a major mistake in other lectures with past lecturers. Some times we are told to cover a topic before we have seen the test yet, so it is possible that I might not cover a topic correctly in regards to what will be asked on the test. I am very conscious of this however, and I will try my hardest not to let this happen in our lecture.)

Most people will purchase the books. It is likely you will not be specifically told when to read what. You have to keep up with the reading on your own. With the non-BASIC topics you can pretty much read the topics at your own leisure as long as you get the reading done before the exams. On the other hand, when it comes to reading about programming, **DO THE READINGS FROM THE BASIC BOOK WHEN THE TOPICS ARE COVERED IN LECTURE.** For your own good try to stay with these readings.

[Jt students: I will probably make up a handout that will clearly show what lectures are given on what days. This can help you plan your reading. This "lecture schedule" will also be posted in various places throughout Loree.]

Tests:

You will have two midterms and a final. **EXAMS will be given at night.** We are sorry we have to do this to you, but it is the only way we can deal with it in a course of this nature. If you can't make the exam due to a conflict, you must give a note to your lecturer a week PRIOR to the day of the exam. Failure to do this will mean you end up with a ZERO for that exam. For students who do have the proper excuse notes, (from another professor, doctor, dean, boss etc ...) a makeup is generally given the first period the next morning. We will give you details when we get your note.

Dates and locations for exams will be announced in lecture well in advance of each exam. If you fail to note these dates, that is your tough luck. You can expect to get a zero for screwing up in this way.

Hw:

You will have to do about one HW assignment per week which you will hand in to your TA. Late HW is generally given only partial points and no HW is accepted more than a week late. In the past HW has counted 25 to 30 percent of the grade, the rest of the grade coming from test scores. In the past, almost all students who have handed in all their HW ended up with at least enough points to pass the course. (This is not a promise, just an observation!)

Homework is generally done on the computer so you can expect to spend much time in the various computer centers. Though no one ever believes me when I say this, HW turns out to be very important. First of all, if you don't do your HW, you will most likely have a difficult time on the exams. Secondly, if you don't do your HW, your final grade will be a grade or two lower because of missing points. The actual drop in grade is dependent on how lax you have been. The first semester I taught, a student failed the course even though he was doing near A work on the exams. He was missing all the points on the HW and this brought his grade all the way down. Do the HW and at least hand in what you have accomplished. You can often earn a lot of points this way.

Don't Depend on Jt's Conversations on True BASIC

This material has been used by thousands of students for several years now. It was a lot of work writing up the notes (some 3/4 of a million characters) and I kinda did a rush job on it. Therefore, errors have popped in here and there. I am continually in the process of getting as many errors out as possible. However, you are first responsible for what is covered in lecture, not what is in this book. Simple fact: students in the past who relied on the the book rather than attending lecture have generally done much worse than students who **came to lecture regularly** along with the doing the reading.

Why Is This Course Important?

Now, what do I want you to get outta this course? Obviously, this is school and most of you are worried about getting credits, grades and degrees. I realize this. In some ways it interferes with "learning". We will be throwing a lot of computer stuff at you this semester and I hardly expect you to remember this material a year from now, especially if you have never seen this stuff before. So what is the point of the course? Or at least, what do I personally feel the point of the course is? Look, it is like this. What you should get out of this course is a feeling such as "Hey, computers aren't that bad — at times a bit frustrating and so on — but I can do this stuff if I try". Hopefully, you'll realize that you can deal with computers and at least use them, if not program them, should the opportunity arise. You should lose any "fear" that you have of them. Remember this: after this course is over and you get over the shock — it might take a year or so — you might come across some project or another and say "Hey, this would be much easier on a computer!" And so maybe you will check into the possibilities of doing it on the computer. Computers can be useful. I am certainly not claiming they are the world. But they are all around us and it is to your advantage to know about them and start feeling comfortable with them. It might take some time. This course might not be enough for you to get comfortable with them. But it is a start. Face it, there are times that computers can really be a help to you. Look, if you would rather use a typewriter than a good word processor, then you are a bit backwards ...

You Can Do It!

Ok, just a final note. The topics you will be learning in this course are really very simplified. Computers can be much more difficult than what you will be learning. If it wasn't for the fact that you had a grade to worry about, you'd look at this stuff and say "Wow, this is so easy!". But as the semester goes on, many of you are gonna start feeling some pressure and thus freak out. Just stay with it and show some patience. You really can do this stuff. Good luck.

Have fun.

-Jt

This book is dedicated to Jennifer.
She threatened me with dishonor
if I didn't dedicate this book to her.
Truthfully though, she deserves this dedication.
Nobody else could put up with me
for as many years as she has.
'Tasy: Think of the the swans!
Have fun, Be Happy, Lotsa Love

FOREWORD

This book started as a collection of lecture notes created for the Rutgers course 198:110 during the spring and fall of 1987. This course was, and still is, a course that introduces students to computers — culminating in a few intense weeks of learning to program in BASIC. While this publication does not contain the complete series of notes, it has a very focused purpose — concentrating on the Macintosh computer and the True BASIC programming language.

A student recently wrote on a course evaluation:

This is one of the few books I have purchased for a class at Rutgers and have actually read!

This sentiment has been echoed by numerous students throughout the many years that this material has been available to students in this course. Clearly a book is worthless unless it is read. This book *is* read by the students that use it. Furthermore, most students claim it is entertaining, easy to understand and informative. The reason for the success of this material is that it is written using a very conversational tone. I have broken many of the rules of good writing style when creating this work — but this was done intentionally. The book is geared towards the audience that is using it. These students don't demand good writing style — in fact, such a style bores them — these students want something they can stand reading. This book is written directly for students in this course and other courses like it.

This book is intended to introduce novices to programming. Only a small part of the True BASIC programming language it discussed here. The purpose is not to teach students everything there is to know about this language. Rather, the purpose is to give students enough straight forward knowledge so that they can create their own simple programs. This book is more likely to encourage students to stick to one particular style of programming instead of trying to broaden their knowledge to include a wide repertoire of ways to write programs. Though at times, for pedagogical reasons, various ways of writing a particular program are discussed. This material is designed to give students a feel for what is involved in programming. It is intended for an environment where diverse students are learning the essentials of programming in a short period of time during which they are being swamped with work from various other classes.

This book does not assume the student possesses a wide body of previous knowledge — it is intended for courses in which students have a wide variety of backgrounds and knowledge. Many of the programming examples use real-world examples calling for the most limited of mathematical expertise.

Thousands of students have used this text over the last few years. Based on course evaluations, it seems that students in the past have treasured this collection of notes. Most comments made about the material have been highly complimentary. However, don't let the popularity of these notes fool you. Although some people enjoy the informal nature of this book, please keep in mind that its informality can at times distract you from learning the material. I hope you will have no trouble weeding through and finding the real — pertinent — information.

Be forewarned that at times these notes can become a little "crazy". In fact, at times I "cross the line" as to what I discuss. But, what can I say—that is part of being "Jt".

Good luck learning to program in True Basic.

-Jt

Contents

Part I

Tidbits About the Macintosh

Chapter 1

The Macintosh, System 7 & the Rutgers Setup

True BASIC is a programming language and as such is not designed to be used on any one type of computer. That is, a person can certainly program in the True BASIC language without worrying about the details of using a particular computer model. And yet, to actually edit, debug and utilize software written with True BASIC, it is of course necessary to realize any particular program on some actual machine. Thus, it makes sense for the programmer to become familiar with the particular computer that is intended to be used, prior to actually initiating the programming process.

One platform True BASIC is available on is the Apple Macintosh line of hardware. This chapter is meant to give you some information on particular details of the Macintosh and how you will be using it. This chapter is specific to students who are learning about programming on the Macintosh. Other computers that you may get a chance to use in the future (or have used in the past) may be very different from the Macintosh with commands and features that are quite dissimilar. Though, in recent years many other computers, emulating the Macintosh's design, have certainly tended to evolve to a point where they clearly are patterned after the Mac's "look and feel". Thus, knowing the basics about the Macintosh can lead to a fuller understanding of many other modern computers.

Furthermore, certainly for students reading this book, understanding the information about the Macintosh contained within this chapter will help a lot in this course when work actually has to be done on the computer. Better still, if one continues to use the Macintosh after this course, this chapter contains a lot of interesting and useful information along with various shortcuts that can help you speed up any work you may wish to perform on the computer. The better you understand the computer you are using, the easier it will be to use that computer to do your work. Since for this course you are using the Macintosh, here follows information that you may find helpful. (Get on with it already Jt)

Most of this chapter will concern itself with the user-interface of the Macintosh operating system. In virtually all software you will find for the Macintosh, most of the following features will be available for you to use. This means, that if you understand how to use the user-interface of the Macintosh, you have a head start on learning *any* program written for the Macintosh. In fact, you will find that by using common user-interface techniques and a little experimentation, you can *figure out* much of the available Macintosh software without ever touching a "user's manual".

Please note that the user-interface and other system software on the Mac is constantly changing. (This is in fact true of most modern computers.) The last major released version to the Macintosh User Interface is known as System 7. This chapter is written with System 7 in mind.

When reading thru this chapter, it is wise to have a Macintosh in front of you.

1.1   Macintosh Hardware:

Before we talk about the operating system of the Macintosh, however, let's talk about the available hardware. There are a number of different models in the Macintosh product line. The actual hardware you are using will depend on which model you have. Also, the actual hardware conditions will vary according to what type of printer you have and whether your computer is a stand-alone or connected into a network.

This is one section of this book that becomes outdated almost as soon as the book is published. Currently, Apple comes out with new versions of Macintosh every three or four months and discontinues old models at about that same rate. As I write this, Apple has just recently introduced several new models incorporating the new Motorola RISC chip called the PowerPC. These new computers are very powerful, seamlessly blending in many multi-media technologies including sound generation, voice-recognition and video manipulation. It is likely that this represents another large step forward in the computer world signaling the direction that many other computer manufacturers will soon follow.

However, it is workable for this book that we pick one moment in time and discuss the associated hardware for a computer, that at that time, was typical. So, let us consider one such possible hardware arrangement. For instance, at Rutgers, new Macintoshes were recently purchased. Place yourself in the Rutgers DCS labs in Spring 1994:

These labs have Centris 610s installed. (Apple had already dropped the Centris "line" months before the publication of this book.) These Macintoshes are rectangular boxes about three inches high and sixteen inches square. Fourteen inch color monitors sit atop the box.

The Motherboard

The main component of most microcomputers consists of the CPU (and other important processors on a circuit board) and main memory. Okay, so what about the main circuit board on these Macs? Well, there are many types of Macs. At Rutgers, you will be using one type called the Macintosh Centris 610. It has a CPU chip made by Motorola called a 68040. Among other things these Macs have 512 kilobytes of ROM, but more importantly these Rutgers Macs have 12 megabyte of RAM. The ROM holds important parts of the operating system, including the boot code used to start the computer. At Rutgers, special boot ROMs have been installed that tell the Mac to look for its operating system out on the network. On the other hand, the RAM is where currently running programs, (including your own) and the data and variables they need are kept for easy access. (Some info is also kept on the secondary memory — diskettes, hard drives, CD-ROM etc. — but remember it takes a lot longer to get information from secondary memory than out of the RAM.). So there is *only* 12 million bytes of easy space on the computer's circuit board to hold the applications you are running, programs that you write up and papers that you enter using a word processor. The term "only" is used tongue in cheek. 12 million is a fairly big number so there should be plenty of space to use if you are simply typing papers. Then again, once you start using many applications simultaneously, manipulating multi-colored images and playing around with sound and "movies", that space can quickly be gobbled up. So far in the history of computing — what seems like a lot of space memory one year ends up being a trivial amount the next.

Standard Input

You will also notice that the back of the Mac has small ports into which a mouse and keyboard can be inserted. Alternatively, you can just plug the keyboard into the Mac and "daisy chain" the mouse by plugging it into a similar port on either side of the keyboard. Even though many other types of input are now available — including voice — the keyboard and the mouse still act as the main devices through which you personally can communicate your wishes to a Mac. There are also a number of other ports on the Mac. You can connect modems, printers and other disk drives (including hard drives) to your Mac with little difficulty. There are probably hundreds of different I/O (input/output) devices that can be hooked up to a Macintosh.

Internal Peripherals

Peripherals such as disk drives, monitors, printers and the like are often separate external pieces of hardware that must be connected to the main unit of the computer by the use of special cables and ports ("sockets" where you can plug things into a computer). On these Macintoshes some peripherals are placed internally. If you were to open the chassis of these computers, you would discover that besides the main circuit board there was also an eighty megabyte hard drive installed. Furthermore, there is also room for a CD-ROM drive which may be installed later. Also, there is a high-density diskette drive with a slot showing through the front of the machine into which diskettes can be inserted. Into this you can insert three and one-half inch, high density, double sided diskettes onto which data can be stored and later retrieved.

External Peripherals

The Macintosh Centris 610 has a number of ports in the back into which you can attach a number of external peripherals. One large port is used to attach the external monitor using a special video cable. Also, you can plug printers directly into the Macintosh. There is a SCSI port which enables you to attach many brands of external hard drives. Another small port allows you to connect a modem which will give the computer the capability to communicate with other computers across phone lines. There is an audio port on the Macintosh so that computer generated sounds can be redirected to other audio equipment, whether it merely be external speakers or more sophisticated devices such as stereo systems. There is also a port with which to attach a microphone to enable sound input. This can be used to load sound effects into the computer or — by using sophisticated Apple software — to give the computer voice-recognition capabilities.

Networking

At Rutgers there is a large network of Macintoshes. Therefore, note that one of the ports on the back is used to cable the Macs to one another. The Centrises in the Rutgers labs are networked together using a protocol know as ethernet. This allows up to 10 million bits per second to be transferred across the cables. From any Mac, you can communicate with any other Mac or other piece of equipment attached on the same local-area network (LAN). The individual labs at Rutgers are also connected together into a larger campus-wide network containing thousands of computers. Rutgers itself is one node on the world-wide network called the Internet. Thus from one of these Centrises, it is possible to communicate with and send info to millions of other computers around the world.

We use our network for a number of reasons. First each lab has LaserWriter II's connected to the network. These act as our printers. They are laser printers. A student can send printouts to the printer from any Mac through the network. Also, the network also has "file servers" on it. At Rutgers, large hard drives are attached to the Centrises acting as file servers. The file servers have all the applications needed by students in the course. Special data — including sample files, lecture notes and examples, HW assignments — are also available on the file servers. Students can access this info from any Mac on the network by using a special utility (or "desk-accessory") called Chooser which allows a computer to attach to a file server and transparently utilize it as if it were an actual diskette or hard drive on the machine.

The network also allows for other activities, including allowing students to send e-mail to one another, their TAs and professors, and friends on other computer systems around the world. Direct person to person conversations — using "talk" software — is also possible. Access to read a common "newsgroup" readable by all students in the class also comes in handy. More generally, having access to the Internet means that students can access, download and utilize information from computers around the world.

Summary

So, the computers we have described are Macintosh Centris 610's with 12 megabytes of RAM and 512 kilobytes of ROM based on a 68040 CPU. The computer has an external 14 inch color monitor. It also has an internal high-density diskette drive and an eighty megabyte hard drive. A keyboard and a mouse are attached to ports on the computer. These Macintoshes are connected together on local ethernet networks into which various other equipment including LaserWriter printers and file servers with large hard drives are attached. Or, that is what you would read in the advertisement brochure.

And that is the **hardware** situation when you discuss these Macintoshes.

1.2   Booting

General Concepts

In any computer, the hardware by itself is useless. Instead, software — or code — is needed to make those hardware components function in some useful manner. Virtually every computer has sophisticated software that it is always running in order to maintain and use the available resources — such as, primary memory, files and devices — and to allow the machine to interact with humans through some type of "user interface". This software is called the "operating system". It is running on the computer at all times, even when other applications — such as word processors, spreadsheets and games — are running "on top" of it.

All software on a computer must be loaded into a computer's primary memory — ROM and RAM — in order to be utilized. Primary memory is the only memory fast enough to keep up with the speed of the CPU. Therefore, each moment a computer is ready to execute another instruction, it will pull that instruction out of the primary memory. With this in mind, it is easy to see why a computer can not run its software directly off of secondary memory devices — such as, hard drives and CD-ROM — because these devices, being in part mechanical, are too slow to keep up with the CPU.

Thus all software, even the operating system, must be loaded into the computer's primary memory before it runs. In actuality, the operating system is a very complex piece of software. The computer does not need all of its parts loaded in order to utilize it. As long as the most important parts are loaded, the computer will be able to do most operations. Other parts of the operating system can be loaded in when necessary. (For instance, possibly the computer will load the code needed to control the printer when you actually get around to trying to print.) Still, the parts it needs can be rather complex and it may take a while to load this information into memory.

This initial loading phase of the operating system is called "booting". This is necessary whenever the code for the operating system is on a secondary device — such as a hard drive — when the computer is initially turned on. In such situations, it is necessary that the operating system be loaded into the primary memory before the computer will become operational.

A computer manufacturer can opt to build the operating system within the primary memory of the computer. To do this, they can encode all the operating system on to its ROM memory. This type of primary memory, being only readable, is created in a factory and will never be modified once placed in the computer. ROM, since it is not volatile, still maintains the same information even when the computer is turned off. Thus, in this case, as soon as you turn on the computer, the necessary code would already be right there in primary memory. Therefore, booting up off of some type of secondary memory would not be necessary. You'd be able to use the computer as soon as you turned it on.

However, there are drawbacks to placing the operating system on ROM. First of all, since the operating system is a very complex piece of code, it can be rather expensive to encode all of it on ROM and include this large amount of ROM memory on the main circuit board. More importantly, if the operating system is built into the computer in this way, it becomes very difficult for the computer company to modify the operating system by fixing mistakes or just making useful improvements. To do so, they would have to ship new ROM chips to each user who then would have to have a professional install these chips inside their computer.

So, for most computers, including the Macintosh, the operating system is instead kept on some type of secondary memory device — often a hard drive. Software kept here can be easily updated by shipping a new version on diskettes and loading it from there. So, when you boot up a computer that has the operating system on the hard drive (or some other secondary memory device) which type of memory is the software loaded into during the booting process? Clearly, the code must be placed in the RAM. You cannot place the code on to the ROM because the ROM is unchangeable ("read-only"). The RAM is the type of primary memory that can be written to. In this case, the operating system can be written on — or loaded on — the RAM.

On catch though. For a computer to do anything, it must follow the instructions written in some piece of software. That is, even to do a task like copy the code from its hard drive to its RAM, the computer must be following some section of code. Did you get that? During boot up – when it copies the operating system to its RAM — the computer is following a program telling it how to do this.

But wait a second. All executing code must be in primary memory already. How can the machine follow the "booting code" if this is part of the code it is trying to boot? Now, you are starting to see why this is called "booting". It comes from the phrase "pulling oneself up from one's own bootstrap". A very circular concept indeed. On the computer it is accomplished in the following way. At least one small section of the operating system code — the "boot code" — is kept in a location other than secondary memory. Usually this code is kept in the ROM, all ready to execute. Remember, the ROM is produced in the factory – and its code will never change during the life of that computer. (Unless, the actual chips are changed.) So, when a computer is turned on, the first thing it does is execute the small section of code it sees in its ROM telling it how to boot. This code then directs it to look at a certain section of its secondary memory and copy the necessary pieces of its operating system into is RAM. Once the operating system is in the RAM (which may take a while), this computer can then start functioning in its usual way. It has been booted.

This has been a lengthy explanation. But it is important that you understand fundamental concepts like the difference between hardware and software, between primary versus secondary memory, between ROM and RAM and what exactly an "operating system" is, in order to truly understand how your computer works and what actually happens when you turn it on.

Normal Booting on a Macintosh

What happens when you turn on most modern Macintoshes? They look at their ROM memory chip which has code on it telling them how to boot up. Following this code, they look on their hard drive for the operating system – usually found in a special "folder" called the "System Folder". They copy necessary parts of these files and code into their RAM. This process can take a while. Once the operating system is loaded into RAM, the Mac will start performing in its expected way. Parts of the operating system code will remain in the RAM as long as that computer is left on. Other applications, data and documents will be loaded into the remaining room in the RAM as you start performing other activities. But the operating system is always there to help manage the resources and devices of that computer.

Netbooting

In large labs, maintaining a number of computers and making sure they all function in a similar manner can be a headache. Any user can change the setups and software on any machine and seriously affect how each machine operates. Illegal software can be placed on hard drives. Necessary software can be destroyed, disabling the machine. Or numerous small settings can be changed to cause the machine to function in various obnoxious ways – whether it be by having special sound effects played or different screen images displayed. For students in an Intro course using such a lab can be confusing. Therefore, it is to everyone's advantage if all the machines in a lab are set up to always function in the same manner when they are originally turned on.

In the Rutgers labs we have been discussing, a different method is used for booting. The normal Macintosh ROM memory chips have been removed and special "netbooting" ROMs have been installed instead. When these Macintoshes are turned on, these ROM chips tell the Macintosh to boot in a different manner. Instead of retrieving the operating system off of their hard drives, these Macintoshes look for the operating system on a special file server hard drive elsewhere in the lab. They boot off of the network. Since all the machines copy and use the same operating system, they all act the same way when turned on.

In a normal lab, the local copies of each operating system can be modified and that is why each machine may act differently. With net booting, there is only one copy of the operating system and it is not on any one of the machines. At the Rutgers labs, only certain individuals have direct access to the operating system folder and only they can change it. When changes are made, that change is implemented on all the Macintoshes the next time they are booted.

Network Benefits

At Rutgers, the Macintoshes are set up so that you can not get on them and use their software until you verify who you are. After netbooting they place a screen on them that asks you to identify yourself. You are expected to type in your "user name" and your "password". The Macintoshes themselves do not know anything about you. But other larger computers have been set up around Rutgers to hold the database of user names and passwords. The main machine is called "Eden" or the "eden-backend". When you enter your username and password, this information is sent across the network to the Eden computer. The Eden computer checks to see if your password is correct. It then sends a message back to the Macintosh allowing you on to the Mac. Furthermore, each student at Rutgers has space on Eden where they can keep files. The login process attaches your Eden space to the Macintosh. You will see your Eden space on the Macintosh screen as a small disk icon. You can use this space just as you use the space on some diskette you place into the machine. Functionally to the Macintosh there is no difference. In actuality, when you place information on Eden or read it off of Eden it is routed through the Rutgers network in order to end up on the right secondary space on the Eden machine located at Hill Center on Busch campus. But to you, it seems no different than as if you were using your own diskette. (However, of course, you don't walk away with the Eden-held information in your knapsack when you leave the lab – which you do with your own diskette.)

Not everyone who comes to one of the Rutgers Macintoshes already has an account on Eden. Thus the login screen on the Macintoshes has an option to lead a student thru the process of building an Eden account. You can follow the directions to set up this account the first time you need to. When doing this, you will have to supply some personal information — such as birthdate and social security number — that will be checked against Rutgers administrative data.

Having an Eden account is useful. Not only does it allow you to get on to these Macintoshes and have special space to save your work but it also enables you to send and retrieve electronic e-mail. Students with Eden accounts can use e-mail software to send each other messages. Any message sent to an Eden user is stored on his/her account until the next time that person gets on a computer and uses e-mail software to read his/her mail. Besides sending e-mail to one another, these students can send messages to professors, administrators and, in fact, millions of people outside of Rutgers. Eden users can also access "newsgroups". These are special message buffers where people can send messages that can be read by anyone else on the system. There are thousands of newsgroups on topics covering everything from aerobics and baseball to yoga and zoology. Students in the Intro course at Rutgers are expected to read a newsgroup (ru.nb.dcs.class.110) that contains important information and announcements pertaining to their course — sent there by the professors, teaching assistants and even other students of the course.

Lastly, since the identity of each Macintosh user is checked so carefully, Rutgers allows any users who have been verified on these Macintoshes full access to the Internet — or "information superhighway". This allows students to transfer data, software, documents and messages from millions of computer systems around the world. For example, students may be interested in using the Rutgers Info system, or exploring hundreds of World Wide Web hypertext pages containing text, pictures, sounds and movies on various topics. This can be investigated with the software called Mosaic. A discussion of the available information on the Internet is too long to include here but it is worth it to note that there is a vast amount of interesting and useful information available and many interesting ways to access it.

1.3 Hardware Usage Secrets

Using Diskettes

Inserting The Diskette

You should note that on a diskette, there is an edge that has metal on it which protects the magnetic surface of the disk and automatically is moved to the side by the computer as the disk is placed into the Mac. You should also note that on one side there is a small metal disc that is centered on the diskette. Great! Got that! I doubt it, if you don't have a disk in front of you. At any rate, insert the diskette into the Mac so that the metal edge goes in first and the small metal disc is face down. If you insert it properly, the drive will pull the disk in. Do not try to force a disk into the machine.

Formatting Diskettes

Unlike some other computers a Macintosh checks to see if a diskette is formatted as soon as you place it into the drive — no matter when you perform this activity. If you are using a diskette you have used before in a Macintosh, it should be recognized as soon as you place the disk in the drive. Depending on what you are currently doing, this will place a "diskette icon" on the desktop or allow you to navigate the file system of that disk through standard operations like the Save or Open dialog boxes.

However, if you insert a new disk, the computer will prompt you asking whether you want to initialize it and, if so, ask if you want to format both sides, and what name you want to assign to the disk. (You should give a different name to all your disks. Unlike other computers, such as DOS machines, you can use fairly long names and use an extensive list of characters within the name.) Answering these questions will cause the disk to be formatted, a process that can take a few minutes. A disk will be formatted as "double density" or "high density" (twice as much info as "double") according to whether there is a hole in its upper left corner. A diskette with such a hole is a high density disk. It usually has the letters HD stamped on it so humans can easily recognize it as a high density diskette too. (You can trick a computer into believing the diskette is only double density by taping over this hole.)

There is also a hole on the upper right of the diskette. This has a tab on it. If the tab is closed, covering up the hole — then the diskette is writable. That is, new information can be written on it. With the tab closed the disk is also erasable and formatable. If you don't want the information on a diskette to change, you can open up this tab. A diskette with an open tab is read-only. New information can not be written on it. It also can not be erased in the normal manner — that is from the disk drive itself modifying the magnetic surface. (Although, activities like placing the disk too close to any external magnetic surface, getting it wet, touching its surface with your hand, getting dirt in it or putting it thru temperature extremes can affect the disk and thus modify its information. This is why you want to be careful with your diskettes and ALWAYS back-up important information so it is on more than one diskette or at least in two separate locations — like the hard drive and a diskette in your desk drawer.)

A disk that has been formatted on another non-Macintosh computer may not be readable by your own Macintosh. Your Mac will not recognize these disks and thus think of them as being unformatted. If you format these disks on your Macintosh, you will wipe out all the information that used to exist on them and the original computer will no longer be able to retrieve that information. In short, do not place non-Macintosh disks in a Macintosh unless you are willing to erase all the information that used to be on the diskette. Fortunately, modern Macintoshes can be easily set up to read disks from the other main type of popular microcomputer — a DOS machine, otherwise known as an IBM compatible or an IBM clone. With the proper software loaded, a Macintosh can easily read DOS diskettes and manipulate their files.

Rejected Diskettes

If you ever stick a disk into a Macintosh that you know used to work and the machine asks whether you want to format or initial it, then the wise thing to do would be to calm down and hit the Eject option on the initial message box on the screen. This will get the disk back out of the machine. Why would a Macintosh do this? There are two possibilities. Either something is wrong with that Macintosh's disk drive, or something has happened to the diskette itself. To check the first condition, find another Macintosh and see if it will recognize your disk. If the disk works fine on this second machine, then something is wrong with the first machine. Plan to have that machine fixed or make sure that the personnel who run the computers in that lab are aware of the situation so they can attend to the maintenance of that Macintosh. If the diskette still does not work in a second or third machine, then something probably happened to your diskette. What should you do? Well, if you don't need the information on the disk, you can reformat it and lose all chance of ever seeing that information again. However, there is special software (such as HFS First Aid) that can be used to try to fix damaged disks. This software can not always retrieve all or even any information off of a bad disk but many times it does succeed. So if you have a bad disk, try to find a copy of this type of software and attempt to fix the disk yourself. If you are in a computer lab, bring your disk to the personnel on duty and have them try to fix it for you.

Diskettes do go bad. It happens all the time. Some times it is negligence on your part — you put the disk through a washer and dryer or you let your baby brother play with it and he bit off one end. There is one wise piece of advice you should follow. **Always have copies of all your important work in more than one place. Back-up your work often.** That is, make backups of your important diskettes so you have two copies of each one. It only costs a dollar or less to purchase another diskette. This is worth it, especially when you consider the amount of time and effort you will have to waste in order to reproduce the hours of work that may be contained on any one diskette. The concept of "backing up" your work does not just apply to diskettes. You should back-up files from a hard drive in some secondary location – whether it be to a library of diskettes or to a DAT tape using some tape backup hardware.

Ejecting The Diskette

One important thing that you will want to know how to do is eject your disk from the Mac. Many other computers have a manual way of ejecting the disk. On the Macintosh, the eject is software controlled. That means that a program has to tell the Mac to eject the disk. There are many ways to get a disk out of the Mac. Here are some.

- Use EJECT DISK from the SPECIAL menu.

  This will work only when you aren't in any application. When you are in an application, the SPECIAL menu will not be on the menu bar and thus it, and its commands, are not available.

- Use command-E when you aren't in any application. (Ah ha, if you look at EJECT in the FILE menu, you will notice that command-E is a short-cut for it. Read about short-cuts and the command key later within this chapter.)

- Use RESTART from the SPECIAL menu. This not only ejects your disk, but it restarts the computer. That means, that it will reboot just as if you were turning it on for the first time. Only use this method of ejecting if your computer is freaking out on you and you want to start over. You will only see the SPECIAL menu when you are not inside of some application.

- Use SHUT DOWN from the SPECIAL menu. This is a lot like doing RESTART. The disk is ejected. The computer then places a message on the screen telling you that you can now turn off the computer. You will only see the SPECIAL menu when you are not inside of some application. (On some computers, this command will completely turn off the Mac and you need not hit any power switch.)

  This is the way you should normally end your session with a Macintosh.

- Use LOG OUT from the SPECIAL menu. This is a special command at Rutgers used instead of SHUT DOWN. **This is the last command that all Rutgers students MUST use when they**

are done using the Macintoshes in the Rutgers labs. Failure to do so will mean a student becomes responsible for any havoc the next user causes from that machine. This command puts the computer in LOG IN mode — meaning the computer will not be fully operational until another person comes along and properly completes the logging in process, allowing the computer to validate who they are through a Rutgers database. Logging in and out is done for security reasons and allows Rutgers students complete access to the Internet.

- Use Command-shift-1. That is, hold down the command key and at the same time you hold down the shift key and 1 key. This method should work no matter what application you are currently in.

- Use the EJECT button from the dialog box that pops up when you use the SAVE or OPEN command. This button EJECTS the disk and allows you to insert another disk in order to save files or read in old files.

Emergency Methods:

Occasionally your Mac may totally bomb on you. Nothing seems to work, you can't get it to do anything. At this point you will want to get your diskette out so you can go home and cry or try again. The following methods work to get your diskette out, but only use them if all else fails.

- Turn off your Mac. Turn it back on and hold the mouse button down at the same time. This will eject the disk.

- Get a paper clip and stick it in the small hole that is next to the disk-drive slot. This is the only "manual" way to get a disk out. **This is your only alternative if your disk is in a Mac when a power failure strikes.** (Yeah right, no one said finding that pinhole in complete darkness would be easy.)

Navigating A Mouse

Moving The Mouse

If you have never used a mouse, you should be warned that there is an art to it. At first it may seem very awkward and you will start saying silly things like "this is so stupid, give me an IBM-PC any day". But after a few days, you will come to your senses and realize that a mouse isn't so bad and can indeed be quite a tool. Hey, let's put it this way, it took a while to learn to drive ... do you think that mouse-walking can be much worse?

A couple hints. Always keep your mouse oriented towards twelve o'clock. A lot of people get freaked out because the arrow pointer is tilted. They start tilting their mouse to try to compensate for the tilted arrow. Forget it, you tilt your mouse and nothing works as it should. Up is no longer up and down is no longer down. You will find that the arrow doesn't go in the direction you want it to.

If your mouse is kept in the right direction, you will find that if you push the mouse slowly up along the tabletop, the arrow will follow. Likewise, left moves it left, right moves it right and down moves it down. The arrow follows in whatever direction you choose to move the mouse.

But what happens if you run out of room on your table? Maybe you want the arrow to go down further and the mouse is already on the edge of the table. Well all you have to do is lift the mouse off the table so that the ball is no longer touching the tabletop. You will notice that you can do all sorts of maneuvers with your mouse in mid-air and this doesn't effect the arrow on the screen at all. So simply pick your mouse up and then place it down in a comfortable location on the desk top. You can now continue moving down and the arrow will follow. This solves the out-of-room-on-the-table problem. In general, whenever you don't like the position of your mouse on the table, feel free to lift it up and move it where you want.

Uses For the Mouse Button

The Macintosh mouse has one button on it. This button can be used in various ways. There are four main operations you can do with the mouse. They are:

Pointing This is done by sliding the mouse without holding down the mouse button. Since the mouse is an interactive device you will generally see something happen on the screen as you are sliding the mouse around. Usually there is a cursor on the screen in the shape of an arrow. As you slide the mouse around the arrow pointer follows you. Pushing the mouse to the left moves the arrow to the left on the screen. Sliding the mouse towards your body ("down") moves the arrow down on the screen. By using the mouse you are able to move the arrow around to select or point at items, tools or objects on the computer screen.

Clicking Once you have located the arrow atop some screen object you can click the button on the mouse one time. This is know as "single clicking". There are various reasons for doing this depending on the nature of the object. For example, if you click an icon once this will "select" it — highlighting it or turning it black. You usually select items because you are about to execute some command to modify that object or information in some way. You can click the mouse button for other reasons too. Another example is clicking a radio button in a dialog box to turn some option on. Usually this places a dot in the middle of the button to show that that option is currently chosen.

Double-clicking Instead of clicking the mouse button once, you can also click it two times in rapid succession. This is known as "double clicking". This operation can be used for various activities. For example, you can double-click on a word in many word processors on the Mac in order to select that word for further editing. A common activity you can do by double-clicking is "opening". You can open up, or start, any application by finding and double-clicking its icon. Double-clicking on a document will load up the application that produced that document (assuming it can be found) and read in that document so it can be worked on. Double-clicking a folder or disk icon will open a window which shows you what is within that folder or disk.

Dragging A more complex operation you can do involves holding the mouse button down as you move the mouse around. This is known as "dragging". For example, you can drag the lower right corner of a window to change its size. Or, you can drag an icon on top of a folder icon to drop it into that folder. Or, you can use the drag operation to draw a rectangle on the screen in many Macintosh graphics packages. You can also drag the mouse over a section of text in a word processor to select it for editing. For example, consider this last activity. It involves going to a location on the screen, *holding the mouse button down and keeping it down*, then simultaneously sliding the mouse to a new location and finally letting go. All the text in the region from the first location to the last will be selected.

1.4   Macintosh Software Features

Many people consider the software of the Macintosh to be well designed. This is evidenced by the fact that many other software systems have been written that are patterned after the Mac. Furthermore, the software has been designed in a consistent manner. This means, the environment seems very similar when you switch from using one application to using another. There are often many similarities between different software packages, making it very easy for a user to quickly understand and utilize any new application they come across. This consistently applies across time also. That is, operations that you could do on the Macintosh ten years ago are still possible nowadays. And this has been accomplished without making the software static. New features and advances seem to come along as quickly as cost-effective hardware is created which is powerful enough to perform the desired operations.

Consider, in 1984, the Mac allowed you to Cut text and pictures from one application — like Macwrite — and Paste that information into another – like Macpaint. Cut and Paste of text and pictures is still possible on today's Macs in the very same manner. Furthermore, it is actually possible to run those original versions of Macwrite and Macpaint, from their original "single density" (400K) diskettes on today's Macintoshes. This is very note-worthy, since one should not assume such compatibility across time is usual in the computer world — especially on a platform that constantly is improving to remain at the leading edge of technology. In fact, the Cut and Paste paradigm has since been expanded to include Sounds and Movies as two other types of information that can be easily moved around. Utilizing this software update seemed intuitive to any user already used to manipulating text on the Mac. Another paradigm called Publish and Subscribe was added to the Macintosh when System 7 came out. Again, although this involved a major system modification allowing changes of information in one document to automatically cause the same change in another document — usage of these new features were quickly learned by anyone already familiar with Cut and Paste.

Before discussing the Macintosh User Interface in detail, let us explore some of the standard features found within the Mac software. Development of many of these features often set a direction that much of the computer world soon followed after the Mac led the way.

The Finder

The Macintosh was the first popular microcomputer to use a graphical method to interact with the user. Though the concept was originally developed at Xerox, few people had witnessed it and realized its potential until the Macintosh came along. Previous to this, computers interacted with users through a "command-line". That is, everything that a user wished to do was announced to the computer by a properly spelled and punctuated command typed out with a keyboard. Often, a new user needed to spend considerable time reading manuals or taking seminars to learn the nuances of these commands. By switching to a "graphical user interface" many tasks can be accomplished on the Mac without worrying about remembering a particular command and its options. This GUI is called "the Finder" on the Mac.

The Finder has a number of features we will explore later. These include "icons" or pictures that represent information or tools, "windows" that partition the screen up allowing the user to view different information in different locations, "dialog boxes" which allow the computer to place messages on the screen and receive information from the user and "menus" which allow users to use commands without typing them into the keyboard.

Desktop

Information on the file system of the Macintosh is also visible on the computer screen. Each segment of related information on a diskette, hard drive, CD-ROM, network partition or some other secondary device is kept in what is known as a "file". This includes applications, word processing documents, spreadsheets, databases, pictures, movies and many other things. On the Mac there is generally an icon associated with every file.

Because files are represented as icons — graphical images — it becomes possible to modify the structure of the secondary memory by manipulating icons on the screen.

The background of the Macintosh screen is known as the "desktop". This is the top level of the Macintosh upon which sits the windows and icons. If you start working with a particular application, it may very well hide the desktop — especially if the window is full-size. Yet, at most times you can see at least a portion of it and easily get back to it if necessary.

One of the activities you can do on the desktop is organize the windows. You can open and close them, move them around and change their size. This will be discussed more in the section below on the "Macintosh User Interface".

Even more importantly, you can manipulate the file icons on the desktop. You can drag icons from one location on the screen to another if you want to organize them in some coherent order. Or, you can place a file into a folder by dragging its icon on top of the folder. You can drag icons from one disk to another in the same manner. This "drag-copying" actually allows one to have information be on more than one physical device. You can also get rid of a file by dragging it into the Trash folder. Other activities you can do to a file from the desktop include changing its name, duplicating it and creating an alias to it.

File Structure

The information on the Macintosh's secondary memory is organized in a structured manner.

Files: As mentioned already, a file is a collection of information stored on secondary memory. Examples include software already written for you, such as a word processor or even the True BASIC editor and translator. Other files include programs you are writing yourself, term papers you are authoring or spreadsheets you have created. You can see these icons on the desktop. Every time you create a new file by doing SAVE AS on the computer, a new icon will be made to represent the new file.

Folders: Some icons will look like folders and might even be labeled with the name "Folder". One "Folder" you have is the "System Folder" explained below. A folder is a collection of icons (files). You can open up a folder by double-clicking it. You can close up a folder by using the close box on the window for that folder. You can place information into a folder by dragging the icon representing that information atop of a folder and letting go. The icon (and associated info) will fall into the folder. You should use folders to organize your files more intelligently. If you placed all your icons on the top level of the desktop it would get confusing rather fast. You would end up with hundreds of icons. It makes more sense to think up some logical categories (like "English papers" and "110 work") and create folders for those categories.

Disks: You will get a disk icon for each diskette you place in the computer. This icon can be double-clicked to open up a window representing the files on that disk. Or the window can later be closed up (by using the close box) and shrunken to icon size. You will also see a disk icon for any hard drive attached to your computer — internally or externally. Likewise, you will get disk icons for any network file servers you attach the Macintosh to. You can open, close and use these disk icons much as you use the folder icons. You can freely move icons around on your screen by doing the drag operation. Thus you can pull an icon from one disk window into another or drag an icon atop a disk and drop the associated file there. The Mac will interpret this to mean you want to copy a file on to another disk. Whenever you use icons from a window that represent a disk not currently in the Macintosh, the Mac will realize this and eject the current diskette, asking for the disk that the file you are about to use is on.

You will likely be using diskettes to save your work during this course. (For example, at Rutgers you can buy a HD diskette at the bookstore for under a dollar.) In fact, it would be wise to have more than one diskette so you can also back-up your work. In case anything happens to your original disk, you may have copied files to the backup disk and thus still have your work. You can copy as mentioned above by dragging icons from one disk window to another and then the Mac will tell you to "swap" disks in and out until the copying is done. However, it is important to realize that a disk you buy at a store is not yet ready to be used by a computer. It must be "initialized". That is, it must be prepared so that it can be used by a particular computer. Each computer uses its own format for storing information on a disk. The disk must be formatted by that computer before it can be used. When a disk is formatted for a particular type of computer, it is not possible to read the information on other computers that don't understand that format.[1] Be aware that the first time you put a blank disk into a Macintosh, the Macintosh will ask you whether or not you want to "Initialize" your disk. On some computers such as the IBM PC, you must remember to issue a command telling the computer to initialize. The Mac looks for an uninitialized disk and prompts you asking if you want to initialize it. This will happen the first time you put a new diskette into the machine. Make

---

[1] Current Macs can read disks formatted for IBM PC's. However, the reverse is not true. A disk formatted for use on a Mac will not be readable on an IBM computer.

sure you have carefully read the section on initializing and using diskettes earlier in this chapter as very useful information is contained there.

Trash Can: There is a special folder on your disk called the Trash Can. You can drag icons (files) into this folder when you no longer want them. (Remember, drag is a select, hold button, slide and let go of button operation . . . you must have the arrow pointer inside of the Trash Can when you let go. The Trash Can will turn black indicating that you can let go.) After a while, you may accumulate a lot of old files that are worthless to you and you may want to make more room on your disk. Throw your files out by dragging them into the Trash Can and you may be happier. **Unlike other computers, files can be retrieved relatively easy on the Mac after they have been trashed** (deleted, erased etc). Since the Trash Can is a folder, you can open it up and pull icons back out of it. **However, the trash can be completely emptied whenever you are ready by using the Empty Trash command from the Special menu.** Once the trash is emptied, the files are gone forever.

System Folder

The files, resources, drivers and code that make up the operating system are kept in a special folder on the desktop. This folder generally has the name "System Folder" which has a small picture of a Macintosh centered on it. The System Folder contains other folders within it so the information is organized more intelligently. Some of these folders include Fonts, Extensions, and Control Panels which are discussed below. Others include Preferences — where files containing default settings for various applications are kept and Start Up Items — where applications and items that you want loaded as soon as you start the computer are kept.

Two of the main items in the system folder are System and Finder. Both of these are very large blocks of code. The first one of these is the main part of the operating system. Code for dealing with much of the resource allocation is contained within this file. The file that says Finder contains the code that supplies the user interface of the Macintosh. Since the System Folder is generally contained on a secondary memory device such as a hard drive, it becomes a simple matter to upgrade your Macintosh to perform new activities by obtaining new versions of the System and Finder when they come out. For example, you can copy new versions of these from diskette or CD-ROM replacing the old versions that exist in your System Folder on your hard drive. Thus, the next time you start your computer, it will begin using this new code and thus the computer will act differently — hopefully with new and useful features.

Even without replacing the System and/or Finder, a knowledgeable user can effect how his/her system performs by manipulating the various folders, files and controls that exists within the System Folder.

Changing the way the system acts can, of course, be a bad thing as well as a good thing. Thus it is recommended that you do not mess around with System Folder information unless you really know what you are doing. However, for anyone who wants to use a Macintosh fully, especially if they own their own machine, it would be very wise to learn more about modifying the System Folder. Knowledge about such changes can be quite powerful allowing one to make many useful and important changes to their computer when necessary.

Application-Independent Device Drivers

One of the useful features incorporated into the Macintosh is the capability to control the attached devices system-wide, rather than only thru certain applications. For example, in the past some computer systems have been designed such that each application had to worry about how to actually send information to the printer. Thus, it was possible for one to purchase a printer to attach to their computer only to find out later that their word processor could not print to this type of printer but the spreadsheet software could. This was not fun. On the Macintosh, the drivers — that is, the code that interfaces between the computer and particular piece of hardware — is a system feature. These drivers are usually added to the system as extensions or add-ons. When you buy the hardware, it will come along with a disk that has the necessary driver on it. You merely have to copy this file to your System Folder. Then, any appropriate application will automatically be able to use that device. For example, most of the time once you have attached a new printer to a Macintosh and loaded its associated driver into the System Folder, it will be the case that applications already existing on that machine should have no problem printing to that printer.

Fonts

Another system-wide feature is Fonts. These are sets of related characters. One thing this can mean is that a particular form is used to design the characters of the Font — for example, they are all tall, narrow characters, or they are short, wide, curly characters. Or it can actually mean that the characters associated with different keys on the keyboard are not what you would normally expect. For example, a different symbol, or pictograph — having nothing to do with the English character set — may appear for each key you type. Examples of useful fonts of this second type include sets of mathematical symbols or character sets from foreign languages.

There are thousands of different Fonts available for the Macintosh. They are designed by various companies who plan out what the particular characters will look like on a computer screen or piece of paper. Any particular Macintosh will only have certain Fonts available. These will be the ones that have been placed into the Font Folder within the System Folder of that machine.

Most programs will allow you to use the available fonts when typing, or, even to change characters to a different font long after they have been entered. This means, you can type a paragraph in a word processor and then easily switch that paragraph into new font formats to see what it looks like. Whenever you want you can print out what you see on the screen and it will generally look exactly the same on the printout.

This capability was unheard of before the Mac. It is now expected by computer users throughout the world.

Desk Accessories

Likewise, another useful feature that appeared on the original Macs that still exists on current Macintoshes — albeit in a greatly expanded role — is Desk Accessories. These are small programs that you can "pull out" and use at any time. Some of the original Desk Accessories included a Calculator, Notepad, Alarm Clock and Puzzle. These were things that you might find on a real desk – and thus the name "desk accessories". The Macintosh was modeled after the paradigm of a desk in order that it would seem easy and intuitive to use by people who were timid around computers.

These desk accessories are available on the Macs leftmost menu – the Apple menu. Generally, at any time you can access the desk accessories. So you may be in the middle of word processing and decide you need to do an elaborate calculation. There is no need to close up the word processor. Instead, you just slide you mouse over to the Apple menu and pick the calculator off the list. This will open up an image on the screen that looks like a calculator. It will appear on the desktop on top of the word processor. You can use that calculator in the usual way, except you press the buttons by using the mouse instead of your fingers. When you are done with your calculation you can close up the calculator to put it away and continue on with your paper. (Or you can even keep the calculator on the screen unused if you prefer.)

There have been hundreds of desk accessories created for the Macintosh. Long ago they stopped being limited to objects you might find on your desk. Instead, software to perform many useful tasks have been turned into desk accessories. Like Fonts, only certain Desk Accessories — or "Apple Menu items" — will be available on any particular machine. They need to be loaded in the same manner you load Fonts. Adding more Fonts and Desk Accessories is one of the many methods a Mac user can implement to customize his/her own machine.

For System 7 Apple broadened the concept of what can appear on the Apple menu. Nowadays it is possible to place **any** application on this menu. Thus "desk accessories" are no longer limited to small little useful programs geared toward one focused task. Since you can now place any program on this menu, the term "desk accessory" is slowly dying out.

Control Panels

Another folder within the System Folder is for Control Panels. These are utilities used for setting options for various software and devices on the Macintosh. There are hundreds of examples. But consider a few. You can use a control panel to set the background color and pattern on your desktop. Another control panel can be used to set the system clock. Still another allows you to set how much time the computer will allow between two mouse clicks in order to count that activity as a "double click" as opposed to two separate single clicks. And another allows you to pick what sound the Mac makes when it displays an error message on the screen. The number of things you can set is quite extensive. These controls panels are usually designed as fancy dialog boxes allowing you to select options thru the use of buttons and menus and other graphical techniques. They are fairly simple to use.

Extensions

Apple allows a method to attach extra capability to the Macintosh without relying on new versions of the operating system to come out. This means that Apple, or any other software company who wants, can create sections of code that can be loaded on to your computer to add new functionality. This code comes in files called Extensions. They can be placed in the Extensions folder of any Macintosh. The computer will then be able to utilize that code as you are using it. Device drivers are one type of extension. Other extensions include code that constantly looks for computer viruses and another that won't allow you to use the Macintosh until you enter a password. Another famous extension is known as Quicktime. This is a whole system of code that allows that Macintosh the capability to display "movies" on the screen.

Types Of Information

Some types of information come in standard formats on the Macintosh. Apple decides the way the information is encoded on their system and includes routines within their software to make this information easy to use and manipulate. Any serious software developer will call upon the Apple routines to use that type of information. By doing this it makes it possible for their applications to easily blend into the Macintosh environment and share the information with other applications. There are several types of information that are easy to manipulate on the Macintosh. These include:

- Text: Collections of characters are the simplest type of information that can be manipulated on the Macintosh. Often associated with the actual characters is a Font as mentioned above. Sometimes the style (bold face, italics, underline) and size of the characters are included as attributes of the text.

- Graphics: Pictures have been one of the standard types of information on the Mac from its very beginning. Originally the images were only in monochrome. Color graphics, using millions of different shades, are now standard. Images can be created on the Macintosh through various software including charting programs, bit-mapped graphical editors and object-oriented software. Various hardware — including scanners, cameras and VCRs — can be used to load images into the Mac.

- Sound: Though not easily manipulated on the original Macintoshes, sound has become one of the major types of information that can now be utilized. Macintoshes generally come with speakers and microphones to make sound input and generation easy. All sorts of different types of software from word processors to database software can now play, manipulate and utilize sound.

- Movies: Moving pictures are now also a standard type of information. On the Mac these are called "Quicktime movies". The images can be any series of continuous images meant to be played during some time sequence. This can be anything from several minutes loaded into the computer from a video tape or camera, to consecutive graphs loaded from a charting program to show the change of some factor over time, to a cartoon drawn with computer animation. Apple has created mechanisms to encode and compress such images easily.

Cut and Paste

Information on the Macintosh can easily be moved around or copied within a document, between two documents of the same type of even between two totally different types of applications written by two separate software companies. The standard information mentioned above can be easily copied across applications. But other types created by a particular software company for a particular task, are usually just as easily transported within documents of that type. This can include formulas in cells in a spreadsheet, data in databases and measures of notes within music software.

This process is called "cut and paste" in Macintosh terminology. It is always a four part operation. Select what you want to move. Cut it. Reposition the cursor to where you want the information to go. Paste. The commands "cut" and "paste" are found on the Edit menu. The processes of "selecting" and "repositioning" can be unique to each application. However, there are common ways for doing these operations. For example, dragging over text often selects it. Likewise double-clicking a word often selects it. Clicking the mouse can be used to reactivate a window and reposition the cursor. Scroll bars help you find a position within a document.

"Cut" actually removes the information from its original location. There is a similar command called "Copy" that leaves the original in its first location but still allows you to Paste other versions of it elsewhere. Cut and Paste will be explained more thoroughly later in this chapter.

Publish and Subscribe

A potential drawback with Copy and Paste is that if you bring a version of the information to a new location, it becomes separate from that original information. This may be fine but maybe not. For example, you may draw a floorplan of a room and decide you want to include it within a letter you send to a friend. You Copy the floorplan and Paste it into the letter. Now you realize the floorplan is slightly wrong and you need to fix it. You go back to the original file with the floorplan and make your correction.

Now what is in the letter? What you originally Pasted is there. That is, the first — incorrect – floorplan. You are gonna have to Copy and Paste it again back into the letter to also correct the letter.

Sometimes it is desirable to attach copies of information to the original so that if the original changes then all its copies also will. Apple realized this and thus added a new feature to System 7. It is called "Publish and Subscribe". Instead of "copying" the original information, you can instead choose to "Publish" it. Then you can "Subscribe" to that information from elsewhere. Then, if you make any changes to the original, all the copies — or "subscribers" — will be automatically updated.

Aliases

Apple also realized that modern file systems have become rather complex. A user may have hundreds, if not thousands, of files on his/her machine. Likewise, a particular machine may have access to many many more files out on a network. You can use folders to organize the information but this still may not be good enough. Sometimes you may have information that seems to fit into more than one category.

System 7 allows the creation of "aliases". That is, you can go to any application and create another second icon for it (or a third and fourth etc.) The second icon can be placed on to any other disk into any other folder that you wish. Now, if you open this "alias", the Macintosh will find the original and use it as if you had gone to it initially.

Multi-tasking

System 7 also allows the Macintosh to have more than one application running simultaneously. Prior to this, you could only do one application (non desk-accessory) at a time. You would have to quit word processing before you could go on and begin a spreadsheet. Now you can run numerous applications at the same time. For example, you can have a word processor, a spreadsheet, a game and an e-mail package all open simultaneously. The number of applications you can open at the same time depends on how much

RAM memory you have in your computer and what the actual applications are. But most Macintoshes will easily let you run two or three applications at the same time.

At any one time only one application is "active". That is, it is the one you are currently communicating with. The others applications are loaded into memory but will be waiting for you to get back to them. Doing so can be done in several ways. Reactivating another will only take a second and it will be back in the state you left it. That is, if you reactivate the open word processor you will find it sitting in the middle of paragraph fifteen of your English paper — if that is where you left it when you switched over to your e-mail.

Each application will have its own windows and thus your desktop can get very cluttered. Sometimes it is hard to tell if you are currently in one application or another. For example, you may look at the screen and see a paper you have written in the word processor. But in actuality the graphics program might be active.

How do you tell what application is currently active? There are two ways. First of all, each application generally displays its own set of menus up on the menu bar. The active application has control over the menu bar and will display its menus there. If you look at the menu bar carefully you should recognize the set of menus and thus realize what application is currently active. Also, the last menu on the bar — all the way to the right – is special. This menu will display the icon associated with the currently active menu. Each application will have its own icon that you will spot when you originally go to start it up. A word processor icon might be a picture of a typewriter. A graphics package might have a paint brush. Noticing this icon all the way to the right on the menu bar will help tell you what application is currently active.

How can you make a sleeping application active again? This can be done in two ways. One way is to find a piece of any window that belongs to that application on the desktop some place and click that window to make it active. This will also make the associated application active and brings its menus up on the menu bar. Otherwise, you can just go to the righthand menu and find the application on the list there. All loaded applications will be on the menu there. You can just select whichever application you want off of the menu and it will become active.

One thing always listed on this menu is the Finder. This is so that if you are running any application and decide you have to manipulate the files that are on the desktop — copy them, move them to a folder, throw them out, or just find where they are — you can get to the desktop to do these activities. As discussed before the Finder is the software that lets you manipulate the desktop. Thus you switch over to this — making the current application inactive — in order to manipulate the file system by playing around with the file icons.

Sometimes weeding through all the windows on the screen can become disturbing. This last menu also has commands to help you decide what is displayed on the screen. For example, you can hide the current application so all its windows become temporarily invisible on the desktop. Or alternatively, you can hide all the inactive applications so they are not in your way. Using this menu you can always make these invisible items visible again when you want them.

Voice Synthesis

Macintoshes also have the capability to produce output in the form of spoken words. With this feature on, that Macintosh can speak — with various different voices and special effects — text that appears on the screen. This feature can also be used to help point out aspects of the GUI as you are using it. This is useful to people who have a visual impairment.

Voice Recognition

Likewise, now that Macintoshes have built-in microphones, it is possible to speak to *them*. Currently Macintoshes have become rather good at associating a sound that you produce (a word or phrase) with some action it should take. Thus you can say "Close All Windows" and it will be able to do the close operation to all windows currently open on the screen.

Don't be misled however. This neither means the Mac understands English, nor that it even understands where one word ends and another begins. It merely can recognize the sound waves formed by the noise you generate as you speak those words. It can associate that wave pattern — within the range of normal human speech variability with considerations for the acoustic properties of human dwellings — with some section of code it should run when it hears a sound that matches.

Soon it is expected that the Macintosh will be able to analyze spoken sound and break it apart into words. With this capability it will become possible to do "voice typing". That is, you speak the words and they will be entered into a text document, spelled correctly, as if you had typed them. If you think about this, it is a rather complex process. Just analyzing a sound by itself, without understanding the context it is being used in is not enough. A computer will need to differentiate between "marry", "merry" and "Mary". We know which to type when we are typing. How do we do that? Certainly we follow some rules. But what are they? Apple and other computer organizations need to discover these rules and then write the code that follows these rules before this capability will be available on the Mac. But this may happen soon — possibly during the lifetime of this book.

1.5   The Macintosh User Interface

Ok, now it is time to get down to the nitty gritty of using a Macintosh. To do this, we should discuss the Macintosh's User Interface — the "Finder".

There are four main features to the Macintosh user-interface:

MENUS are collections of commands that can be pulled-down from the Menu Bar at the top of the screen.

ICONS are pictorial representations of information that can be manipulated and tools that can be used to perform tasks. Icons can represent documents, applications, folders or disks. Likewise they show tab settings on rulers and locks on windows.

WINDOWS are sections of the screen that can be independently moved around, resized, opened or closed. Windows are used to display different types of information within an active application. Alternatively, different windows can be operated by totally separate applications. Windows act as mini-screens.

DIALOG BOXES are special screen displays that can be used to communicate information between the computer and the user. Simple dialog boxes will display a message on the screen for the user to read. Complex dialog boxes allow the user to click various buttons to pick desired functions. They also allow the user a way to supply needed text — such as the name of a file when you do the SAVE operation.

We will learn more about these features as we go on.

This software that lets you interact with the windows, menus, icons and dialog boxes — the FINDER — provides the visual user-interface of the Macintosh operating system. You can actually see an icon representing the FINDER code inside of the System Folder.

The Desktop Level

Unless it is set up to automatically load some application, once a Macintosh has been booted various menus, icons and windows will appear on the screen. At this point, you will now be looking at what we call the desktop.

Do you remember how it got its name "desktop"? Well, to reiterate what was said before, the reason it is called the desktop is because Apple realized they could sell more computers if they advertised their computers as being very familiar and thus easy to use. They tried to pattern the user-interface of the computer after what many people are used to — their own desk top. Thus there are various things that you can "pull out" on to your computer *desk*, including calculators and note pads. You even have a little trash can next to your desk. Isn't it adorable. Okay, okay, it may seem k...da dinky, but it is in fact all very powerful and fairly easy to learn. Some people hate the Macintosh because it seems like an insult to one's intelligence. Other people really like it because it is very simple to learn. Personally, I like it because it seems ingenious to me that programmers came up with this visual environment rather than the old-fashioned command-line operating system of that mega-giant IBM.[2]

And what should you see on your desktop when you first get on the Mac? Well most of the screen will be filled with whatever the current background pattern and color is. There will be several features that are easily identifiable. For instance, across the top of the screen you will find the Menu Bar. Each word on this bar marks the location of a menu. For instance, you will see an apple to the left, then File, Edit, View, Label and Special. These are the menus usually found on the typical Mac desktop screen when you are at the Finder level. Keep in mind that most commands that you can issue to the computer are found on the menus. Since each application will have its own commands and thus menus, these *particular* menus will only be visible when you are using the Finder to manipulate items on the desktop. Therefore, the only time you will find commands such as Eject, Shut Down and Restart is when you are at the Finder level. **When in an application you will have to use Exit from the File menu or, alternatively, select Finder from the rightmost menu in order to get back to these main menus and find these commands.**

In the upper right, you will see a little picture (icon) of a disk. This represents the start-up disk. In actuality, this will probably be your hard drive. However, it can also be a diskette or a network volume (like at Rutgers.) The "start up" disk is where the computer found the System Folder as it was booting up. This is considered to be a special disk since the operating system needed to control the computer is kept there. There may be other disk icons below this as soon as you start up. Or, more may show up as you are using the computer during that session. In the lower-right, you will see an icon of a trash can. You will also see a little arrow. This arrow can be called the *pointer*, the *cursor* or the *arrow*. It represents where on the screen "you currently are". (The reason I quote that is because it is a pretty weird concept ... *you* aren't on the screen and neither is there any place in the computer where you currently *are*!) You can move around to other parts of the screen by repositioning this arrow. And how exactly does one do this? By using the mouse. (Remember the chained input device?) A mouse is a great tool for manipulating a visual user interface.

Interacting with the Desktop Using the Mouse

So great, you can move this rodent all over your tabletop and this arrow will track along on your screen. Now isn't this a useful computer? Why? Why? You ask. Why the heck did I take this course? No, No calm down. There actually are some valid reasons why you would want to slide your mouse over a gooky, gooey, grimy top of a Rutgers table and it doesn't solely have to do with striving for a grade.

The mouse is useful for a number of different tasks such as:

1. Selecting an icon

2. Opening an application/file (icon)

3. Dragging an icon

4. Manipulating a window (now doesn't that sound kinky)

5. Selecting a command from a menu

6. Selecting options in a dialog box.

So let's delve into this more:

---

[2]It took a while, but IBM eventually realized that a visual operating system was worthwhile. IBM personal computers can now run a number of visual operating systems, including Windows and OS/2.

Selecting Icons (Clicking)

Well in case you haven't noticed, there is also a button on a mouse. (If you are gonna dress a mouse then the proper fastener to use is a button. It would be too confusing for a mouse to have a fly.) Yes, this button does have some uses. No, I hope you didn't just click it? Did I tell you to click it? Oh great, you went and did it anyway. Did you destroy your disk? Oh terrific. Okay, for now on just read through this whole thing first and then — after you have mastered all the fine details — then, and only then, should you attempt to use your Macintosh. Okay, so now, just slowly release your finger from that mouse. **Slowly** I said ... okay much better. Now just pay attention.

One of the uses for the mouse is so that you can select an icon. To select an icon, slide the mouse on the table until the arrow pointer is atop of the icon. Then, click the button once. This will select the icon. You will know it is selected because it becomes highlighted. Depending on the setup of your computer it will turn black or some other color.

Why do you want to select an icon? Oh, there are several reasons. For instance, many of the commands on the menus work on the selected icon. For instance, we will see that commands such as Get Info and Duplicate from the File menu do this.

Many icons often have some text under them to identify their use. It is also possible to click within this text. Doing so causes a typing cursor to appear allowing you to enter new information from the keyboard. The current name of the icon will be highlighted. Typing will replace the current name with whatever name you want to give to the icon. For example, if you wrote a paper but picked a name for the document file that you now want to change, you can use this method simply by clicking on the name below the icon for that document and typing in a new name.

Unless you are meaning to change the text, remember that when you go to select an icon, make sure you click on the actual picture rather than the text under it.

You might want to know that on the Macintosh if information is selected — including an icon — you can *deselect* by clicking anywhere on the background of the screen. If you don't want an icon to be black any more then do this.

Double-Clicking / Opening a File

Another operation you can perform with the mouse is called double-clicking. Double-clicking is generally used when you want to open or start a file or program. You should slide the mouse until the arrow is atop of the icon (representing the particular application or file) and click the button twice in row, rapidly. The reason you must do this fairly quickly is because if you do two slow clicks, the Mac may think you have done two separate single clicks rather than a double click. How rapidly must you do this double-clicking? Well fairly quickly. But don't worry, if your fingers don't work fast enough, there is a way to change the double-clicking rate. We will learn about this when we talk about the control-panel.

So in short, if you want to start an application, such as the TRUE BASIC editor, you will have to slide the mouse on the tabletop until the arrow pointer is atop the icon for that software and then you must click the mouse button twice rather quickly.

Note, when you open an application, this means that necessary code to cause the computer to function as intended is loaded from some secondary memory device — like a hard drive — and placed into some section of the RAM of the computer. Once there the computer will begin to function in the proper way to perform the tasks associated with that application — such as allowing a person to type in a paper inside a word processing application. Copying code from secondary memory to main memory can take a while. Thus you may have to wait a bit when after you double-click on an application icon.

When you open a data file (document, paper, spreadsheet, picture, etc.) an extra step is performed. In this case the computer will look for the software that created that data file and open that application. Then the data is read in. Why is this? Well consider a document you create with a word processor. This is merely a section of text — such as your English paper. This text does not tell the computer how to act like a word processor. Instead, software companies write sophisticated code to do this task. The computer needs some software, such as the applications MacWrite or Microsoft Word, to cause the computer to behave like a word processor. Thus, when your paper is double-clicked the computer must first go and find the actual word processor. Once it is loaded, the computer will then pull your paper into memory also and allow you to continue working on it.

If you understand this, then you realize that if you double-click a data file — or document — it might be the case the computer can not find the application that created it. Then what happens? The answer is that the computer is at a loss over what to do. It doesn't know how to act like a word processor and so it can not let you use your paper. In this case a message will come up on the computer screen telling you that "The Application Is Not Available". For example, you may begin some work at a computer center — like the Rutgers labs — using software such as Microsoft Word to create a paper. You may save your work on a diskette and leave the lab. Later you might find another Macintosh elsewhere — such in your friend's dorm room — and wish to continue your work. You double-click your paper and get the offending message. The problem will probably be that Microsoft Word does not exist on your friend's computer. However, for many people, if they don't understand what is going on, they get confused when they see the message and think that something dreadful has happened to their paper and that they have lost many hours of work. They may believe that they now must type everything all over. This is not the case. One merely has to go find a computer that has Microsoft Word on it and continue the paper on that computer.

Dragging

A further operation you can do with a mouse is called dragging. (No, no, this isn't some sadistic way of reducing the Rodent population.) Dragging is when you move the mouse across the table until the pointer is atop an icon (or some other tool) and then you push the mouse button down **but don't release the button.** You can now continue to move the mouse around on the table and the icon will follow the pointer around on the screen. You are dragging the mouse on the table and the icon on the screen. You can eventually release the mouse button and the icon will end up precisely at the location it was when you let go of the button. So to move an icon around from one spot on the screen to another, you must do this act called dragging. (Slide mouse to find icon, push and hold button, slide mouse some more, let go of button).

About now, you should be shaking your head and exclaiming. "What the heck is this hippy talking about?!" Chances are, what I am talking about might not be so clear to you. The reason is, this is all very hard to visualize without a Macintosh in front of you. It will all make a lot of sense after you have used a Mac. So maybe go back and read this then. Until then, if you are having problems visualizing this, just read along and try to get the major ideas. The Macintosh was meant to be very visual. It doesn't work out well when you try to describe how to use one by writing up some chapter in a book. You have to see it to believe it ...

Selecting Commands From A Menu

Another action you can do with your mouse is select commands from the various menus. The way to do this is move your arrow (slide your mouse) across the screen until you reach the menu bar. Slide until you are directly atop one of the words on the menu bar. (There will be one word for each different menu ... like Edit or File or Special).

Once on top of the menu, push down the mouse button and *hold* it down. When you do this, you will notice that the menu itself actually appears. In fact, this is called a "pull-down" menu. You can think of the menu as being pulled-down from the menu bar. As long as you keep holding the mouse button down, the menu will appear on your screen.

How do you select commands from the menu? All you have to do is keep your finger pressed on the mouse button and slide down the menu by moving your mouse down. Various commands will be selected when you have moved down far enough. As with anything that has been "selected" on the Macintosh, the menu item you are currently passing will be highlighted. That is, it will turn black. When the command you want turns black, you can let go of the mouse button and the Mac will do the command you just selected.

You will notice that the choices on the menu will be written in one of two ways. Either the command will be printed in dark black, or it is typed using a grayish shade instead. These gray choices are said to be *dimmed*. You will not be able to select those dimmed commands. The mouse will slide right by them and not ever highlight them. If a command is dimmed it generally means that that command is available in the program but not at the current moment. For instance, you can't Empty Trash if you don't have anything in the Trash Can to empty. So that command is generally dimmed on the Special menu until you put something in the Trash, then that command becomes activated. Or many times, you can't use Open or New on the File menu because you are already working on a program or file. So those commands are dim. To activate those commands, you would have to do a command such as Close to close up your current work allowing you to Open up something new.

Sometimes the items on a menu can get a checkmark placed in front of them. These type of menu items are called **toggles**. A toggle is switch that can be set in one position or another. Likewise, a toggle menu item can either be "on" or "off". The check mark in front of the item means that that command has been selected and is currently in effect. The checkmark is a reminder to you that that command is currently being used. If you want to turn that command off, then select that item from the menu again and the checkmark will disappear indicating that that option is now off. For instance, in many Mac programs you can cause text to appear on the screen in italics. The command to do this is generally a toggle. When you want to type in italics, you select this item from the proper menu and a checkmark appears in front of the command. When you are done typing in italics you select this command again, getting rid of the check mark, and turning the italics option off.

Similar to this are **inverse commands**. A particular location on a menu may have one command listed there. When you select that command you cause a certain action to take place. Simultaneously, the menu gets changed to show the inverse command in that location. If you pick this command, some type of inverse action will take place. As an example, many Mac word processors have commands such as Show Ruler or Open Header. Using either of these commands will cause its inverse to show up — namely, Hide Ruler or Close Header.

It is also possible for software to have **submenus**. A submenu is a menu that you get to by choosing an item off of another menu. In particular, you first slide down the main menu to the submenu you want and then slide slightly to the right. When you do this, a submenu will open up and you can then work your way down thru the items on that menu. One advantage to having submenus is that it allows an application to contain many more menus, and thus commands. Another advantage is that by using submenus, the designer of computer software can organize the commands in a more meaningful manner. For instance, a program may contain a main menu (on the menu bar) called Text. Off of this menu there may be four submenus: Style, Size, Font and Color which allow a user to describe the text he is using. Each of these menus may have a number of options. As an example, Style may contain Bold, Italics, Underline, Outline and Shadow. You can see how such an organization makes it easier for the user of a program to understand how to use the software.

Macintosh menus can also "scroll". To scroll, means to make information that is not currently visible become visible in a uniform manner. Generally, you don't notice this feature because most menus only have a few options on them. But sometimes a menu will have many options on it. In particular, it may have more options than can appear on the screen. This is likely with a Font or Desk Accessory menu (see below), when you are using a Mac with a large hard drive and a large customized system folder. You may have dozens of choices on these menus. A scrollable menu will notify you that more commands are available by placing a small down arrow as the last item visible on the screen. If you slide completely to the end of the menu you will notice that you can continue sliding down. As you do so, new commands will come into view forcing all previous commands to move upwards on the screen and making some disappear from the top of the list. It is almost as if the top and the bottom of the Mac are ends of a scroll of paper that someone is rolling in front of you.

Some programs use **tear-off menus**. With this type of menu, it is possible to slide all the way down past the last item on the menu and as you keep sliding down, the whole menu will then be pulled off the menu bar, remaining open. This menu now acts as a small window of commands. You can drag the menu to any handy location on the screen and use it from there. You can close up the menu (usually it has a close box) when you no longer need to use those commands. Having a menu always available on the screen is handy because you save a step in your command selection — you no longer need to pop open the menu to pick the command. The disadvantage is that each available menu takes up working space on the screen. Plus, it helps to add to the clutter on the Macintosh screen. Having tear-off menus allow the user to decide when the advantages outweigh the disadvantages.

One thing that seems annoying about the Mac is that it always seems that in order to do *anything* you have to steer your mouse all over the table top in order to find the freakin' menus in order to find some dinky command. After a while, searching around the menus gets to be a pain. **Well it turns out that there is often a short cut to get a command from a menu.** Often when you look at the choices on a pull-down menu, you will see next to some of the items a funny-looking character (let's call it a "clover-leaf") followed by another character. If you look on your keyboard, you will notice that you can find this clover-leaf-like character on each side of the space bar. This key is called the *command key*. As an example of what I am talking about, you will notice that there is a clover-leaf and then an E on the Special menu after the Eject choice. What this is telling you is that the short-cut way of doing an Eject is by doing "Command E". That is, without even using the mouse at all, you can just hold down the command key on the keyboard and at the same time hit the E key. This will do essentially the same thing as going to the menu by using the mouse and selecting Eject from the Special menu. In general, many of the most often used commands will have a short-cut attached to them. So, if you want to save yourself some command-finding time, you can use the short-cut method. But you must be smart enough to notice these short-cuts staring at you when you pull down the menus.

Window Manipulation:

Windows are one important component of the Macintosh visual operating system. Many applications use one or more windows. For instance, TRUE BASIC typically supplies you with three windows. In order to use the Mac successfully, you should understand how to manipulate the windows by using the mouse. There are five main "controls" on a standard Macintosh window. They are:

1. **CLOSE BOX** The first thing that a new Mac user wants to do is close up the window. This is because of the standard get-me-out-of-here mentality of a new user. At any rate, whether you are a new user or not, you will eventually want to close a window. There is a control on the window called the close box. This is the little white box in the upper left corner of the window. To use it, move the arrow pointer until the tip[3] of the arrow is actually *in* the white box. Then click the mouse button. This will close the window. (Which means it will then shrink down into an icon or disappear altogether.)

2. **ZOOM BOX** Since it is possible to have many windows on the screen at one time, there may be a reason why you want to concentrate on one particular window. One thing you might want to do is make the window full-size so that it takes up the whole screen (possibly covering other windows). There is a little white box with a line through it in the upper right of the window. If you click this box with the mouse, the window will become "as big as necessary to show everything". If there are only a few things to display, the window may not be too big. However, if there is a lot, the window will be considerably bigger. In fact, there may be so much in the window — for example, a 50 page paper — that it is impossible to fit it on the screen. In this case, "as big as necessary" will be as big as the screen itself and, yes, not everything will be visible but the computer will be doing the best it can do. The Macintosh remembers the original position of the window and its former size so that when you click this box again, it will shrink back to the size and position it had before. Thus, the zoom box is a toggle control allowing one to easily switch between two window setups.

---

[3] This really means "tip". If nothing happens, you don't have the tip of the arrow in the right place.

3. **TITLE BAR** Another action you might want to do to a window is move it. Since you may have a number of windows on the screen at once, you may like to position them so that they are easier to see. The way to move a window is by using the title (or header) bar. This is the bar across the top of the window that has a number of horizontal lines across it. It also has the title of the window on it. You can move a window by placing the arrow-pointer on this title-bar, pushing down the mouse button, *holding it down*, then dragging the mouse some place else and finally letting go. **That is, do the standard drag operation on the title bar and you can reposition a window.**

4. **SIZE BOX** Another action you might want to do to a window is to resize it. If it is large, you may want to make it smaller; if it is small, you may want to make it large. If it is long and thin, you may want to make it short and fat. Zoom will let you make it full size, but this might not be what you want. Full-size windows will cover up all other windows. You may want a number of windows on the screen at once. Thus, you may have to play around with their sizes so that they all fit. The way to do this is to use the size box. This is the control in the lower-righthand corner of the window. To use this control, place the arrow in the size box, push the mouse button down and hold, then drag the mouse. You will be repositioning the lower-right hand corner of the window. Let go of the mouse button when the window is the desired size. In this way, you can resize/reshape the window. So drag the size box when you want to resize a window.

5. **SCROLL BAR** At any one time, a window may only be displaying a portion of what there is to see. For instance, a program may be rather long and it would be impossible to show it all in one window. A part of the window that we haven't discussed yet is called the scroll bar. You may see these on the bottom and sides of a window. They are bars that have a dotted pattern in them. The scroll bars also have arrows at each end and a small white square in them. If there is more to see than what is currently visible in the window, the scroll bars for that window will be activated. You will be able to spot this because the arrows along the bottom or side of the window will turn black, the white box will appear and the gray dotted pattern will be obvious. They can now be used. Use the arrows to see other parts of the window. For instance, there is an arrow on the right hand side that points up. If you click this arrow you will see what is above the current window-full of information. Thus, in an application, if you want to see previous parts of your information, then click the up-arrow on the righthand scroll bar. In general, a window may have an up-down scroll bar on the righthand side and a left-right scroll bar on the bottom. You can use the arrows to go in whatever direction you want. The arrows scroll rather slowly. If you want rapid motion, you can try to move to any spot directly. The way to do this is to move the white box to any position along the scroll bar. For instance, if you want to go to the end of your program quickly, then drag the white box all the way to the bottom of the righthand scroll bar. One other way to scroll is by displaying one window-full at a time. If you click a scroll bar on the pattern between the white box and the arrow, it will scroll in that direction exactly one window-full of information. So remember, there are three separate ways to use a scroll bar. Either use the arrows, drag the white box, or click between the white box and the arrow.

Besides the five controls on its framework, there are two other operations you can perform to a window.

- **OPEN** Well, how the heck do you get a window to show up in the first place? One common way is to double-click an icon. Many icons represent some application and when this software is "opened", or loaded, it opens up a window. Another way is to look for a special Window menu (or some-such menu) that lets you put windows on the screen. Possibly there is some icon-tool that lets you do it. Various applications do it in one or more of these standard ways.

- **REACTIVATE** One other thing you can do to a window is to reactivate it. There is no tool for this. At any one time, although there may be many windows on the screen, only one window is active. That is, if you type information or issue commands then the task running in the active window processes what you have done. If you want another window to be active instead, then slide the arrow so that it is some place in that window and click the mouse button. This will reactivate this other window. The active window will "come to the top of the screen". That is, if it was covered in part by another window, it will no longer be obscured. Sometimes you can not find a piece of an inactive window that you want to reactivate because other larger windows are overlapping it. Thus, you will have to move these other windows out of the way or change their size in order to find the hidden window. Alternatively, it is sometimes possible other mechanisms, such as commands off of a menu, may be available to reactive windows.

So, given a window, you should now be able to open it, close it, reactive it, toggle it to full-size, resize or reshape it in any manner, move it anywhere and scroll around within it.

Dialog Boxes

As has already been mentioned, a dialog box is one of the main ways in which information can be passed back and forth between a Mac and a user. A dialog box is a stationary fixed-size screen-section that gets displayed whenever information needs to be given to or requested from the user. In this box may be various controls, called "buttons" that a user can utilize to make various option selections. The mouse is used to click these buttons. Often a dialog box will also contain small segments into which the user can supply text. When a dialog box is in the screen, you usually can not use any of the other Mac features (such as windows and menus) until you make the dialog box disappear.

If they are well designed, you should understand most dialog boxes. Essentially, click buttons in front of the different options you want. Some buttons turn black when you click them. These are generally oblong in shape. Sometimes, selecting one of the buttons finishes off the dialog session with the computer making the dialog box disappear. Other buttons are small squares which display an X when they are clicked. This X reminds you that you have chosen that option. You can click the box again to make the X disappear. Similarly, some buttons are small circles. They may get a dot in their center when you select them. Often you can click them again to make the dot disappear to show you no longer desire that particular option.

Like menu commands, buttons can be dimmed (or grey). This means you can't use the command at that time but may be able to later if you do something else first. For example, the Eject button in a dialog box might be dimmed if there is no diskette in your machine.

A couple buttons are quite common. An OK button will appear on many dialog boxes. Clicking this button means that you are finished using the dialog box and satisfied with any selections you have made. Error messages, warnings or general information often appear in a dialog box which solely contains one OK button. This button is there so you can indicate when you are done reading. To make the dialog box disappear you must click the OK button. Stay calm if you see such a dialog box. Just read the information and click OK and the Mac should continue to work. If it is some type of error message, try to correct your work accordingly. As an alternative to OK, you may see a QUIT button. This too may make a dialog box disappear. If neither of these buttons are there, there should be some similar type of button to end your session with the dialog box. Another important button is the CANCEL button. Sometimes you will accidently select a command and cause a dialog box to show up. You might not want to proceed with the command. For instance, the Print command from the File causes a dialog box to show up before you attempt to print. If you selected this accidently, then you don't want to proceed. Rather, you would prefer to back up. A button entitled CANCEL appears in most dialog boxes. Clicking this button will close up the dialog box — the effect being as if you never selected that particular command in the first place. Sometimes you purposely make a dialog box appear, play around with the options for a while and then realize you are creating a mess. You may wish to restart the dialog. Clicking the CANCEL button will get you out of the dialog and you can reselect the proper command to get a new, fresh dialog box to appear.

Most dialog boxes have one particular button that is the main button in the box. This button is likely to be the main reason you are using the dialog. Most people, most of the time will use that command. To indicate the importance of the command, that button will be emphasized with outlining. This is called **the default button**. It turns out that often when you are in a dialog box, you can hit the return key on your keyboard to select the default button. In some situations this can be a time-saving shortcut. One common default button is PRINT in the print dialog box. SAVE in the SAVE AS dialog box is an especially convenient default button. After you have typed in the name of your file in this dialog box you merely hit the return key and the SAVE option is automatically done without you having to hit the SAVE button in the box. This beats having to take your hands off the keyboard and using the mouse to pinpoint the button and click it.

One other feature of dialog boxes are the **text areas**. These boxes allow you to supply some necessary information by using the keyboard. For instance, you might supply a name of a file when you are using the SAVE AS dialog, or type in a number to specify the number of copies you want when using the PRINT dialog box. Keep in mind that you can use the standard Macintosh editing features when using these text boxes. You can select parts of the text by sliding over it with your mouse turning it black; you can use CUT and PASTE; you can move the cursor around; you can use the delete key to fix errors; when text is black you can replace it by typing new text on the keyboard and so on. More about this will be explained when we explore "editing".

There is one hint to remember about dialog boxes that have more than one text area. The **TAB** key can be used to jump from one text area to the next as you are entering information thru the keyboard without having to resort to using the mouse.

1.6 Some Common Menus

Remember when I discussed menus? Well it turns out there are some common menus on the Macintosh that you will often see in the various applications.

1. FILE

2. EDIT

3. VIEW and SPECIAL

4. FONT or SIZE or STYLE menu

5. APPLE (otherwise know as the DESK-ACCESSORY menu)

File Menu

Most programs give you a FILE MENU. It is here that you will find common commands such as SAVE, PRINT, NEW, OPEN, CLOSE and QUIT.

OPEN: Besides being able to open a file by doubling clicking on it before you enter an application, there is also a way to access a file once you are inside of some software. The OPEN command allows you to open a file from within an application. You will be given a list of files and you should select one with the mouse. You may have to look through a number of folders and/or disks to find the file you want. Many applications only allow you to have one file open at a time ... other software may have a limit as to how many can be opened at once. Usually each file is placed in another window.

When you choose OPEN from the FILE menu you generally get a typical OPEN dialog box. In one section will be a scrollable list of files. Above this list will be a "title menu" showing you the name of the current disk or folder that the files in this list are placed. If the file you are looking for is not in the current folder (or top-level of the disk), then you will have to sift your way through the folder hierarchy to find the proper file. If a folder name is one of the items in the list, you can double-click on the folder name. That folder's name will now be placed in the title menu and the list will now be showing all items in that folder. As you get deeper and deeper into the folders, you may decide you need to back-up out of a folder, to see the items in a surrounding folder or disk. You can do this by using the title menu. If you place your mouse on the title above the list and hold the mouse button down, a pull-down menu will appear with the name of all enclosing folders and disks. You can back up to the level you want, by just choosing the proper name. Besides the usual CANCEL button to make the dialog box disappear and the default button OPEN, there generally are a couple of other buttons. One says EJECT. This button will eject the disk currently in the drive, allowing you to insert another disk. Doing so will enable you to open files on this other diskette. Macs often have several disk drives and other secondary storage devices attached to them, and with the use of network software such as AppleShare you can also attach to several file servers. You may wish to open files off of any of these drives or file servers. You can easily get to the top-level showing you a list of the currently available disks by clicking the DESKTOP button. For example, if you are looking for a TRUE BASIC program you have saved on your diskette and use the OPEN command it may start out looking at your hard drive. This is not useful to you. To make things easy you can click the DESKTOP button which will then show you a list containing the name of your diskette. You can then click this name and the dialog box will jump down into the information on your diskette and show the files stored there, including the program you are looking for.

Sometimes, the dialog box allows you to specify a particular type of file you are looking for, if the program can handle more than one type of file. (For instance, possibly text files, and picture files.) Sometimes, the program can read files created by other programs, converting them into the correct format as it reads them in off the disk. An option such as IMPORT FILE might be available for this purpose.

When at the desk-top level, another way to open a file rather than double-clicking its icon is to click its icon once and use OPEN from the FILE menu. **You will want to use OPEN (or double click) when you are working on an old file (program) that you want to modify.**

CLOSE This command allows you to close up a file. That is, you will no longer be able to work with it until you do an OPEN again. A CLOSE may ask you whether you want to SAVE.

NEW This command allows you to start a new file or document. A blank window usually appears and you can start entering any necessary information. Often when you start an application it will assume you want to do a New and thus come up with a blank window. For instance, you can start on a new program in TRUE BASIC by double-clicking the TRUE BASIC icon. Or if you are in the middle of working on an old program and decide you want to start a new program you can use NEW from the File menu.

SAVE AS This command saves your work (program or file) on a disk or some other secondary memory device. Your work is not secure until you do this. You will be asked to supply a name for your file. Remember your data, document, picture, etc. is in RAM as you work. Information in RAM is forgotten when a computer is turned off. You want your information stored on a secondary memory device such as a disk so that you can keep it from session to session. This command asks for you to enter a name for your file. It also needs to know exactly what disk you want to save on (in case you are using a number of diskettes, hard disks or file servers at the current time.)

The typical SAVE dialog box contains a title menu placed above the list of folders and files appearing in the current folder or list. Before you SAVE, you can double click folders, or backup using the title menu to get to the folder you want to save your file into. An EJECT button exists so that you can eject the current diskette and insert another if you would rather save your work on another. Like with the OPEN command you can use the DESKTOP button to back up to the top-level where you can easily view the available list of attached disks.

As you Save you want to be sure of two things. First be very clear what disk you are saving it on to. It is very possible to Save on to another device when you think you are placing it on your diskette. You will be very disappointed if you leave with your diskette and later place it into a machine elsewhere only to discover your work is missing. Therefore, make sure you see the name of diskette (or the name of whatever you want to save on to) right before you hit the SAVE button on the dialog box to actually save your work. The second thing you want to be careful with when you save is to make sure you pick a unique name for your work that you can easily remember. Do not save with a name of something already on the diskette or you will wipe out what used to be on the disk with that name. That is, don't call your word processing assignment "My HW" and then a week later call your spreadsheet "My HW". If you do, you can kiss your word processing assignment goodbye.

The file that will be saved is shown in the dialog box. There is a text area in the dialog box to allow you to enter a name. If the file has already been saved at least once, the text area will already contain the current name of the file. You can use this name again, wiping out what used to be saved under that name or you can supply a new name if you want to save multiple versions of your work. A CANCEL button exists. The default button is SAVE. (Remember, default buttons can be activated by the return key.) If the current application can save a file in a form that can be read by other software or computers, there may be an option such as Export.

Students at Rutgers should be careful they are saving on to their diskette and not on one of the other drive options like the hard drive of the machine in the lab they are using or one of the file servers.

SAVE The same as SAVE AS, except you are not asked to supply a name. The computer will use the old name again. (It knows this name from the last time you did an OPEN or SAVE AS).

The very first time you try to SAVE, you must supply a name, so a SAVE AS is done no matter what. You will usually want to use SAVE after you have already supplied a name previously by using SAVE AS. It is strongly recommended that you save every 5 or 10 minutes. If you work on the computer for an hour and a half and never save your work and then the computer dies ... well then you lose everything you have done for the last hour and a half because you never placed it on your disk. Warning: you should get into a habit of saving automatically very often. If you don't do this, you are likely to end up very upset like millions of computer users before you who relied on the RAM to hold their work and then lost hours of important work. Information in RAM is at risk because RAM is volatile. This means when the power is shut off, the info is lost. Don't get burned by a power failure, or an accidental nudging of the reset switch or by a frisky friend who feels like smacking your computer. And don't forget, software being rather complex is full of bugs. This means that at any time your computer can get hung. At that point the only way to get it to work again is to turn it off and reboot it. You will not be able to save before doing this — so you will lose everything you entered since your last Save.

Some people may like to save several versions of their program: for instance **Hw1.Version1**, **Hw1.Version2** and **Hw1.Itworks**. You can pick new names by using SAVE AS whenever you want. Then you will still have the old files but also newer files. This is in case you want to go back to the way a program used to be before you started messing around with it.

Normally, when you do a SAVE, the previous version of your program is lost forever. This might be disastrous. For instance, let's say you called up an old program to fix one line. As you were fixing that line you accidently wipe out 100 lines of your program but fail to notice this. Up to this point this tragic mistake will only be within the RAM of the computer — not on your diskette. However, what if you then SAVE. Then that one line will be placed into the program on the diskette, wiping out the better version that used to be there. Now the copy of your program on the diskette is missing those 100 lines ... oh NO!

Fortunately, any normal person would notice that they deleted 100 lines of their program. If you are working on a program and accidently mess it up badly, all you need to do is QUIT out of TRUE BASIC (or whatever you are working on) and **don't** do a SAVE, (it will ask if you want to. Click "NO"!) Then you can just open up the version of the program that is still on the disk ... this will be the old unmessed-up version since you never saved the messed-up version. This is great.

Remember, if you mess up your file or document badly and can't fix it then Quit without Saving. Sure you may lose a little work that you did. Possibly you had entered a new paragraph after the last time you saved but before you accidently wiped out the whole fifty-page paper. You will be happy to

Quit without Saving. Yes, you will be able to get back the whole paper without that one paragraph. But I doubt you will care about the missing few lines at that point.

QUIT Hey, this is how you get out of an application. You will want to do this eventually. You won't be able to do a **SHUT DOWN** until you quit out of all applications you are in.

PRINT This is how you get a printout of your work.

The typical PRINT dialog box varies depending on what type of printer you are sending your work to. Laser printers have different features than dot-matrix printers. There are many options that you can choose from when you print. Often all you need to do is hit the Print button on the dialog box in order to get one copy of everything to print out. However, you can opt to print more copies by typing in a number after the option **Copies**. Or you can specify that you only want certain pages to print. You can have the complete document print by hitting a button that usually says **All**. But to print some pages you can specify a range by clicking the button in front of **From** and typing in a number for your first page (From) and your last page (To). Laser printers usually contain a stack of paper in them so you'd specify that the paper source was **Paper Cassette**. Other times, if you bring your own fancy paper to use in the printer, you may specify **Manual Feed**.

Clicking the OK or PRINT default button allows the printout to be sent. Using CANCEL gets you out of the PRINT dialog box without sending something to the printer.

Printers may be networked to many Macs. To print to network printers is slightly more complicated than just selecting PRINT from the file menu when you want to print. One of the very first things you will have to do is use the CHOOSER desk accessory at least once every time you get on your Mac (see below). If you forget to do this, you won't be able to print.

PAGE SETUP Depending on the type of printer you are using and the particular program, there may be a number of options you can use in describing what your printout should look like. This command allows you to specify the necessary options. Any options you set using PAGE SETUP will remain in effect until you use the command again. You need not ever use this command if you are satisfied with how your printouts are coming out. Or you may use it once to specify things exactly as you want them. But you shouldn't have to specify this command every time you print. The PAGE SETUP dialog box has the usual OK and CANCEL buttons. Often, you can specify what type of paper you are using. There are several standard sizes including US letter, US Legal, Computer Paper, A4 Letter, and International Fanfold. You may be able to specify any custom size, specifying a certain Page Width and Page Height. You should be able to specify the orientation of the text on the page. Do you want the text across the wide part or narrow part of the page? There are the usual helpful icons to help you specify these options. You may be able to reduce or enlarge the printed material by any specified percentage, much like on an expensive copying machine. You may have an OPTION button to show you a larger list of available options. These might include Flipping the picture Horizontally or Vertically on the page or Inverting the image (changing black to white and vice versa). There may be a number of options that affect the appearance of the output or how quickly it prints. These options include Font Substitution, Text and Graphics Smoothing, Faster Bitmap Printing, Precision Bitmap printing, Unlimited Downloadable Fonts, and Larger Print Area. It is not important to understand these options at this time — just realize that they affect the speed or quality of the printouts in various ways.

Particular programs may allow you to specify how much space to use for the left, right, top and bottom margins. You may also be able to specify material which should be placed on each page, such as a page number or headers and footers by using this dialog box. There may be options allowing you to specify whether certain material should be printed or not, such as Row and Column numbers or Cell Notes from a spreadsheet.

In general, it is a good idea to check what options are available under Page Setup for each individual application. You may never have to use this command but it is good to know what is available. If you ever are attempting to make some special modification to a printout, the first place you should look is under Page Setup.

Simple Editing:

Editing is the process of entering (typing) information into a computer and rearranging or modifying that which is already there. You need to edit when you enter a program or a document into the computer. You can get a file to have the proper information if you know how to do three easy operations.

1. Position your typing cursor.

2. Type.

3. Delete the character before the cursor.

POSITIONING: When you are in a window that allows typing, you will have two cursors. One will be the standard arrow pointer. The other will be a thin vertical bar. This bar is the typing cursor. Anything that you type will appear after this cursor. You can position this cursor anywhere you want by just moving the mouse arrow and clicking the button once. The vertical bar arrow will move to where the arrow pointer was when you clicked the mouse. Often, you can also use the cursor keys — arrow keys which you see on the keyboard — to help you move the typing cursor around. Some Mac software has other ways to position the cursor, too.

TYPING: Sitting at a Mac, you will see all those characters in front of you on the keyboard. So use them! Remember, use the shift key if necessary. Many Mac word processors automatically skip to the beginning of a new line when you reach the right margin. (So you use return only when you get to the end of a paragraph!) Also, most of the time the window will automatically scroll for you if you run out of room at the end of the window. TRUE BASIC scrolls for you, but you must hit return to go to a new statement. If you want extra lines between things, then hit a lot of returns. If you type in the middle of an already existing line, the Macintosh will reflow the document for you. That is, it will make space where you are typing, pushing existing words further to the right on that line, or, if necessary, down on to new lines.

DELETING: There is a key on the Mac called DELETE. This key erases the character that is before the typing cursor. How can you delete blank lines if you so desire? *Well how did they get there?* They got there because you typed in RETURN characters. (As far as the computer is concerned, a RETURN is just another character or keystroke, even though to us humans a return seems to cause an action rather than to leave a mark on the screen.) So how do you get rid of them? Simple! Use DELETE. Put the cursor on the beginning of the line *after* the blank line and hit DELETE and you will erase that extra RETURN. (Is that simple enough? Believe it or not, most people don't understand how this works.)

You can now insert characters anywhere on the screen and delete them. So you can go anywhere you want and fix them. You may have to use the scroll bars to get to parts of your file that you can't currently see on the screen.

Edit Menu

Sure you can do just about anything using the simple editing steps but it may take a long time. Think how much hitting of the delete key you would have to do if you needed to wipe out 1000 lines from your program. The EDIT menu supplies you with short cuts.

To use the EDIT menu, you must first "select" some text to be edited.

Selecting Text:

The way to select text is to drag your mouse over the text. That is, kinda wipe over the text you want to edit while you hold the mouse button down. This will turn the text black. **Selected text is highlighted in black so you know it is selected.** Selecting can be a pain until you are used to it. Just try this. Go in front of the first character you want to select, push your mouse button down and *hold it.* Now for each line you want, slide down slowly until that line turns black. On the last line, slowly move to the right and one character at a time will turn black. When just the right characters are black, let go of your mouse.

There are a number of ways you may want to manipulate selected text.

Deletion: When text is selected, hit the DELETE key. This will erase all the selected text for good.

Replacement: Type anything else when text is selected. This will replace the selected text with what you have typed!

So be careful! If you select text and touch any key on the keyboard, that will wipe out the selected text forever. (Well maybe not ... read about UNDO.)

Common Edit Commands:

UNDO Often the EDIT menu has a command called UNDO. If you make some drastic error like wiping out a fifty page paper, immediately go up to the EDIT menu and select UNDO. This may undo the last thing you did (the mistake). Lots of times this works and sometimes it doesn't. So don't count on this command but remember it is here if something awful happens.

SELECT ALL will select all the text in your file.

COPY will place a copy of selected text into a special location or buffer in the computer's memory. On the Mac, this location is known as the *clipboard.* (This wipes out what used to be in the clipboard.)

CUT will place the selected text in the clipboard and *also* delete it from the screen. (What used to be in the clipboard is lost.)

PASTE will copy all that is in the clipboard and place it after the current cursor position on the screen.

SHOW CLIPBOARD will give you a window showing you what is in the clipboard in case you forgot.

Steps For Simple Copying Of Text:

Often you may want to repeat information within a file (for example, a paragraph in a document) into another part of that same file or even into another document altogether. To do this follow these steps:

1. Select your text by dragging your mouse over it.

2. Use COPY from the EDIT menu.

3. Reposition your typing cursor to where you want the selected text to go.

4. Use PASTE from the EDIT menu.

Alternatively, you might want to *move* the selected information. This can be done by using CUT instead of COPY in the steps listed above. At any rate, whether you get the text into the clipboard by using CUT or COPY you then can use PASTE numerous times and get versions of this information in many other locations.

View And Special Menus

The VIEW menu is only found when you are at the Finder level. It allows you to look at the files in different ways within the disk windows. For instance, you can make the icons smaller. Or you can have the files listed in a way more common on other computers (like alphabetically by name).

THE SPECIAL menu is also only found when on at the desk-top level. Here is where you can Eject, Restart, Shutdown, Log Out or Empty Trash. You can also have your icons rearranged on the screen in a more organized manner by doing CLEAN UP.

Font, Style, Size Menus

One of the neat things about the Macintosh is that the letters (and characters) you type on the screen can come in all sorts of shapes, sizes and styles. Characters will also print out any way that they appear on the screen. There will be menus to allow you to choose a particular size for your characters or a particular style. **Size** generally is listed as *point* size. You will just have to play with this to see how big various letters are — typically people use 10 or 12 point for normal typing. **Styles** are modifications to lettering such as boldface, italics or underlined used to emphasize a section of text. Fancier choices such as *outlined* and *shadowed* are available. You just have to see these things to know what I am talking about. You will no doubt find such features very interesting.

Then there are **fonts**. Fonts are sets of characters that have been designed in a certain related way. For instance, maybe the letters are very rigid and thick . . . or maybe they have a lot of curves. Fonts, in fact, might not even be English characters but rather a foreign alphabet, mathematical symbols or even a set of small pictures. There are hundreds of fonts available on the Macintosh. Any System Folder will come supplied with some common ones. There are programs that let you design your own fonts. It is possible to modify the System Folder so that you can use fonts designed by other people. There is a desk accessory called KEY CAPS that helps you look at the various installed fonts and see how particular characters match up with keys on the keyboard. Such keys as OPTION, SHIFT and SHIFT-OPTION can be used in conjunction with other keys to let you access characters you don't see displayed on your keyboard. You can access the extra special keys no matter what software you are using. For instance, if you are writing up a paper and need some symbol such as π [Pi: 3.141], it is probably available for you to type. Maybe by holding down option as you hit the character "p". If you don't know one way or the other, you can use KEY CAPS to find out.

There are two ways to go about selecting FONTS, SIZES and STYLES for your text.

1. Select the options from the menus **before** you type.

2. Go back later and SELECT text (turn it black) and then use the options on the menus. (This affects only the selected text!)

Apple Menu (Desk Accessories)

Another interesting feature of the Macintosh is that there are special small applications called *desk-accessories* that you can pull-out (open up) and use at any time . . . even if you are inside of other software. Just like there are many many fonts, there are many many DESK ACCESSORIES. Your System Folder may only have certain of these. You can always modify your system by adding more desk accessories to your disk. You can access the desk accessories through the "APPLE" menu. This is generally the very first menu on the lefthand side of the menubar that is marked by a small apple.

Common desk accessories are:

1. **Alarm Clock:** Lets you see the date and time. Also allows you set an alarm to beep at a certain time.

2. **Calculator:** Places a window that looks like a calculator on your screen. You can use it with your mouse or keyboard.

3. **Key Caps:** Allows you to see the various FONTS on your disk and the special characters they have.

4. **Scrapbook:** Allows you to store (by PASTEing) and retrieve (by COPYing and CUTting) various pictures and portions of text that you would like easy access to no matter what application you are currently in. Used to transfer information from one application to another. For instance, lets you use a drawing program like MacPaint to draw a picture that you want to place into a word processor file.

5. **Chooser:** Must be used in order to attach other devices on a network to your Macintosh. This can include printers and network partitions from a file server.

1.7 Chooser

There are generally several steps you must follow in order to use CHOOSER to connect the Macintosh you are using to a file server and printer that is available on a network. CHOOSER can also be used to get access to other network features. Rather than go into all the details, let us just look at one example of using CHOOSER. Again, place yourself in a typical Rutgers computer science lab.

As has been previously mentioned, many of the computer centers at Rutgers contain LANs of Macintoshes. Each of these LANs usually has at least one printer and one file server. Furthermore, many of the LANs are now connected to each other so it is now possible, for instance, to see the printers and file servers at the Hill lab when you are over at the Loree facility. When you get on a Mac it is important to specify which printer you will be using and what file server you prefer. You may need to be connected to a file server so you can get the main software we are using throughout the course, such as ClarisWorks, Mosaic and True Basic. You can also access the file server to find your TA's folder or access information left by your Professor such as homework assignments and lecture notes. The desk accessory called Chooser allows you to specify your printer and file server.

You will get a series of dialog boxes if you select Chooser from the Apple menu. The first dialog box is a four section box. In the upper left of the box you will see several icons. One should say AppleShare and is a picture of a file server. (AppleShare is the program that allows the sharing of software off of the file server.) The other icon is a picture of a printer and says Printer. Below this will be a list of AppleTalk Zones. Each available LAN at Rutgers will be listed on this list. If you wanted to, you can scroll thru this list and explore what is available on the other LANs. But for the most part, you want to use the LAN you are currently on. Usually this LAN will already be selected. If not, then select the proper one. For instance, at Loree use the one that says Douglass-DCS-Loree, at the Satellite use Cac-DCS-Satellite and so on. Off to the lower right it says User Name and AppleTalk. AppleTalk should always be active so *do not* click the Inactive button. You can specify your name for user name if you wish but this is not important for students in this course.

Selecting a printer is rather simple. Click the Printer icon. Off to the right will appear the list of available printers on the selected Zone (Lan). Now all you need to do is click the name of the printer you want to use. This name will turn black indicating that you are done selecting your printer. This needs to be done before you attempt to get any printouts. *You MUST do this each time you get on to a Mac. After you log on it would be wise to do this as your first activity.* It makes sense to pick the top printer that shows up on the list. This printer is the one that is attached to your local LAN. Sending your printouts to this printer will be much more reliable and will speed up printing immensely.

If no printers show up, this can mean several things. Possibly no printers are on. You should turn the printers on with their power switch if they are not currently on. They will then show up on the list. If this isn't the problem then it is possible that the cables forming the LAN have been accidently removed or loosened. It is not up to you to fix this problem if it happens — you should find someone in charge in order to get it fixed. In fact, you best not be caught fiddling around with the cables for the LAN. However, often a loose cable is obvious. Look around for knocked out cables at the back of a Mac or a loose cable on the printer. If it isn't obvious where a loose cable should go, please don't attempt to fix it but at least point it out to the person in charge of the computer center.

To pick a file server takes a few extra steps. First of all, you may not need to pick a file server. Currently at Rutgers you only need to do this if you want to get to material not on the hard drive of your machine. Most necessary software will be on the hard drive. However, if you want to get to some other software or class materials then you should know how to use Chooser.

If you do need to attach to a file server, select CHOOSER from the Apple menu and click the icon in the upper left that says AppleShare. (Again, you will usually want the Zone to be set to your local computer center before you do this.) After you have clicked this icon, a list of various file servers will show up on the righthand side of the screen. You can choose any of the file servers listed there by just clicking their name black. When you click the name, you will then be able to confirm your choice with the OK button that appears. (Alternatively, you can just double-click the name of your choice.)

Another dialog box will appear on the screen. This dialog box is asking who you are. You are considered to be a guest in this course. So click the button that appears in front of the GUEST option and click the OK button.

A third dialog box will now appear. This is telling you the list of network partitions that you can attach to on this file server. For our class, there are two choices, one called Course Materials and the other called DCS Course Support. A small box appears next to this name. Clicking this box will cause the file server to be loaded up automatically the next time you get on a Mac. You almost definitely do not want this to happen. So in the Rutgers labs, don't click this box. (This is more appropriate for a someone who always uses the same computer attached to a larger network. Such as a professor with a Macintosh in his/her office.) However, on this last (third) dialog box just click the actual item on the list you want and then click the OK button. (You click on the words, highlighting them. You can select more than one item by holding down the shift key on the keyboard as you click the second, third, etc. items that you want.)

Use DCS Course Support to get to all the software that is available for you in this class. Click Course Materials if you would like to get to the HW assignments, lecture materials, examples, or TA folders.

Having done all these steps you will be back at the CHOOSER dialog window. When you are done picking the file server and/or the printer, your last step should be to close up this dialog window by using the close box in the upper left. If you used CHOOSER to pick your file server, you should now see new disk icons in the upper right of your screen, below the icon for your disk.

To complete this subject, know that you can disconnect any file server by just dragging its icon into the trash. Also, if a certain file server is always loaded when you get on to a Mac and you don't want this to be so, throw out that file server by dragging it into the Trash Can. Then, go through the steps of reloading it by using CHOOSER and when you get to the third dialog box, make sure the square button after the server name is not selected with an X in it. (Getting rid of this X will keep this server from being automatically loaded.)

As a review, you can pick your printer by:

1. Make sure the printer is on and the cables are ok.

2. Use CHOOSER from the Apple menu.

3. Click the Printer icon black.

4. Select the top printer on the list on the right, turning it black.

5. Close the CHOOSER dialog window.

In short, this is a review of the steps to attach to the file server:

1. Use CHOOSER from the Apple menu.

2. Click the AppleShare icon.

3. Double-click the file server you want from the list on the right.

4. The second dialog box shows up. Click the button in front of Guest.

5. Click OK.

6. A third dialog box shows up. Select "Course Materials" or "DCS Course Support" or both depending on what info you want access to.

7. Click OK again.

8. Close up the CHOOSER dialog window.

1.8 Learn This Chapter

A lot of material has been presented here. It isn't meant to be testable though you may see some of the important terms show up on an exam. However, the real reason all this material is here is to make your life easier. The more of this chapter you understand and can utilize, the easier your life will be when you actually use your Mac! Be wise and use your computer in the easiest manner possible. This is one chapter you might want to read several times.

Have fun and don't let these computers get you down. You have to learn to be patient when you use computers. In the long run they can make your life a little easier once you are used to them.

-Jt

Part II

Programming in BASIC

Chapter 2

BASIC : An Introduction

2.1 You Become A Programmer

From this day forth, you can all consider yourselves to be programmers. That is, at least to a certain degree. Many of you probably have had some programming in the past. Others might be looking forward to their first "hands-on" experience. And then, there are those of you who probably are terrified at the thought of doing actual programming. Fear not. Programming need not be difficult. Much of the programming you will be doing will be quite straightforward and simplistic.

That is not to say that you won't run into some problems. Most of you will have days that you feel like burning all computer labs to the ground and banning all computers from mere existence on Earth. However, just keep in your mind that the key to programming is patience. With some patience you can eventually get the job done. Remember at all times, as you are making mistakes, try to learn from your mistakes. Any knowledge you gain will be helpful on future programs. Don't be afraid to play around with your program and try to figure out why you are getting the weird results you are getting. Once you grasp the key to the chaos, you will have greatly improved your knowledge of programming. Just be patient and think of it as a puzzle. When your programs finally do work, many of you, even though you might be afraid to admit it, will feel a deep sense of satisfaction bordering on immense pride. That is not to say that you are gonna walk away from this course loving computers or anything about them. On the contrary, after this course is over, you may need a long break. But there will be some satisfaction in learning the material. So as you are crawling along on your assignments, just show a little determination and patience. All of you have the necessary intelligence, so don't feel threatened by the mystique of computer programming and the story of those intelligent little nerdy beings, the computer hackers. You can do this stuff. So just hold on.

2.2 What is BASIC

If you want to program on a computer, you need a language with which to work. You will be using a language called BASIC, for Beginner's All-purpose Symbolic Instruction Code. This language will be translated into the Macintosh machine language by the TRUE BASIC interpreter that you use to run your program. BASIC is an interesting little language. It is the first language that I ever learned and I have a small place in my heart for it. However, no one ever claimed that it is the "best" computer language. It does in fact have its limitations. But many beginners seem to pick it up quite quickly. I am sure you will have little difficulty.

2.3   Writing A Program

Every time you sit down on the computer, you will have to go thru a sequence of steps in order to develop a program. Hopefully, before you have even gotten to the computer, you will have written down what you believe is the necessary program for the task you are trying to complete. This of course will be your first mistake, as no one ever gets a program right on the first try (except me of course). But, you need a starting point. So before you head over to the computer lab, make sure you sit down in your room, as you listen to your Yngwie Malmsteen tapes, and come up with a written program to solve the homework assignment. Then head over to the computer center. Once there, yell "fire", causing all current users to flee the room, and grab yourself a computer. Turn it on and insert your disk and you are ready to go. To develop your program you will have to execute certain steps over and over until you get it right. These steps are:

1. Get into the editor of TRUE BASIC

2. Type your program

3. Get out of the editor (saving your program of course)

4. Run your program

5. Notice what mistakes exist

6. Figure out how to fix these mistakes

7. Get back into the editor

8. Modify your program

9. Go to step 3

Eventually on step 4, you will realize that there are no mistakes and you can thus print your program and get outta there. Printouts can of course be made at other times if you need a printed copy of your program with which to work.

To do all these steps, you will need to know where the computer room is, how to get onto a computer, how to get off a computer, how to get printouts, and where to pick up printouts. Most importantly, you will need to know how to use an editor and run your program. Don't worry, you will acquire all these skills before it becomes time to write your first program.

The point is, these are the main steps you are expected to follow as you work on your programs. Failure to do these steps properly can make you look like a village idiot. For instance, printing your program before you have typed it into the computer or forgetting to save it while leaving the editor, or trying to run it without supplying the input is going to cause all sorts of confusions, frustrations and embarrassments. Stay cool. You'll get it right eventually.

2.4   Syntax

In order to use BASIC you must know the precise rules needed to create a program. A program is made up of values, variables, expressions, statements and other components. You must know what makes up these various units and how to build the actual units you want in your program. To build the components you must follow exact rules. These rules form the SYNTAX of a computer language. The computer will only be able to understand programs that follow these syntax rules exactly. Every time we learn something new in BASIC, new SYNTAX will be explained to you. If you follow those rules exactly as you create your own programs, you will have less trouble developing your own software. Be clear on necessary punctuation and keywords. Follow the correct formatting requirements. (For some types of statements, you must start a new line for different components of the statement.)

2.4.1 Following The Syntax In This Book

In this book, each time a new statement is introduced, the syntax of that statement will be presented in precise terms. When looking at that syntax, you will see that some words and punctuation are typed in **boldface** letters. This is an indication to you that these elements must be included exactly as is, any time you use this statement. Other parts of the statements will be in *italics*. This is an indication to you that you must supply something for these parts of the statement BUT that something is something you think up. These are the parts of the statement that you must supply to meet your particular needs in the program. For instance, if a syntax rule has a part that says *number*, then you must supply a number. The actual number you supply depends on what you are trying to do. On the other hand, if the syntax rule has something in bold face, for instance maybe a keyword like **print**, then you must actually type in the word "print" as you construct the statement. You have no freedom as to what you type in that part of the statement, it MUST be that word. (However in our BASIC, you can type it in small letters, capital letters or a mixture.) Keep in mind that these italics and boldface styles are only there to help you understand the syntax. You need not (and in fact can not) actually use bold face and italics when you are creating your TRUE BASIC programs.

Throughout this book, you will also see many program examples. To make these program examples easier to understand, I have tried to follow certain conventions. For instance, all keywords that I type are in all capital letters. On the other hand, variables will start with a capital letter, but all other letters will be small. This will make it easier for you to tell what must be there and what can be there in a different form. Consider, if I have "INPUT" in my program, then "INPUT" must be there. On the other hand if I type a variable like "Apples" you can create another program that works exactly the same by replacing all occurences of "Apples" with "Bananas". In other words, if you had thought up your own program and it was exactly the same as mine but you had "Bananas" everywhere I had "Apples", then you actually thought up the same program. But if you had "PRINT" where I had "INPUT" you would have a different program. There are other conventions I follow when I create the example programs, for instance indentation. I will not explain all of these but the consistency among programs should make the examples easier to understand. You need not follow my conventions when you create your own programs. Programs will still work if your keywords happen to be in small letters and your variables in all large letters and you use absolutely no indentation. Nevertheless, I will try to stick with these conventions.

2.5 The Fundamentals Of Basic

Unfortunately, before we can start doing anything useful or interesting in BASIC we have to weed through a few of the fundamentals. Even the smallest of programs will have a number of different components in it. Until we learn some of these essentials, it is very hard to create any working programs or examples. So, try to stick with me through the introductory concepts presented in this chapter. Some concepts won't be clear until you see how they connect to other aspects of BASIC. Much as you'll hate to do it, this may be a good chapter to come back to reread later, to make sure you have caught all the fine nuances discussed here.

There are a number of different components to a program written in TRUE BASIC. Let us discuss them.

2.5.1 Line Numbers

If you know what line numbers are, forget about them, you don't need them in TRUE BASIC so don't bother using them. (In case you don't realize this, this is an advantage of TRUE BASIC over other BASIC's).

2.5.2 Values

In BASIC there are essentially two types of values that you can work with.

Numbers These can be in many forms, integers both positive and negative and real numbers. Here are some.

- 10
- -120
- 1.204
- -34.6587156

Other books explain this in more detail if you need to see all the possible types of formats for numbers.

Strings are collections of characters. Characters, if your remember, are that which you can type on a keyboard. Characters have ASCII code representations in the computer. When using strings, surround them by quotes.

Here are some strings:

- "Timothy Tulip"
- "Hello mom"
- " $%^&%)*^&_()1980984jkdhjkhkjh';+_(&*^"

2.5.3 Differences Between Numbers and Strings

Now this is important.

The number 10 is not the same as the string "10". One way, you end up with a binary number in a byte of memory. The string "10" is represented in the computer as an ASCII code in one byte for 1 and an ASCII code in another byte for 0. So, a number is not the same as a string that has the same characters as that number. It is easy to tell one from the other, the quotes around "10" give it away.

(You can refer to Chapter 2 in the supplementary material **Part I of the Jt's Lecture Notes** if you don't understand the terms "ASCII" and "binary numbers".)

2.5.4 Variables

A computer language wouldn't be very powerful if you could only work with set, stationary, constant values. Instead, you need variables. Variables can hold values but these values can change if necessary. For each variable you have in your program, you can imagine there is a little box in RAM (a byte or several bytes) holding the current value of that variable. When you send a new value to this location in RAM, it will wipe out the old value. A value can be read and used as often as necessary from RAM.

Most of your programs will have a number of variables. You will be using these variables to hold on to the different values that the programs work with. For each variable, you will want to be clear on exactly what that variable is being used for, and what type of values it will be holding (either numbers or strings).

Much as the variables in algebra have names, such as "X" and "Y", so too, you must give BASIC variables names. (Ahhhh, I hope placing a scary term like "algebra" in here has not sent you fleeing down the hall, screaming at the top of your lungs.) For you to be able to use variables while programming, you need to decide upon their names.

Variable Names

BASIC is somewhat more flexible when it comes to variable names than you may be used to from Math class. Still there are rules you must follow. When you pick these variable names, you can only use letters and numbers. The first character of the name must be a letter. The name can't be too long but you will find that in our dialect of BASIC, variable names can be quite lengthy. You can use an underline (_) in the variable names, but not spaces. Thus if you want to use two words to make up your variable name, separate those words by an underline. Finally, and most importantly, a variable name can end in a dollar sign ($). However, this has a special meaning. If a variable name ends in a dollar sign, this means that that variable is going to be holding string values. All other variables are considered to be numbers.

There are certain variable names that you can't use because they already have meaning in BASIC. These are called reserved words. It turns out that TRUE BASIC has very few reserved words. I don't happen to know the exact list but I would think you can't use things like PRINT and READ since they are already used by BASIC. If you discover a word that definitely can not be used as a variable name then let me know. (For instance, the last BASIC we used couldn't use the variable name COUNT.) I will keep you posted as I find them out. At any rate, it is usually a good idea not to use a word that seems common. It is hard to try to catch the problem with your program when you happen to be using a reserved word for a variable name. So be wise about the names you choose. For instance, I use KOUNT instead of COUNT when I want a name like that.

Finally, the actual name has no meaning to the computer. You may call a variable APPLES and it may in fact be keeping track of the number of oranges. It is the programmer's fault if something like this happens, not the computer's. If computers could understand English, they wouldn't need people to program them.

Examples of variable names:

- X

- Y

- NUM_HITS

- MY_NAM$

- X12X

- thedate$

2.6 Tracing Programs

Throughout much of this course, you will have to trace programs. Tracing a program means to look at a program and follow it one step at a time. By hand, you simulate exactly what happens when the computers executes the program. Everything that the program does is carefully followed. Input statements use up the available data. Output statements are followed by writing down what the program prints out. Any time a variable gets a new value, its new value is kept track of.

Before tracing a program, it is a good idea to write down on a piece of paper all the variable names that that program uses. One style you might utilize is to write down all the variables in separate columns and then draw a line under them. Each time that variable gets a value, cross out the current value and write the new value under the older value.

You will be expected to TRACE programs on the tests for this course. So be prepared.

2.7   Statements

To write a program in BASIC you need to know the available *tools* that you have to work with. In a programming language, you are given a certain vocabulary with which you can write a program. The words that make up this vocabulary are called **keywords**. **A statement** is a programming command that allows a program to cause a computer to do some action. A statement can be created out of single keywords or groups of keywords. Often statements need other values (strings, numbers or variable names) that you must supply in order to give a meaningful request to the computer. Each statement has a certain **syntax** or allowable format. That is, you must follow precise rules when creating a statement in BASIC. A computer lacks intelligence, so when describing an algorithm to a computer, you must speak precisely. Computer languages are not nearly as flexible as human languages (such as English). Thus, when using BASIC statements, you had better include any words, commas, semicolons, etc., that the syntax calls for.

Before we look at an actual program, we need to know some BASIC statements. Today we will look at

REM

END

INPUT

READ,DATA

PRINT

2.7.1   REM statement

Used to make remarks.

A REM statement is not really part of the program. That is, the BASIC interpreter just skips lines with a REM. It has no meaning to the computer. **One thing this means is that when the program is run, the remarks will not appear as output on the screen!** A REM should consist of the word REM and then a space and any message you want. You use REMs to help describe your program and what it is doing. Most of the programs we are doing are small and thus you don't need many REMs. However, a professional programmer relies on REMs throughout his/her code. We want you to include at least enough REMs (usually at the beginning of your program) so that we know your name, section and TA. A short explanation of the program indicating which programming assignment it is would be nice, too.

Examples:

```
        REM             Jt the lecturer
        REM             Sections 48-55
        REM             TA Ted McClure
        REM             A lecture example
```

You can also add remarks to the end of any line by first putting an exclamation point and then the remark.

Example:

```
print X     ! This line prints something....read on
```

2.7.2 END statement

Marks the physical end of your program. The last line.

All programs must have an END statement or else you will get an error when the BASIC interpreter tries to read in your program when you RUN it. It uses this line to indicate the last line of your program file. So make sure it is there. Likewise, don't put any lines after the END. Statements after END will be ignored. (We will explain why and how to break this rule in a later chapter.) The BASIC interpreter just stops reading in lines when it sees the END. So when editing programs, you might want to type in the END all the way at the end of your file first and then type your other stuff above this line.

EXAMPLE:

```
END
```

(Duh! see me at the end?)

Now sure we can do some structural things with a program such as mark the END and put in some remarks, but how the heck can we actually do something useful. Well one important thing a program should be able to do is get a value into a variable. (Assume variables start out with an undefined value until you actually give them one!) One way to give values to variables is to ask for the value from the person using the program. An INPUT statement stops a program and waits for a user to supply a value (usually from a keyboard) that the program can then use as a value of a variable.

2.7.3 INPUT and INPUT PROMPT statements

Used when you want to ask the user of the program to supply you with a value for a variable.

SYNTAX

INPUT *list of variables separated by comma*

or

INPUT PROMPT *"the prompt"*: *list of variables separated by commas*

EXAMPLES

```
INPUT X
INPUT X,Y
INPUT Name$

INPUT PROMPT "What is your name?":Name$
INPUT PROMPT "How old are you?":Age
INPUT PROMPT "Give me two numbers --- ":Numm1,Numm2
```

Generally, for this course, you should use the prompt form of this statement. Also, you will usually want to have only one variable per INPUT or INPUT PROMPT statement.

MEANING

An input statement does the following. First it prints the prompt on the computer screen (if it is the prompt form of the statement). The program then stops and waits for the user. The user is expected to type in a value. After the user has hit the return key, this value gets placed into the particular variable and the program goes on to the next statement. (For the INPUT statement, a question-mark is used as the prompt.)

You use INPUT statements when you want to request information from the person using the program (the user). In virtually all the programs you write this semester you will want to ask some questions of the user. The answers to these questions are stored in variables. These values can then be used throughout the program to solve the various problems that program is working on.

POSSIBLE ERRORS

Always remember to place your quotes around the string that represents the prompt. (When you get better at programming, you'll see that instead of supplying a string constant in quotes to the INPUT PROMPT statement, you can in fact give a string variable instead!)

When supplying the program with a value, make sure you are giving the proper type. For instance, if the variable name has a dollar sign at the end, you are expected to type in a string. If the variable name has no dollar sign, it is considered to be holding a number. Thus when the program stops, you are expected to supply a number. If you supply a string instead, the program will stop and complain.

USEFUL EXAMPLE

Suppose you need to ask a user what his/her name is and the three grades s/he got on various tests. You might do it as follows ...

```
INPUT PROMPT "What is your name, partner?":Name$
INPUT PROMPT "What did you get on the first test?": Tes1
INPUT PROMPT "What did you get on the second test?": Tes2
INPUT PROMPT "What did you get on the third test?": Tes3
END
```

Note that a name is a string of characters and thus the variable name ends in a $. The test scores are numbers and thus there are no dollar signs. Also note that the prompts (question in quotes) actually have a question mark included. Some BASICs automatically add a question mark on to your own prompts. For TRUE BASIC, if you want a question mark to print out after the prompt in an INPUT PROMPT statement, then you must supply it within the prompt (within the quotes).

2.7.4   READ,DATA

Another way to give values to a variable is through the use of the READ and the DATA statement. The READ statement works a lot like the INPUT statement, but the program gets the values from DATA statements rather than stopping and waiting for a user to supply values.

SYNTAX

READ *list*

The list is made up of one or more variable names separated by commas. (That says *names*. You can not put values on the READ list.)

DATA *list*

Here the list is made up of values separated by commas. The values can either be numbers or strings (in quotes).

If your program has one or more READ statements, then it should also have at least one DATA statement.

DATA statements usually appear in one of two places. Either they appear on the line after the READ statement they are associated with or all the DATA statements in a program might be grouped together at the end of the program just prior to the END statement.

EXAMPLES

READ statements:

- READ A
- READ Name$
- READ X,Y,Z
- READ Place$,Count,Zip$

DATA statements:

- DATA 23
- DATA 23,67,43,23,11
- DATA "James","Jake","Joe","John"
- DATA "Steak",23

MEANING The meaning of the READ statement is to look up the value for a variable. For each variable in the list use the next piece of data as a value. When deciding what DATA to use, start at the very top of the program and find the first piece of DATA that has not yet been used. Thus, several READs may use DATA that is all listed on the same DATA line.

TRACING When tracing a program that uses READ and DATA you can do the following steps as you trace the program. When you come to a READ statement, assign a value to each variable in the list after the READ. To assign the values to the variables, start at the top of the program and look for a DATA statement in which there is still unused DATA. Use the first unused piece of data on that line (the most towards the left) as the value of the variable. The value will be the string or number that is between the two commas (or up to the end of the line if there are no commas). To keep track of what DATA is used and what is still unused, cross out any value as you use it from a DATA statement. Thus, the next time you use a piece of data, you can use the first piece that hasn't yet been crossed out.

ERRORS

- **Not enough data.** The program has more variables on READ lines than there are available values on DATA lines. Thus, at some point it tries to supply a variable with some value but all the data has been used up.

```
READ X,Y
READ Z,Q,R
READ B
DATA 2,6,4
DATA 9
END
```

If you trace this program, variables will receive values in the following order. X will get 2. Y will get 6. Z will get 4. Q will get 9. But all the data is used up and the program can't give a value to R or B.

- **Wrong Type Of Data.** At some point, the next available value on a DATA line does not match up with the type of variable used. That is, either the next piece of data should be a number because you have a numeric variable, or it should be a string because you have a string variable. If this isn't true, you have a type mismatch.

```
READ Cost
DATA 23
READ Price,Age,Name$
DATA 19,"Joan",21
END
```

If you trace this program, variables will get values in the following order. COST will get 23. PRICE will get 19. But then the program comes across an error. It tries to read a value in for the variable Age. Age is a numeric value so it is looking for a number. The next piece of data is "Joan" which is a string and the program freaks out, generating an error.

USE Use READ and DATA when you want to have values that will always be the same every time you run the program. Alternatively, you may have values that very rarely have to be changed for a particular execution of the program. Also, you can use READ and DATA when you have many variables that you need to give values to. This comes in very handy later when we learn about loops and arrays.

Often a program performs a calculation based on some values that must be supplied. Usually you want the user to supply these values when the program is run. In such a case you will want to use an INPUT statement, not a READ statement. On the other hand, some times there are values that you as a programmer know as you are writing the program. These types of values may be supplied by using READ and DATA statements.

At any rate, a program will run exactly the same whether the value is originally supplied to a variable by an INPUT or a READ statement. The only difference is that if you rely on INPUT more than READ than the user has to supply more values when the program is run. (By the way, in effect and use, READ and DATA statements are very similar to straight assignments statements which we will learn about in the next chapter.)

SAMPLE Consider you were writing a program that did some type of analysis on words using a set alphabet. Usually that alphabet would be "ENGLISH" with 26 letters, 5 of which were vowels. You might have the following lines in your program.

```
READ Type$
READ Amount
READ Numvowels
DATA "English",26,5
```

Now you can write the whole program using the variables Type$,Amount, and Numvowels wherever you need them. Later if you switch the program around for a different alphabet, you might have to only change the DATA line and make no other change in your program. This illustrates a case where you are using variables that rarely change from one execution to another of the program. However, there is a potential that for some reason in the future you may want to change the values. This is good reason for using READ and DATA.

The alternative here would be to use INPUT (or INPUT PROMPT) which would force the user to supply the values once the program is run. Hopefully the user would know the correct values and not mind that he/she has to type them in every time the program is run.

2.7.5 PRINT

Used to place information on the computer screen.

SYNTAX

PRINT *list*

The list is made up variable names, values or expressions separated by commas or semicolons.

MEANING

Each value in a print statement is displayed on the screen at the current cursor location. The value of variable names are looked up and these values are placed at the current location. Any direct value (either a number or a string) in the statement is displayed exactly as is. Expressions are calculated and then displayed. We will learn more about expressions in the next chapter. Commas cause the computer to tab to a new tab stop. Tabs are about 8 places apart. Semicolons cause the cursor to just stay where it is and not tab or print any extra spaces. If semicolon or a comma ends a print statement, the print statement will not "return" to a new line. Otherwise, after every print the cursor will move to the first position on the next line. Subsequent prints will be on this new line.

EXAMPLES

```
PRINT 10,23,45
PRINT 2;3
PRINT 2;" + "; 3;" = ";2+3
PRINT "The answer is ";675
PRINT "The answer is "; X
PRINT "Column 1","Column 2","Column 3"
END
```

If you run the above program, the following would be displayed on your screen. (What you are about to see is called **output**. Notice how output from a program is not the same thing as the program itself.)

```
10              23              45
2 3
2 + 3 = 5
The answer is 675
The answer is 0
Column 1    Column 2  Column 3
```

Some things to remember.

When tracing what a print does:

1. Anything in quotes will print out exactly.

2. Numbers are printed exactly.

3. Expressions are calculated and then these values are printed. (The 2+3 at the end of the third line is an expression. Notice how 5 got printed out. This really doesn't belong in this chapter since we have not talked about expressions, but since this seems to be a simple enough example I have included it here.)

4. Values of variables are looked up and these values are used either directly or as values in equations.

In short, how do you decide what will print out? The most important thing is to note whether or not what you are looking at is in quotes or not. If it is, just print it exactly. If not, all variable names are converted into their values and expressions calculated much as if you were doing algebra.

2.8   Programs

2.8.1   A 110er's First Abuse Of The Computer

Several years back, at a University not so far far away, a program that looked a lot like the following program existed on the computer.

```
INPUT PROMPT "What is your name?":Nam$
INPUT PROMPT "What class are you?":Year$
INPUT PROMPT "What is your student number?":Stu
```

$$\vdots$$

and so on

$$\vdots$$

```
PRINT "Welcome ";Nam$;".  Hope you enjoy your ";Year$;" year."
END
```

The first time students logged on to their computer account, this program would run, asking some questions and welcoming the student to the computer. In the part of the program not displayed here, the information was stored in a computer database for later use. For instance, a run of it might look as follows: (Let's say that the stuff in caps after the question mark is what the user replied).

```
RUN
What is your name? Jt
What class are you? GRADUATE
What is your student number? 0
Welcome Jt.  Hope you enjoy your GRADUATE year.
```

Simple, huh? If you look back at the program you should see how each item in this output was generated by the program.

Well, as you will soon find out, even with simple straightforward programs, things can go wrong. This was the case with this particular program. One day while I was working as a student consultant, a 110er came running in all upset. He had just used his account for the first time and something went wrong. I went to look at his screen it said the following:

```
What is your name?  DICK
What class are you?  FRESHMAN
What is your student number?  I DON'T GOT IT WITH ME CAN I PLEASE GO GET IT
?ILLEGAL DATA IN THIRD LINE
```

Well, the truth is, I had a hard time trying not to laugh in this guy's face. I doubt he ever did make it thru the course. But he does have the distinction of being the only person I know who screwed up this program.

What went wrong? Well, go back and look at the program. In the third line you can see the input statement is expecting a number. Its variable is STU, there is no dollar sign on that variable. Thus when the guy typed in the entertaining string that he chose (that collection of characters starting with I DON'T), the computer could plainly see this was not a number. So it complained, displaying an error message and stopping the program which of course, worried this valiant 110er immensely.

And if you think that is funny ... wait until you see your own mistakes.

(In actuality, you may be thinking to yourself how stupid this 110er was, but actually, it was the programmer who was rather inept. The programmer should have anticipated that some user might accidently enter a string instead of a number, and should have written his program to handle such an event without dying. The programmer did not do this. Unfortunately, for the time being, since you lack more sophisticated knowledge of programming, you can not prepare your own programs to guard against such errors. Since you are the only one using your programs anyway you will just have to compensate for this lack of programming ability by becoming a **smart program user**. That is, enter the right data when your program asks for it!)

2.8.2 Toxic Crunch Program

We don't have much to work with, but let us go through the motions of writing a very simple program. Let's say that you want to write a program that will generate a report for a NJ fast food chain named Toxic Crunch. There are four restaurants in NJ, all named after the manager of that particular location. The program should ask the manager's name, the town the restaurant is located in, the number of customers who ate there last year and finally the profit made. The report generated should list the restaurant's profit, name, address and customer tally in separate columns, properly headed in this precise order. There should also be a title on the report.

This whole program can be done with just INPUT PROMPT and PRINT statements. First we should decide what variables we want to use for the various pieces of information. Let us use Manager1$ for the first manager's name, Profit3 for the profit made by the third restaurant and Num_Customer4 for the number of customers who ate at the fourth restaurant and so on. Since the values for the manager's name and the town are collection of characters, or strings (rather than digits), the variable names for these items end in dollar signs. I think you get the general idea. Next, you should decide exactly what questions the program should ask, such as "Who is the manager in the first restaurant?" and "How many customers did the third restaurant serve last year?" For the last step in designing this program, you should plan out exactly what the output should look like. The program problem doesn't specify exactly what the column headers should say, nor the title, so you are free to pick appropriate text. I haven't gone through the trouble of specifying every variable, question and aspect of output here, because this would surely bore you. However, as you design your own programs, you should carefully lay down all these details.

Once you have the preliminaries planned, you can start working on the program, building actual BASIC statements. For instance, you can combine the variable you selected for the third town and the question together to make an INPUT PROMPT statement. This would look something like:

```
INPUT PROMPT "What is the name of the third town?":Town3$
```

And the line of output that generates the title could look like:

```
PRINT "TOXIC CRUNCH SALES REPORT: 1989"
```

Why don't I just show you the whole program and point out some highlights. Here it is:

```
REM The TOXIC CRUNCH Program
REM Jt
REM New Program for Fall 1990 book

READ State$
DATA ", NJ"

INPUT PROMPT "Who is the manager of the first restaurant?":Manager1$
INPUT PROMPT "Who is the manager of the second restaurant?":Manager2$
INPUT PROMPT "Who is the manager of the third restaurant?":Manager3$
INPUT PROMPT "Who is the manager of the fourth restaurant?":Manager4$

INPUT PROMPT "What town is the first restaurant in?":Town1$
INPUT PROMPT "What town is the second restaurant in?":Town2$
INPUT PROMPT "What town is the third restaurant in?":Town3$
INPUT PROMPT "What town is the fourth restaurant in?":Town4$

INPUT PROMPT "How many customers did the first restaurant have?":Num_Customers1
INPUT PROMPT "How many customers did the second restaurant have?":Num_Customers2
INPUT PROMPT "How many customers did the third restaurant have?":Num_Customers3
INPUT PROMPT "How many customers did the fourth restaurant have?":Num_Customers4

INPUT PROMPT "What was last year's profit in restaurant one?":Profit1
INPUT PROMPT "What was last year's profit in restaurant two?":Profit2
INPUT PROMPT "What was last year's profit in restaurant three?":Profit3
INPUT PROMPT "What was last year's profit in restaurant four?":Profit4

PRINT
PRINT
PRINT "TOXIC CRUNCH SALES REPORT: 1989"
PRINT
PRINT "Profit (dollars)","Store Name","Location","1989 Customer Total"
PRINT "----------------","----------","--------","-------------------"
PRINT Profit1,Manager1$;"'s Toxic Crunch",Town1$;State$,Num_Customers1
PRINT Profit2,Manager2$;"'s Toxic Crunch",Town2$;State$,Num_Customers2
PRINT Profit3,Manager3$;"'s Toxic Crunch",Town3$;State$,Num_Customers3
PRINT Profit4,Manager4$;"'s Toxic Crunch",Town4$;State$,Num_Customers4
END
```

While we are at it, we should look at what this program generates when you run it. Everything you see after the question marks are items I have entered as input. Here is the output (exactly what comes on the screen when you run the program):

```
Who is the manager of the first restaurant?Ziggy
Who is the manager of the second restaurant?Tony
Who is the manager of the third restaurant?Trish
Who is the manager of the fourth restaurant?Zola
What town is the first restaurant in?Newark
What town is the second restaurant in?Trenton
What town is the third restaurant in?New Brunswick
What town is the fourth restaurant in?Grover's Mill
How many customers did the first restaurant have?140123
How many customers did the second restaurant have?117844
How many customers did the third restaurant have?455111
How many customers did the fourth restaurant have?233199
What was last year's profit in restaurant one?150419
What was last year's profit in restaurant two?114423
What was last year's profit in restaurant three?62429
What was last year's profit in restaurant four?287145
```

```
TOXIC CRUNCH SALES REPORT: 1989
```

Profit (dollars)	Store Name	Location	1989 Customer Total
150419	Ziggy's Toxic Crunch	Newark, NJ	140123
114423	Tony's Toxic Crunch	Trenton, NJ	117844
62429	Trish's Toxic Crunch	New Brunswick, NJ	455111
287145	Zola's Toxic Crunch	Grover's Mill, NJ	233199

Okay, what is there to notice about this program?

Well, first of all, what is the last statement? END! All programs must end like this. And yes, we have the customary REM statements here, even though these have no effect on the output.

One of the most important things to notice is that there are really two parts to this program. There is an INPUT section and a PRINT section. It makes sense to design your program into a number of separate subsections. This makes it easier to read and debug. Later, when we learn about calculations, you'll see that most programs can be broken into three main sections. The INPUT and PRINT sections are usually the easiest sections to work on. If you don't have a good idea how to design your program, at least get started on the INPUT PROMPTs and PRINTs and see if ideas come to you as you are working on these simple sections.

Actually, this program has another small introductory section. We can call this the INITIALIZATION section. In this we set up the state name. A READ and DATA statement is used to accomplish this. Why bother asking the person using the program for the state name? We know it is NJ. So we don't want to get this information from the user of the program by using an INPUT PROMPT statement. On the other hand, at some future time, we may want to take this program and use it in another state. So there is a potential that the state name might change at some future time. So we take this one item which we consider a constant, the state name, and change it into a variable. We localize its value at the top of the program and initialize the variable here by using READ and DATA statements to give it a value. Throughout the program, instead of using the value ", NJ", we instead use the variable State$. Thus if the program ever changes to be used in another state, we just have to change the DATA statement. We don't have to go through the whole program, looking for wherever we typed ", NJ" and change this into some new state. We only have to change it in the one place! This is highly desirable. Notice, that we include a comma at the beginning of the state name. This is because in this program we always plan to place the state name right after the town's name separated by a comma in the output. So why not just stick this comma in here and never worry about it again?

By the way, as you know, there is a bit of flexibility as to where you can place the DATA statement itself. We've decided to place it after the READ statement here but as you know there are various other conventions that are used. Technically, the DATA statement could be anywhere here (before the END) and the program would work fine. It turns out that in this program, we also have some flexibility as to where we can place the READ. It can in fact be anywhere prior to the final PRINT statements. All we have to be sure of is that the varaible State\$ gets its value some time before we try to use it (that is, PRINT it out). It is only used in these last four PRINT statements, so the READ can be placed any time before this. Of course, it would seem kinda silly placed in the middle of the INPUT PROMPTS or between the PRINT for the column headers and the other PRINT for their underlines. The program would still work the same if you placed this READ in these other places, it would just be kinda awkward to humans reading the program. It would upset the smooth flow of reading through the program. We generally try to place initialization statements (statements that give variables their initial value) at the beginning of the program some place.

As for the structure of the program itself, notice there are blank lines interspersed throughout the code. This is just to make it easier to read. Notice that these blank lines, as also the REM statements, have absolutely no effect on the output. In other words, blank lines are NOT printed in the output when you leave a blank line in the program.

A choice was made to include all similar INPUT PROMPT statements in one group, thus creating four groups in all. The program could have been done in a slightly different way. We might have chosen to include all the questions pertaining to one restaurant in a group and still accomplished the goals set down by the program problem. For instance, an INPUT section that began as follows would have been fine also (though the questions in the output would have been likewise rearranged when we ran the program):

```
INPUT PROMPT "Who is the manager of the first restaurant?":Manager1$
INPUT PROMPT "What town is the first restaurant in?":Town1$
INPUT PROMPT "How many customers did the first restaurant have?":Num_Customers1
INPUT PROMPT "What was last year's profit in restaurant one?":Profit1

INPUT PROMPT "Who is the manager of the second restaurant?":Manager2$
INPUT PROMPT "What town is the second restaurant in?":Town2$
INPUT PROMPT "How many customers did the second restaurant have?":Num_Customers2
INPUT PROMPT "What was last year's profit in restaurant two?":Profit2
```

When I ran the program and it was time for me to enter information to the INPUT PROMPTS, notice I did not enter commas or dollar signs in the numbers. I just gave the digits. When entering text, just give it exactly and hit a return, you should not surround it with quotes. The only time you must surround string values with quotes, is when you are WRITING a program, not using it.

Notice that the PRINT section begins with two solo PRINT statements on lines by themselves, with no list of items attached to them. PRINT statements like these cause a blank line to be printed in the output. That is why you see two blank lines between the questions and table in the output. Notice how the title is printed, then a blank line, and then the column headers. Notice how strings are picked for each column header, and these strings are separated by commas in the print statement. This is to cause each column header to start at a new tab stop. Notice how the column headers are underlined by actually supplying four strings of dashes of the appropriate size by placing them in another print statement immediately after the header line, making sure commas are used to place these underlines in the appropriate column.

The rest of the PRINT section consists of four print statements, one for each restaurant (and thus line in the table). The main gist of these statements is to print the profit, manager's name, town's name and number of customers for each restaurant. These items are separated by commas to cause them to appear in the correct column. Notice, none of these variable names appear inside of quote marks. Because they are outside of quote marks, the value of the variable (which the input prompts filled previously in the program) are printed. Obviously, you can see that embellishments have been made based on this theme. In particular, the manager's name is printed out as one part of the restaurant's name. The rest of the restaurant's name is printed out by following the manager's name variable in the PRINT statement with a semicolon, and then printing the string **"'s Toxic Crunch"** (yes that apostrophe being inside of the quote marks, is printed out in the output). In the same way, the state name is added to the towns name to give the overall address. The state name you will remember was originally set up to be , NJ (yes, including that comma). By following the Town name variable with a semicolon and then the string variable that holds the state name (its value actually precedes the state name by a comma) you end up with the town and state attached in the address. Make sure you understand these aspects of the program, as these are the only not completely obvious events taking place here.

Just as one further comment, you should note that there are often many ways to write the same program. As has already been mentioned, you could have chosen totally different variables here and the program would still run in the same way, generating the same output. That is, the variable for the first manager's name could have been X\$ and as long as you put X\$ everywhere that Manager1\$ currently exist, the program would be the same. Another change here that could have been made would be to break up the print statements into several lines. For instance, the final PRINT of the program could have been broken into pieces such as:

```
PRINT Profit4,
PRINT Manager4$;"'s Toxic Crunch",
PRINT Town4$;State$,
PRINT Num_Customers4
```

Notice we have four print statements here. In particular, note that I didn't just break the line off and start a new one with the remaining material from that original PRINT statement. Instead, I actually made each continuation here into a new BASIC statement by starting it with the keyword PRINT. If I didn't do this, I would have a line that is not a legal BASIC statement. It might be clear to an English speaking person what is intended but a computer needs to see some keyword like PRINT or INPUT at the beginning of the line to figure out what is meant to be done.

Breaking the PRINT into four lines like I have done here will have NO effect on the output. You say, "but won't this information now be spread over four lines in the output rather than all being on one line like before? After all, each new PRINT statement starts at the beginning of a new line in the output. Surely this is a change, and this program is thus different!" Well, that is almost a valid point, but you have missed one tiny detail. Notice that the first three PRINTS here end with a comma. What does it mean when a print ends with a comma or semicolon? As mentioned previously, this means the following PRINT will continue right where this PRINT left off — no new line is started! So all these four PRINTS end up on one output line. (By the way, notice that the final comma, or semicolon can not be in quotes — that is inside of a string — otherwise that semicolon or comma is printed out in the output and not interpreted as a separator of items in the PRINT list.)

Well, hope this detailed explanation of this simple program is enough to prepare you for writing all INPUT and PRINT statements in all future programs. As has been stressed, INPUT and PRINT sections of programs are easy to write. So try to grasp these few simple concepts before advancing to the future lessons.

2.9   Using the True Basic Software

We have now started to learn to program in TRUE BASIC. This is thus a good time to explain the TRUE BASIC software you will be using on the Mac. (Rutgers Students: I apologize if this information is slightly different than what you'll be using during Fall 94 and Spring 95 semesters, but I am writing this months prior to the beginning of the school year and can not anticipate new software that might be installed on the Macs at the last moment.)

In order to work on a program in TRUE BASIC, you need to be able to do several things:

1. Create and EDIT a program.

2. Run a program.

3. Debug a program.

4. Print a program.

5. Save a program.

In order to do this, TRUE BASIC supplies you with a special environment. TRUE BASIC is software that acts as an editor and language translator built into one package.

In order to start programming using TRUE BASIC, you will need to find the TRUE BASIC software on your computer. [For Rutgers students, the software is on the file server. As with the other software you have used this semester, it is located in the **110 Folder**. In particular, you want to open the folder entitled **True Basic**.] When you find it, you can double-click the appropriate icon to get things started.

Once you get into TRUE BASIC you will see the following features. Across the top will be a menu bar containing an APPLE, FILE, EDIT, CUSTOM, RUN, WINDOWS and HELP menu. The main part of your screen will be the editing window which has a scroll bar.

There are a number of different windows available in this program. One window, the editing or **Source** window , is used to allow you to enter and modify the program. The **Output** window is where you will see the output that your program creates when it is run. Finally, a third window, **Command**, can be used to allow you to enter commands — though for our purposes, you usually don't need this window since you can get the commands from the menus above.

Normally, TRUE BASIC has the editing window showing when you are editing and the output window showing when you run your program. You should realize that there is a big difference between what you type into a program when you edit or create it and what the program puts on the screen when you RUN it. Thus, the editing window is for the programmer to modify a program. The output window is for the program (computer) itself to use when it is running. All prompts from INPUT PROMPT statements will go into the OUTPUT window. If a program does an INPUT, the program will sit and wait for a user (you) to type in the necessary data and hit a return. All output that the program generates (by PRINT statements) will also go to this screen! Thus, in normal mode, you will either be looking at the program as you edit it **or** looking at the output as you run your program.

However, TRUE BASIC lets you do things differently. You can have more than one window on the screen at one time. In fact, you can have up to three main windows at once: the editing window, the output window and the command window. To get the output window and command window to show up, you can use the Windows menu. Choose Source, Command or Output to get the particular window you want to show up on the screen. If the output screen has been placed on the screen along with your editing screen, then no windows will disappear when you run the program. If you choose to place these two windows on the screen at one time, you will undoubtably want to use the usual Mac window techniques to position and size the windows in the manner you prefer.

2.9.1 Editing Window:

Here is where you type in your program. You can use the standard editing techniques to type in your program. Also, you can use the usual commands from the EDIT and FILE menus. There are commands on both the EDIT and SEARCH menu which we haven't discussed. Some allow you to attach a name to portions of your program (called blocks) so that you can edit or find them quickly. Some more familiar commands, such as Find, Find Again and Change, allow you to find any particular word or phrase quickly and change it into another. For instance, you might decide when you are nearly done with your program, that you want to change a variable name into something more meaningful. These commands would be helpful to ensure that you do indeed change all occurences of the old variable name. Another menu, CUSTOM, can be used among other things, to indent your program in a way that is easily readable. (The command DO FORMAT on this menu lets you do this. Other commands of this menu use linenumbers which we don't need.) For the most part, you don't need all these special commands. All you usually need are the most minimal of editing techniques you learned while word processing. In general, you use the editing window to enter or modify your program in order to make it a correct BASIC program.

One note though. You will notice there is no left/right scroll bar. However, some lines you type when entering your program may be rather long. It turns out you can use the cursor (arrow) keys on your keyboard to scroll the text left and right.

2.9.2 Output Window:

Into this window goes the output when you run the program. You can run a program by using the RUN command on the RUN menu. If you want to stop a program before it is done (like maybe it is in an infinite loop and isn't going to stop on its own), then use the STOP command on this same menu. You can also use the PAUSE command to stop the program temporarily and the CONTINUE command to let is restart where it left off. PAUSE and CONTINUE are used for debugging purposes which we shall not go into now.

Sometimes, the output window stops displaying new information and the computer just seems to wait for you. This probably means your program has come to an INPUT or an INPUT PROMPT statement. If you wrote the program intelligently, then on your screen will be some question that you are expected to answer. The program won't continue until you answer that question and hit the return key.

If only the Output window is on the screen, then when the program is completely finished, the Output window will stay on the screen so you can read any final results. When you are done looking at the output window, clicking the mouse or hitting any key on the keyboard will hide the Output window, and bring the editing window back into view.

2.9.3 Command Window:

If you are familiar with other BASICs you may want to actually type commands into BASIC. A command is much different than a BASIC statement. A statement is done when a program is run. A command is something you want done immediately! The options you are selecting from the menus are **commands**. For instance, SAVE, PRINT, QUIT etc. These commands don't effect the logic of your program. You can get commands from the menu or type them into the command window. Another purpose for this window is to aid debugging. Let's say your program doesn't work. One way to see what is happening is to check the values of your variables after different times in the program and see if they have the values you expected. For instance, let's say that you have a variable called FLOWER$ that is suppose to have the value "ROSE". You can stop your program with PAUSE command and then place the command PRINT FLOWER$ into the command window ... this will cause the current value of FLOWER$ to print out and if it isn't "ROSE" you have narrowed down one of the problems with your program and you can go try to figure out why FLOWER$ has the wrong value. If FLOWER$ does have the right value, that is probably a sign that you are looking in the wrong spot for your error, so you will want the program to go on. The way to do this is choose the CONTINUE command.

2.9.4 Printing

Eventually you will have to get a printout of your program. [In fact, Rutgers students are expected to turn in both a copy of their program and **a copy of the OUTPUT from the program** to their TA.] Printing the program is rather straightforward. When the Source (editing) window is on the screen, just use PRINT from the File menu.

Printing the output is a bit more complex but still rather easy once you get used to it. There are a number of ways to do it, but we'll only mention one way here. When you finally get your program working and want to get a printout of the Output, do the following steps:

1. Open up both the Output and Editing windows at the same time.

2. If the Output window is not currently displaying the correct information, then Run your program again to generate good output.

3. Now, drag over the section of the output that you want printed to turn it black (select it). (You may have to scroll back in the Output window to get to the beginning.)

4. Use Copy from the Edit menu.

5. Click in the Editing window after your END statement.

6. Use Paste from the Edit menu.

7. Use Print from the File menu and now both your program and its output will be printed together.

8. Finally, if you plan to run the program again, you must remove all information from after the END statement. (Remember the program will not run with information after the END statement.) Turn all the output after the END statement black by dragging over it and hit the backspace key to delete it.

Unfortunately, only so much information is saved in the OUTPUT window. Thus, if your program generates a lot of output, you will not be able to print all of it. The TAs are aware of this flaw however, and you will not be penalized if you can not get the beginning of the output to print for some programs.

2.9.5 Possible Errors:

SYNTAX When you go to run a program, there will no doubt be errors. One type of error is called a SYNTAX error. These errors happen when you type in statements that the computer doesn't recognize. Maybe you forgot your right parenthesis **or** maybe left off an END. Or you forgot the keyword LET. BASIC will try to pinpoint where you goofed up and give you some meaningful error message on the bottom of the screen. If this is the case, then look carefully at what you typed and try to find out what the statement should **look** like.

LOGICAL These are errors that happen when your program runs. All statements you typed are legal but they are in a rotten order. Some logical errors stop the program. For instance, you try to divide by zero. Other logic errors cause the program to **never** stop. You are in an infinite loop. (Here, you must remember to use the STOP command.) But most times when you have logical errors, the program does something . . . but it isn't what you wanted. Maybe the output is wrong or it didn't do things you wanted it to do. This means you wrote a valid program **but** it isn't the program you were trying to write. You will have to find out why your logic is wrong.

SYSTEM There is one other error that can happen at *any* time, not just when you run a program. This is called a **system error**. If this happens, you might have to restart your Mac. *System errors generally aren't your fault*. Most of the time you can just go back to working on your program and things will be okay. System errors are caused by hardware problems (disks, mouse, printer, RAM?) or some type of *"bug"* that the programmers who wrote the Macintosh operating system, or TRUE BASIC failed to get out of their software. The first semester we used the Macs, we experienced many system errors. This is due to the fact that we are using TRUE BASIC in a very sophisticated manner — over a LAN. **Because of this, we strongly recommend that you SAVE your work often.**

2.9.6 Scenarios

Generally there are two possible situations that can take place when you sit down to work on TRUE BASIC. You are either starting a new program or working on an old one. You should generally adhere to the following steps: (I assume you can start a computer and enter your disk.)

NEW PROGRAM

1. Double Click the TRUE BASIC icon.

2. Do a SAVE AS and pick a name. This essentially saves a blank program for now but at least you have a name.

3. Setup the windows as you want them. Open those you want and position/resize them as you like. Set their font size.

4. ENTER/EDIT your program.

5. SAVE your work frequently.

$$\vdots$$

Keep entering and saving until you think your program works.

$$\vdots$$

6. RUN your program

7. If you are notified of SYNTAX errors then go back to step 4.

8. Supply any input your program needs.

9. Look at the output, is it right? If not, your program has logical errors. Debug it! Upon figuring out possible changes in your program to be made, go back to step 4.

10. Your program is fine. Print it out.

11. Quit (make sure you save if necessary).

You may want to QUIT early before you printout or debug your program totally so that you can come back another time. You can get a printout any time you want even if your program doesn't work. This can be used to help you debug or to save a record of the work you have done so far in case your disks gets destroyed or lost.

OLD PROGRAM

1. Make sure the File Server is attached to your Mac (use Chooser if necessary) and find and OPEN the TRUE BASIC Folder (not the program!).

2. On your diskette, double-click your program icon. (As opposed to the TRUE BASIC icon on the File Server.)

(Or alternatively, instead of these first two steps, open up TRUE BASIC like before by double-clicking its icon. Then once in True Basic, use the OPEN command from the FILE menu. On the OPEN dialog box, use the Drive button, and open folders as necessary until you find your program's name on your diskette. Finally click the OPEN button.)

3. Setup windows

4. EDIT

5. SAVE

6. RUN

7. Syntax errors? Go to step 4

8. Supply input

9. Logical errors? Debug. Go to step 4

10. Print.

11. Quit (make sure you save if necessary)

Have Fun,
-Jt

2.10   Problems

Throughout this book there will be problems at the end of each chapter. In particular, there will be three main types of problems. With "Find the Syntax Error" problems you are expected to look at the segment of code supplied and find out what mistakes were made when creating the statements for the program. Most of these mistakes involve an error in the "wording" or punctuation of one of the statements. Other errors involve components that are missing from the program. You are expected to circle and correct the errors. The second type of problem is called "Tracing". For this type of problem you are supplied with a program and you are expected to determine exactly what that program prints out. The final type of problems are "Programs". For these, you are told the nature of a problem that is to be solved on a computer. You are expected to write a program to solve the problem.

You will find answers to these problems in the back of the book, in the section called "Answer Key".

Syntax Errors

There is at least one syntax error in each of the following programs. A syntax error is a mistake made in the structure of a statement. It has nothing to do with how the program works, or what it is supposed to do. Rather, syntax errors exist when you don't write the statement using the proper rules and formats or you have left out necessary statements in your program. See if you can find the main syntax errors in the following programs.

Because this is such an early chapter, it is hard to include complete programs here. So statements have been left out and marked with three dots (...), don't let this bother you. Just assume that something more interesting happens in that part of the program.

1.

```
PRINT "Throughout this book, we will try to stick"
PRINT "with problems that have some relationship to the real world"
PRINT "rather than abstractions that don't make any sense."
```

2. The following code might begin a program that was being used to conduct the census.

```
PRINT "I have to ask you these very important questions."
INPUT "What is your name?":Name$
INPUT "When were you born?":TheDate$
INPUT "Were you on America's Most Wanted last week? (yes, no) ":Answer$
...
END
```

3. A good adventure game might ask you how many opponents you want to challenge.

```
PRINT "Welcome to Ghoulies GraveYard"
PRINT "Answer the following questions to set the level of difficulty"
PRINT "for the game. You get more points the more opponents you challenge."
PRINT "However, too many opponents and you won't have a chance to survive."
INPUT PROMPT "How many zombies do you wish to challenge?";Zombies
INPUT PROMPT "How many sadistic madmen do you prefer?";Madmen
INPUT PROMPT "How many vultures are circling overhead?";Vultures
...
END
```

4. A program to replace a doctor's receptionist

```
PRINT "Welcome to Dr. Hacksaw's office."
INPUT PROMPT "How will you be paying for this?": Payment Source
INPUT PROMPT "What exactly is ailing you?": Patient Ailment
INPUT PROMPT "Are you currently on any medication?": Current Medication
...
PRINT "Please take a seat and the doctor will be with you --- eventually."
END
```

5. A program used by a golfer.

```
PRINT "This program will analyze the golf data."
READ HoleOneScore
READ HoleTwoScore
READ HoleThreeScore
...
DATA "Par","Birdie","Par"
END
```

6. Program to generate payroll checks.

```
READ Employee$
READ WeekSalary
DATA "Jones",550
PRINT "Pay Mr. ":Employee$:" a check made out for $":WeekSalary
END
```

7. Program used by bookies.

```
READ Team1$
READ Team2$
READ Odds$
PRINT Team1$; " are playing ";Team2$;" this week. The odds are ";Odds$
DATA "The Giants","the 49ers"
END
```

Rewrites

Another type of problem is called a "Rewrite". With this type of problem, you are given a perfectly good program but asked to rewrite it in a certain way. Often, the new version of the program should do the exact same thing as the old version when it is run.

Change the following program in the way mentioned so that the new program will run EXACTLY the same way.

1. Rewrite the following program using FOUR different PRINT statements to replace the *LAST* PRINT statement in this version. This program mixes up the words that are given to it.

```
PRINT "Enter three words."
INPUT PROMPT "What is the first word?":Word1$
INPUT PROMPT "What is the second word?":Word2$
INPUT PROMPT "What is the third word?":Word3$
INPUT PROMPT "What is the fourth word?":Word4$
PRINT "The four words, placed on one line, separated by spaces but shuffled are:"
PRINT Word2$;" ";Word4$;" ";Word3$;" ";Word1$
END
```

2. Rewrite this dietician's program in three different ways. You are only allowed to change the READ or DATA statements. (Do not change the variable names to accomplish these differences.)

```
READ Food_1$,Protien_1
DATA "Chocolate",23
READ Food_2$,Protien_2
DATA "Cookies",45
READ Food_3$,Protien_3
DATA "Jello",5
...
END
```

3. This program will be used to keep records at a raceway. Rewrite with better variable names. It is important to realize that the program works the same NO MATTER what the variable names are, but it is easier to read and work with if you pick good variable names.

```
INPUT PROMPT "Who is driving car number 1?":A$
READ B$
INPUT PROMPT "Who is driving car number 2?":C$
READ D$
INPUT PROMPT "Who is driving car number 3?":E$
READ F$
DATA "Porsche","Ferrari","March"
END
```

Tracing

What exactly does each of the following programs print?

1.

The input to this program is: "Red", "Green", "Blue"

```
INPUT PROMPT "Give me a color:":Color$
INPUT PROMPT "Give me another color:":Color2$
INPUT PROMPT "Give me some third color:":Color3$
PRINT Color3$;" was entered after ";Color2$;" which came after ";Color$
END
```

2. Input to this program is: 17

```
REM Get some INPUT
DATA 23,55,77
INPUT PROMPT "What is the cost?":Cost
REM Read some data
READ A,B,Cost
REM Print here is the answer
PRINT A;
PRINT B
PRINT Cost
END
```

3.

```
READ C1$,C2$,C3$
READ P1,P2,P3
READ A1,A2,A3
PRINT "Country","Population","Area"
PRINT C1$,P1,A1
PRINT
PRINT C2$,P2,
PRINT A2
PRINT
PRINT C3$,
PRINT P3,
PRINT A3
DATA "USA","Sweden","Japan",260,23,225,1014,53,72
END
```

Programs

1. Write a program to print out a newspaper advertisement. This advertisement can sell anything you want. The top line of the ad should have the newspaper's name towards the left and the date towards the right. Because this ad may appear in various newspapers on various dates, have the name of the newspaper and the date be input to the program. You can have other input to the program if you want to specialize the ad in other ways. (As an example, maybe you want the phrase "There is an sale on XXXXXX" to appear in the ad, where "XXXXXX" should be filled in by some day of the week depending on which day is supplied to the program.)

2. Write a program to print out customized menus. Each day a particular restaurant has its regular meals. But it also has three specials: one soup, one main meal, and some dessert. Have the program ask for the names and prices of these specials. A menu for that day should be printed. Besides the specials, this menu should at least have names and prices for two appetizers, two soups, three main meals and two desserts. Also make sure there is an appropriate name for the restaurant displayed. You can make this menu be as fancy as you want.

3. A particular business wants to make money selling mailing labels to customers. In order to do this, it wants to have a variety of mailing labels for the customers to choose from. Write a program that asks for different pieces of information about a person and displays three different types of mailing labels. The program should ask for at least eight peices of informaiton on each person (various parts of their names, their address, their zip code, their social security number, etc.). Have the program print out three types of mailing labels — with the parts displayed differently on each one. Each mailing label does not have to include all the information on each person. But all pieces of informaiton should be used on at least one of the mailing labels.

4. There is a safe with a three number combination — something like 23-78-12. This safe has been set up to allow you exactly six tries to open it. After this many tries, if it doesn't open a siren goes off. You don't know the combination but through some clever spying you have determined the three numbers. You just don't know which order they belong in. Because you don't want to goof up when you try to open this safe you need a program that will print out for you all the possible combinations you can make from the three numbers you supply. Write this program. Do it in TWO different ways. For the first verison, use INPUT PROMPT statements to get the three numbers. For the second version, build these numbers into the program by using READ/DATA.

5. Write a program that will allow you to fill in a Mad Lib. For those of you who don't know, Mad Libs use short "stories" that are written with some key words left out. To complete the Mad Lib you are expected to supply various words before you get to see the story. First, you might be asked to supply a plural noun. Next, you might be asked to supply an adjective. And so on. Use what you know about TRUE BASIC to computerize this process. Your story should be several sentences long. It should have at least six blanks that you are expected to fill in when you run the program.

6. Write a program that will generate a form letter to send out to your fellow students. This letter should attempt to convince these students to take 110: Introduction To Computers next semester. You should ask for the student's name, address, major, year of graduation and favorite activity. You should build the answers to these questions into your form letter. By doing so, the program should generate output that is personalized for that particular person.

7. Write a program that will create a formatted version of a limerick for a friend. (A limerick is a five line poem in which the first, second and fifth lines end with matching rhymes and the second and third line end in another ryhme. A famous one starting with "There once was an old man from Nantucket.") The format is simple. The limerick should be double-spaced. (That is, place a blank line after every line of the limerick.) And, the second and third line of the limerick should be indented somewhat from the lefthand margin. (An inch or so would be good.) The other three lines should all start directly at the left of the page. Use READ/DATA. There should be five strings of DATA — one string for each line of the limerick. Make up your own limerick, borrow one from a book or ask your instructor to supply you with one. The program should start off by asking for a friend's name and then print a line dedicating the limerick to that friend — for instance, if you type in the name "Betsy", the output should say something like "This limerick is dedicated to Betsy."

8. Write a program that prints out a customized greeting card. Have the person using the program enter the name of the person the card should be addressed to and the date. Other input should include the name of the holiday or occasion and a saying. All this information should be placed on the card. Also, include other general wording on the card that is appropriate for any occasion — this should not be supplied as input by the user. Finally, include the cost of the card on the lower right corner. This cost should be obtained by using READ and DATA.

9. Write a program that produces a wedding invitation. Input should include the name of the bride, groom, time, date and location. Make the wording similar to what you would expect on a real invitation. One important consideration of this program is to make the output look attractive. You will want it planned well, so no matter what is entered as input, the invitation still looks fine.

Chapter 3

Assignment Statements

3.1 What We Already Know

Last time we learned about several different BASIC statements. There was: REM END INPUT READ DATA and PRINT.

REM and END were used for structural purposes.

PRINT is used to type output on the screen.

INPUT is used to give values to variables. This statement causes the program to ask a question of a user and then assigns the answer to that question to a variable.

READ/DATA were two statements that were used in conjuction in order to give variables some values. By using this method, variables can be given values without the program stopping to ask the user to supply the actual values.

So far we can assign a value to a variable and print it out. This does not allow for much flexibility. For instance, there is no way to combine values together in order to create new values. Most of the time, we want a program to calculate certain values. These calculations are dependent on certain input values but are not supplied as inputs themselves. Otherwise, if these values were already known, what would be the point of a program to calculate them?

3.2 The Assignment Statement

We will spend the rest of the chapter discussing assignment statements. In particular, we will be discussing assignment statements that do numerical calculations. That is, **math**.

SYNTAX
> **LET** *variable-name* $=$ *equation*
> NOTE: The equation is always on the right and the variable name on the left of the equal sign.

MEANING

Evaluate the equation. If that equation has any variables in it, the values for those variables must be looked up. These values are used. After the equation has been reduced down to one value, this value replaces the current value of the variable on the left-hand side of the equation.

EXAMPLES

```
LET   X=25
LET   Fruit$="banana"
LET   A=1
LET   B=2.5
LET   C=7
LET   X=A
LET   Z=1+4+5/25
LET   Avg = (A + B + C)/3
LET   Index = Index + 1
END
```

3.3   Simple Assignment

The simplest form of an assignment statement is when the equation is just a straight value.
Such as

```
LET X=25
```

When tracing this assignment, you would cross out the current value of x and replace it with a new value of 25. It is rather straightforward.

If you think about it, this is equivalent to using READ/DATA statements.

```
READ X
DATA 25
```

One time you might want to use a straight assignment is when you are initializing (or re-initializing) a variable. Initialization is when you give a variable a starting value. Such as :

```
LET HOURS=12
```

Some other examples of a simple assignment are:

```
LET   X=0
LET   Y=1
LET   Product=1
LET   Kount=0
END
```

So now you know there are at least three ways to give a value to a variable. First there is INPUT, then READ/DATA and finally straight assignment. (LET)

INPUT is used when you need to get the value from the person using the program.

READ/DATA is used when you have many variables or when you have values that might be changed very infrequently. This comes in very handy when you use arrays and loops.

Straight-assignment can be used when you want the program to supply the value (or figure it out). This is especially useful for initialization. It is also used when your program needs to give a value to one (or a few) variables. Finally, it can be used whenever the program must give a value to a variable and there is no conceivable reason you would want to change that value in future versions of your program.

3.4 Simple Assignment Statement Using a Right-hand Variable

```
LET X=10
LET Y=X
```

Here, in the second line, we see that x gets assigned to y. Does that mean that the value of y becomes the letter x? NO! Rather, you have to look up the value of variable x and assign this value to y. Thus if you trace this program, both x and y will end up with the value 10.

By the way, when tracing a program it is important to take the lines one at a time, in order. So in this example you would first do everything on line 1. This means X gets the value 10. Then after this is done you can move on to line 2. Then y gets the value 10. When tracing programs, it is important to work on small pieces at a time. Often people screw up because they don't take the tracing task one step at a time but rather try to do a lot of things at once. This is a major mistake. Train yourself to do these small tasks one at a time.

Ok, if this all seems easy, then what does the following program print?

```
LET X=10
LET Y=X
LET X=20
PRINT Y
END
```

It does seem rather easy right? I mean, after all, it looks like the second statement makes the computer know that X and Y are the same. So later when X becomes 20, you know Y does, and so in that last statement, when Y is printed a nice big 20 gets placed on the screen? Right? What could be more simple?

WRONG! WRONG! WRONG! WRONG! WRONG! WRONG! WRONG! WRONG!

The problem is, you are thinking too much like a person. People can see the overall program at one time and thus they can see TOO much. A computer sees and uses one line at a time. You have to do what a computer does. Trace it carefully and see what happens. In line 1, X gets the value 10. In line 2, Y gets the value 10 – that is it copies the value that X currently has. Are you really tracing this? You know, make your columns, put the current value under the variable names. Like:

```
X    Y
--   --
10   10
```

And so what happens in line 3. Well, X gets the value 20, so our tracing looks like:

```
X        Y
--       --
-**-     10
20
```

(Sorry for the funny way I cross out the 10 under the X, but I think you know what I mean). Now the fourth line says PRINT Y, so we do and what gets printed out? Look up the current value of Y, it is 10 — so on the screen 10 would get printed out. **20 is not printed out, 10 is!**

3.5   Mathematical Operations

Ok, so now, how do you "combine" values in calculations in order to form new values? This, as I have said before, is often one of the main chores of a program. The way to do it is to use mathematical operations in order to create equations for the right hand side of an assignment statement.

What mathematical operations are available?

- Addition is represented by +

- Subtraction by −

- Multiplication by *

- Division by /

- Exponentiation by ^

- Grouping by ()

Great, so now you can create all kinds of equations such as:

```
LET X=A+B+C
LET The_Ans=(Zzz+45)/97 * 2^3 - 51*X
```

But, when it comes time to tracing that program, how do you calculate what value that equation gives? Follow these steps:

1. Look up all variables in an equation and replace their name with their value.

2. Always do mini-equations inside of parentheses first.

Inside mini-equations or the whole equation:

3. Do all exponentiation first. Calculate the result of raising the particular number to a power and replace this part of the equation by the calculated value.

4. Do all multiplication and division next, starting from the left hand side of the equation.

5. Do all addition and subtraction from left to right.

6. Assign the calculated value to the variable on the left hand side of the equal sign.

Thus here is a reduction of the following complicated equation:

```
LET A=3
LET B=10
LET C=15
LET D=20
LET Result = (A^2 - 8)*B + D/5 - 15
PRINT Result
END
```

Tracing the equation goes as follows:

```
result= (a^2 - 8)*b + d/5 - 15
result= (3^2 - 8)*10 + 20/5 - 15
result= (9 - 8)*10 + 20/5 - 15
result= (1)*10 + 20/5 - 15
result= 10 + 4 - 15
result= -1
```

Now, some of you may look at this and scream: "Too much nonsense math for me – this rots!" (To put it sweetly!) And, in a way you are right. In a lot of programming examples, such as the one above, we get far too abstract and lose total contact with the "real world". I am going to try to stay somewhat connected to the world throughout this book and use some semi-realistic examples to keep you interested. However, I reckon that I really should stress the prefix "semi" here. I frequently will have to stretch things to serve various pedagogical purposes. (I am but a teacher first, a human being a distant second.)

Unfortunately, it is hard to come up with a real world example that uses exponentiation. Like we all really walk around all day exclaiming "Hmmmmm, two to the power of four is sixteen — how utterly useful!" Nevertheless, here is my attempt to be semi-realistic. Now, stay cool okay. The equation we will finally end up with may seem rather convoluted — but in reality it is rather straightforward. Yes, you are going to have to remember a few infantile geometry equations — but please, don't allow this to cause you to turn to my computer graphics caricature at the front of this book hissing obscenities and slashing out with your penknife. Enuf said.

Ok, so imagine you are an architect and an eccentric client comes to you asks for the following: "I need a home with three small rectangular rooms (bedrooms) of exactly the same dimensions and two more larger rectangular rooms — again, these two should be of the same dimensions. As its one unique feature, the house should have a nearly circular livingroom. Though, a rectangular notch should be cut out of this room in order to take away from the monotony of a perfectly symmetrical room. I don't care about the cost, but I do want the work completed as quickly as possible so please design some homes and get back to me as to how long it will take to complete the construction." As an architect, you know that the construction of a rectangular room takes about .25 hours per square foot. Specially shaped rooms take .55 per square feet. You of course know that the area of a rectangular room is its length times width. A circular room's area can be calculated from its radius using the equation πr^2; though you will have to subtract out the rectangular notch from the area of the special room in this house. You decide to write a program to calculate the estimated construction time of a house of the above-mentioned design. This program should ask for the chosen dimensions of rooms, and then print out the estimated time for construction. The first part of the program was easy for you to write and so it is not given here. It merely involved some input statements to get the size of the small room (LenSR and WidSR), the large room (LenLR, WidLR), the diameter of the livingroom (Diam) and the size of the notch (LenNot WidNot). And now you must decide upon the calculation section of the program. The following is your very insightful code to calculate the necessary values.

```
LET PI = 3.141
LET Smallarea = LenSR * WidSR
LET Largearea = LenLR * WidLR
LET CircleArea = PI*(Diam/2)^2
LET NotchArea = LenNot * WidNot
LET AreaOfAllSmallRooms = 3 * Smallarea
LET AreaOfAllLargeRooms = 2 * Largearea
LET AreaOfRectRooms = AreaOfAllSmallRooms + AreaOfAllLargeRooms
LET AreaOfSpecialRoom = CircleArea - NotchArea
LET ConstructionTime = .25*AreaOfRectRooms + .55*AreaOfSpecialRoom
```

This is pretty good. It certainly should be fairly easy to read and understand. You might want to note that the circle's area was based on the radius, not the diameter, that is why we divided the diameter by 2. Also, note that the area of the special room was decided by subtracting the area of the notch from this circle area. The rest should be very straightforward. Of course, we did introduce a number of temporary variables, like AreaOfRectRooms and NotchArea, to help us construct an answer. Some people, may complain about all these extra variables we created and the number of statements it took to arrive at the final answer. I will not condemn this practice. If you are the type of person who prefers to do things in small steps — keeping each step easy — then this is how you should attack this problem. Let me just show you a couple of other ways this problem could have been attacked. Look at this:

```
LET PI = 3.141
LET Area = LenSR * WidSR            !Area of one small room
LET Time = .25 * 3 * Area           !Time to make all small rooms
LET Area = LenLR * WidLR            !Area of big rooms
LET Time = Time + .25 * 2 * Area    !Add on time to make big rooms
LET Area = PI*(diam/2)^2 - LenNot * WidNot  !Area of special room
LET Time = Time + .55*Area          !Add on time to make special room
```

The general idea with this method was to figure out the area for one type of room, then accumulate on to a total the amount of time to make all rooms of that type. In particular, notice that the second and third equation in which Time is calculated adds on to the amount that previously was calculated for Time. (That is, read the last equation as follows "The final amount of time needed is equal to the amount of time we already calculated plus the amount of time needed to make the special room".) Accumulating some total is a method that is used a lot while programming.

Also notice that the variable Area is used with three slightly different meanings. First it means "the area of one small room", then "the area of one big room" and finally "the area of the special room". As these lines are executed, each new value for Area will wipe out the previous value — which will be lost forever. Thus, we must use an old value of Area before we replace it with a new value. So, for instance, we use the area of the small room to calculate the time before we replace this area with the area of the big room. Any time while programming that you have used a particular value of the variable for the last time (you know you don't need it any more) you can then reuse that same variable for ANY other desired purpose. That is, technically you can do this. However, it is not recommended to use the same variable name later in a program for a totally different purpose. It makes it too hard to read and understand the program. Here we have only slightly changed the meaning of the variable — at least it still is an area we are working with. If this variable was called X instead of Area — then what we wouldn't want to do is use X again way later in the program to calculation something like "cost". This would probably be too confusing.

This version would calculate the exact same answer as the first version. Do I like this version of the code better? Well, I won't comment on that. One version is very slow and understandable — the other version uses less lines but might be less clear for some people. I suggest you use whichever method you feel most comfortable with. There are further improvements that could be made to this second version. For instance, instead of using Area three different times, why not use the same statements, but use SmallArea first, then BigArea the second time and finally SpecialArea the last time. This might be easier to read. It is up to you however — though the TAs who are grading may encourage you to do things in "better" ways.

As a final version, this whole calculation could be done at once. For instance:

```
LET Time = .25 * (3*LenSR*WidSR + 2*LenLR*WidLR) + .55 * (3.141*(diam/2)^2 - WidNot*LenNot)
```

If you followed the previous version, you can pretty quickly see that this version is correct. But then again, if this was how I started off this example — this particular equation would probably — well let us say "disturb" you. Well what do I think of this? I wouldn't recommend doing everything in one line, unless you are very sure of the equation. It is too easy to make some silly mistake, like missing parentheses, when you try to do everything at once. It is also harder for people reading the program to understand what is going on.

However, do you believe the whole reason of me doing this example was to come up with some lengthy equation like this that seems to have some meaning behind it (again I stress "Semi"-realistic) as opposed to that first example I gave you which seemed like I pulled it from a hat.

Anyway, let us use this example to trace a complicated equation and make sure you can grasp the order of mathematical operations involved. Assume that previously in the program we got the information that LenSR=12, WidSR=10, LenLR=16, WidLR=14, Diam=20, LenNot=4, WidNot=4. Now let us trace this one-liner.

1. The original statement is.

   ```
   LET Time = .25 * (3*LenSR*WidSR + 2*LenLR*WidLR) + .55 * (3.141*(diam/2)^2 - WidNot*LenNot)
   ```

2. Replace variable names by their values.

   ```
   LET Time = .25 * (3*12*10 + 2*16*14) + .55 * (3.141*(20/2)^2 - 4*4)
   ```

3. There are two mini-equations here. Let us work on the first one. It has only multiplication and addition it. Multiplication comes before the addition.

   ```
   LET Time = .25 * (360 + 448) + .55 * (3.141*(20/2)^2 - 4*4)
   ```

4. Now the addition in this mini-equation.

   ```
   LET Time = .25 * (808) + .55 * (3.141*(20/2)^2 - 4*4)
   ```

5. Now let us work on the second mini-equation 3.141*(20/2)^2 - 4*4. There is a small mini-equation 20/2 inside of this equation, so let us do this first.

   ```
   LET Time = .25 * 808 + .55 * (3.141*(10)^2 - 4*4)
   ```

6. Now this second mini-equation has exponentiation, multiplication and subtraction it. Exponentiation first.

   ```
   LET Time = .25 * 808 + .55 * (3.141*100 - 4*4)
   ```

7. Now multiplication in this mini-equation.

   ```
   LET Time = .25 * 808 + .55 * (314.1 - 16)
   ```

8. And the subtraction here

   ```
   LET Time = .25 * 808 + .55 * (298.1)
   ```

9. No more mini-equations. Only multiplication and addition left. Multiply first.

   ```
   LET Time = 202 +   163.955
   ```

10. A simple addition left.

   ```
   LET Time = 365.955
   ```

So the computer would calculate that it would take about 366 hours to build this house.

I'd suggest that you jot down the original statement and the variables' values and try tracing this yourself without looking at the book. If you can get the same answer, you understand this material.

3.6   Incrementing and similar operations

Often you will be using a variable that keeps track of some value where each time this variable is changed, the new value depends on the old value. For instance, maybe you are writing a game to play backgammon and you want to keep track of the current value of the doubling cube. Whenever you "double", you need to know the current value of the cube and then multiply it by two. This means you end up with an assignment statement that has the variable on both sides. Things are no longer like algebra....

LET Cube=Cube*2

This may look illegal as far as algebra goes (unless CUBE = 0) but there is no problem if you remember how BASIC works. Just solve the equation on the right hand side and once you get a value, place this value in the variable on the left hand side. You can read this equation as "The new cube is equal to the old cube times two". Notice how I use the phrases "new" and "old" to show that cube has two separate values; one before the statement takes place and a new one afterwards.

This is used in many cases. For instance, if you are keeping track of the total amount of something. You will have to have a variable to hold the current total and then when you find out some new value that must be added to the total, you can update the total. Like this, for instance:

LET Total = Total + New

Another task you will be doing a lot is adding one to a variable. This is called **incrementing**. For instance, if you are keeping a count of something, you might have the following line in your program:

LET Kount=Kount + 1

In all these examples, a particular variable is on both the left and right hand sides of an equation. Ok people. So you get the general idea by now.

3.7   Writing A Program

Suppose you want to write a program that calculates gas mileage for your car for two months. (Let's say January and February). You want the program to print out the miles traveled, gas used for each month and then the gas mileage (miles per gallon). At the end of the program you want the total miles traveled, total gallons of gas used and total gas mileage for the two months to print out. How can you write this program?

You really can handle this problem, and many other problems, in three steps. First work on handling the input, then handle the calculations that have to be made and finally handle the output. Part of this process will involve picking variables in which to store our various values. Another part of this process will involve deciding what BASIC statements we want to use.

So what about the input? Well, for this program we have to supply at least 4 separate pieces of information: miles traveled in January, miles traveled in February, gas used in January and finally gas used in February. When working on a program it is a good idea to at least know in your mind, if not written down on a piece of paper, the variable names you are going to use and their precise meaning. For this program we could have.

variable name	meaning
Miles_Jan	distance traveled in January (miles)
Miles_Feb	distance traveled in February (miles)
Gas_Jan	gas used in January (gallons)
Gas_Feb	gas used in February (gallons)

Ok, and what values are going to be calculated? Well, we are going to have to calculate the mileage for January and February. Also we are going to have to calculate the total miles traveled, the total gas used and the total overall gas mileage. Thus

variable name	meaning
Mpg_Jan	gas mileage (miles per gallon) for January
Mpg_Feb	gas mileage (miles per gallon) for February
Tot_Miles	total miles traveled in the two months
Tot_Gas	total gas used in the two months
Overall_Mpg	the overall gas mileage for the two months

A further problem when worrying about the calculation sections is to decide how to calculate these values.

Mpg_Jan equals miles traveled in Jan divided by gallons used in January. Look up what variables will be holding these values and rewrite the English equation above and you get:

    Mpg_Jan = Miles_Jan / Gas_Jan

Likewise

    Mpg_Feb = Miles_Feb / Gas_Feb

Tot_Miles equals miles traveled in January plus miles traveled in February .... that is

    Tot_Miles = Miles_Jan + Miles_Feb

and likewise

    Tot_Gas = Gas_Jan + Gas_Feb

Overall_Mpg is the total miles traveled divided by the total gas used or

    Overall_Mpg = Tot_Miles / Tot_Gas

Notice how for that last equation we relied on previously calculated variables rather than inputed values. Another thing to keep in mind is that you must stay with the variable names all thru the program. Don't try to change a variable name half way through the program. **This is a very common error. Switching to a different variable name for a particular meaning often causes problems. If you so much as add an extra character to your variable name, things will get screwed up.**

Now when thinking about output, decide what you want it to look like. Often the programming problem as stated will tell you exactly what values need to be printed out. It isn't enough to just print out values (numbers) though. For the person using the program it is important to "label" your values. That is, the program should print out some meaningful statements, not just a lot of numbers. In this course, you MUST do this always in your programs. Otherwise points will be taken off. For this particular program some reasonable output might look like:

    You traveled 400 miles in January on 40 gallons of gas.
    Your gas mileage in January was 10 miles per gallon.
    You traveled 260 miles in February on 13 gallons of gas.
    Your gas mileage in February was 20 miles per gallon.
    In the two months together you traveled 660 miles on 53 gallons.
    Your overall gas mileage was 12.45 mpg.

The numbers used here are just a sample. The program should work for any set of numbers that are supplied as input.

Now that you have all the pieces that you are going to work with, you can start writing the program. For our first attempt let's use assignment statements and actually build the values into the program. Don't forget your END statements at the end of the program.

```
REM A basic program to demonstrate assignment statements.

REM Initialize
LET Miles_Jan = 400
LET Miles_Feb = 260
LET Gas_Jan = 40
LET Gas_Feb = 13

REM Calculations
LET  Mpg_Jan = Miles_Jan / Gas_Jan
LET  Mpg_Feb = Miles_Feb / Gas_Feb
LET  Tot_Miles = Miles_Jan + Miles_Feb
LET  Tot_Gas = Gas_Jan + Gas_Feb
LET  Overall_Mpg = Tot_Miles / Tot_Gas

REM Output
PRINT "You traveled ";Miles_Jan;" miles in January on ";Gas_Jan ;
PRINT " gallons of gas."
PRINT "Your gas mileage in January was ";Mpg_Jan;" miles per gallon."
PRINT "You traveled ";Miles_Feb;" miles in February on ";Gas_Feb;
PRINT " gallons of gas."
PRINT "Your gas mileage in February was ";Mpg_Feb;" miles per gallon."
PRINT "In the two months together you traveled ";
PRINT  Tot_Miles;" miles on ";Tot_Gas;" gallons."
PRINT "Your overall gas mileage was ";Overall_Mpg ;" mpg."

END
```

And that is all there is to it. This program follows pretty easily from the discussion we had before we attempted the program. We really should modify this program to make it more flexible. The way the program currently stands, we have to change the program itself to get it to work on other numbers. To do this we would edit the program and modify the initialization section. It would work. However, why not use a different method to get the "initial" values for the variables? In fact, why not use several INPUT PROMPT statements? This way, we could keep running the program and every time we did, we could supply it with different numbers.

Thus, the lines in the initialization section could be replaced by an INPUT section. (Instead of the LET statements.)

```
REM Input Section - Ask the User for the necessary values.
INPUT  PROMPT "How many miles did you travel in January?":Miles_Jan
INPUT  PROMPT "How much gas did you use for January?":Gas_Jan
INPUT  PROMPT "How many miles did you travel in February?":Miles_Feb
INPUT  PROMPT "How much gas did you use in February?":Gas_Feb
```

Now the program will stop and ask these questions at the beginning of an execution. After we supply the four answers, it will then move into the calculation section and finally the output section. Since both of these sections are unchanged, the output generated will be the same (provided we supply the same numbers that appeared in the LET statements before.)

So, now you see how to write a program. Are you ready for your own programs now?

Have fun,

-Jt

3.8 Problems

Syntax Errors

1.

```
INPUT PROMPT "How many do you have?":Count
INPUT PROMPT "How many do you want?":Want
LET Want - Count = Missing
PRINT "You need ";Missing;" more."
END
```

2.

```
INPUT PROMPT "What is the capacity?":TopSize
READ CurrentSize
DATA 47
LET PercentEmpty = ( (TopSize - CurrentSize) / TopSize * 100
PRINT "There is still ";PercentEmpty;" percent left."
END
```

3.

```
READ ANumber
DATA 10
PRINT "This number is:";ANumber
ANumber = Anumber + 10
PRINT "Ten more is ";ANumber
ANumber = Anumber * 2
PRINT "And twice this is ";ANumber
END
```

Tracing

1.

```
READ X,Y,Z
DATA 10,20,30
LET X=Y+Z
PRINT Z,Y,X
LET X=Z+Y
PRINT Z,Y,X
LET Answer=X/5 * (Z-Y)
PRINT Answer
END
```

2. The input to this program is: 3

```
INPUT PROMPT "What is the power?":P
DATA 10,15
READ A,B
LET C = A^(P-1)-B
LET Result = (A + C / 5 - 2 ^ P) * ( (B - A) / 5 + P /  P)
PRINT Result
END
```

3.

```
LET Sum = 1 + 2 + 3 + 4 + 5
LET Sum = 10 + 3 ^ 2 * 3 + 2
LET Sum = Sum + 1
PRINT Sum, Sum * 2, Sum
END
```

Programs

1. Quatra is a country that consists of four separate regions. Two in the North are called Highland and Edgementon. In the South is Botolonia and Fludplain. Quatra is holding an election to find out who should be the leader of the country. There are two candidates: Big Jen is a supreme court justice who also happens to have a Nobel Prize in Physics and be the holder of the world record in the mile. Squeaky Otis is her opponent. Write a program that asks for the total population of the country and the number of males and females that voted for each candidate in each of the regions. (That is, there are 8 voting tallies.) The program should print out the total number of votes each candidate received so we can tell who won the election. Then the program should calculate and print some statistics. In particular, how many male votes did each candidate get? How many female votes? How many votes from North regions were there for each candidate? And, how many from South regions? Finally, the percentage of the population that actually voted should be calculated and displayed.

2. A new state law has gone into effect protecting certain animals kept in zoos. In particular, due to extreme weather during the winters, it has been decided that gloves, boots and hats should be purchased for these animals to keep them warm. The animals protected are as follows: elephants, who need 4 boots and one hat; centipedes who need 100 boots and 2 hats (one for each end); egrets who need two boots and one hat; octopuses who need 8 gloves and 1 hat; and finally monkeys which need 2 gloves, 2 boots and one hat. Currently gloves cost $7 a piece, boots $27 and hats $8. (Build these numbers into the program so they can be easily changed in case prices vary in the future.) Write a program to ask how much a zoo has earmarked for clothing and how many elephants, centipedes, egrets, octopuses and monkeys live there. Calculate the amount of money left in the clothing fund after all these animals are supplied with their winter outfits. (If this number comes out negative, then we will know the zoo must close down for lack of funds.)

3. Recreation World hires many students as summer workers. This amusement park is open for 200 days a year. These students are paid an hourly wage. The number of workers at any particular time is kept at a constant value. There are a certain amount of clowns, clean-up workers, ride operators, ticket sellers and food vendors. Write a program that tells how much money is needed to pay these workers for a year. The program should ask how many of each type of worker there are working at a given time and what their hourly pay should be. The program will also need to ask how many hours the park plans to be open during the day.

4. Write a program to help out in a bowling league. In this league bowlers play each other in head to head competition. Each week, they play two games against a new opponent. Each bowler has a handicap determined from subtracting his/her average from 300 points. (Thus, if a bowler has an average of 175, the handicap for this person is 125.) The winner of a game is determined by adding the handicaps to the raw scores and comparing these new adjusted numbers. The winner is the person with the largest adjusted score. Your program should ask what numbered week this is in the tournament. Then it should ask for each of two bowler's names and averages. Finally, it should ask for the scores that each of these bowlers got in the games they played. For both games, the program should determine and print the adjusted scores (with handicap) for both players. Then the program should display the new average for each bowler. From the information provided above, the new average can easily be calculated. (Hint: think about it. Let us say a bowler had an average of 150 in the prior 12 weeks of bowling. This week he bowled 175 and 187. Then prior to this week this bowler had knocked down 150*24 pins or a total of 3600. Adding this week on you get 3962. Divide this by the number of games the bowler has now played — 26. This gives you a new average of 152.38.)

5. Write a program to calculate the yearly tuition for students at a major university. This university has two different colleges. In order to determine how much the university should receive in tuition money, the program will total up the expenses for the university and then subtract any funds that will be used to pay these expenses. The left over amount will have to be supplied through tuition payments. Getting more detailed, the program will need to know how many students are enrolled in this university. Then, for each college, the program should ask for the cost of the faculty salaries and the cost for the staff salaries. As a third expense, the yearly operational cost (telephone bills, heating etc) of each college should be requested. A fourth consideration is the yearly cost for supplies (everything from chalk and books to testtubes and tables). Besides these expenses for the two colleges, the university also has one overall amount that it plans to earmark for research — the program should ask for this figure also. After asking about the expenses, the program should get the amount in endowments the univerisity will be receiving from outside sources (grants are one example). The program should print several results including the overall costs for each college, the total amount of expenses for the whole university and finally the yearly tuition cost that each student should pay in order for the college to break even.

6. Mark VandeWettering has just purchased a fancy automobile. He is new to NJ and needs some help in budgeting his expenses. Help him determine how much he should set aside each month to pay for his car. The program should have him enter the three main monthly expenses he can expect to pay. These includes his car loan, repair/maintenance costs and finally car necessities (fuzzy dice, maps and jumper cables). He should be asked to enter what he plans to spend weekly on gas (assume four weeks per month). Finally, have the program ask him to enter his yearly car insurance payment. Don't forget that all cars must pay a yearly registration fee. Build this number ($85) into the program instead of asking Mark to supply it — but make it easy to change this number in case it changes in future years. Have the program print out how much Mark should budget for each month — make sure you convert all non-monthly amounts into monthly amounts before you attempt to determine this total. Besides printing this value, the program should give Mark some advice on whether or not he should continue to live in this state.

7. A general store deep in the heart of Oregon only sells three items: rice, corn and jelly beans. It buys these items in bulk. Write a program to calculate how much money this store makes from one customer. The store buys a certain amount of each product for a certain price. (For instance, it may get 400 pounds of rice for $700.) Use READ/DATA to find out how many pounds of each item the store purchased and what total price it paid for each of these products. From this information, the program should calculate the unit cost for each product. To make a profit, the store multiplies the unit cost by the factor 1.73 to get the unit price. Your program should also calculate this unit price. Now the program can deal with the customer. For each product, the program should tell the customer what the sales item is and print out the unit price for that item. It should then ask the customer how many pounds of that item s/he wants to buy. From this information the program should notify the customer how much the bill is. As a final task, the program should calculate and print how much money the store made in profit from this customer. (Do this program one small step at a time and you will find out it is not very difficult.)

8. Write a program that allows you to type in how many calories you had for breakfast, lunch, dinner and snacks and lists how many minutes of aerobics you should do to burn off the extra calories in order to maintain your weight. Also list how many minutes of biking, swimming or hiking you can do instead to burn off those same calories. Here are some numbers you can use. A person of moderate activity will maintain their weight if they eat 15 calories for every pound they weigh. Anything above this is extra calories. These can be burned off at a rate of 4.5 a minute when biking, 5.6 a minute when doing aerobics, 6.6 a minute when hiking and 7.9 a minute when swimming. Only worry about entering data such that your total caloric intake is excessive – more than enough to maintain your weight. (Example: a person who weighs 150 pounds can maintain his weight with 2250 calories. However if he eats 600,800,1000, and 250 calories for breakfast, lunch, dinner and snacks respectively, he ends up with 400 extra calories which he can burn off from about 89 minutes of biking or 71 minutes of aerobics or 61 minutes of hiking or 51 minutes of swimming.)

9. Write a program that helps you calculate how much money you earned from investing your money in three different mutual funds. For each fund the program needs to ask how much you initially invested in it and from this it will subtract a three percent commission and then calculate how many shares you purchased from the remainder given the initial buying price per share. (That is, let us say a share costs $10 and you invest $1000. After the commission — .03*1000 = $30 — you are left with $970 which buys you 97 shares.) Then for each type of mutual fund the program should ask what its final selling price was, calculate how much you got back from the fund, and what your capital gain was. (Continuing this example, let us say the share later sold for $15. Your 97 shares would bring you $1455 for a gain of $455.) To complicate matters, you have to pay the government a 40% capital gains tax on the money your investment earned you. (Here: 455*.4 = $182) From this the program will tell you how much your investment actually placed in your pocket – that is the money you earned when you sold the shares minus your initial investment and the taxes you paid. (In our example:1455-1000-182 = $273.) Your program merely has to print the total earned after taxes from all three mutual funds combined. The input is how much you invested in each fund and for each fund, the beginning buying price, along with the final selling price. Although not necessarily true in real life, you can assume the final selling price is larger than the original buying price.

Special Chapter 1

The mixture of students in this course is rather diverse. Because of this, it is hard to write a book that is useful and interesting for all people. In particular, people who have never written programs before may feel a special need to see a whole program written from scratch, seeing how each decision is made, in order to help them design their own programs. For this reason, I am including several "special" chapters in this book. These chapters will contain no new material (hopefully) and can be skipped by people who feel the regular chapters were adequate enough for them to grasp the subject matter. I intend for these special chapters to be short, but thorough, explanations of writing particular programs. I hope that these chapters will be used by people who feel they need some extra help writing programs.

It is probably too early to include a special chapter here. After all, in the last couple of chapters I have been fairly thorough in explaining the necessary steps needed to create the programs I have presented. Still, some people might like to see another example at this time. Furthermore, this chapter will present you with an introduction to the nature of these special chapters. You'll be able to judge for yourself how helpful these special sections will be for your purposes.

The Movie Theatre Ripoff Probe Program

Movies Galore is one of those converted movie theatres. Back in the good ol' days, it used to be quite fancy, with balconies and comfortable seats. Movies used to cost a nickle and you even got to hear live music from an accompanying piano player. It was quite pleasant to watch a movie. The popcorn was edible — even tasty, the audience was rather civilized. It wasn't like nowadays where your fellow movie-goers all seem to have learned their movie-watching techniques at the Rocky Horror Show Academy Of Cinema Audience Etiquette. Movies Galore has since been split into three theatres, one of which has a screen which is skewed off to the lefthand side of the room, so that the necessary fire door could be squeezed in along side of it. Samuel Droneon the manager of Movies Galore is an elementary school science teacher by day. Lately, he has noticed that the customers of his theatre have been rather ill-behaved. From the historical perspective presented here, we are not at all surprised. But he was not about to put up with it. In particular, he suspected that customers were sneaking into the theatre through the fire doors, or using the bathrooms between shows to upgrade their single ticket purchase into double-feature opportunities. Rowdy crowds he could tolerate, after all he didn't watch the movies with the hordes but rather would view the movies with his close associates at special private previews he could arrange when he so desired — so if they wanted to be disrupted, what did he care. But a loss of profit was unacceptable. He has decided to use the powers of modern day computers to calculate the extent of the free-movie problems. Of course, he has hired the cheapest programmer possible to help him with his problem. You! A former 110 student.

The situation is this. Each day he can easily note his daily ticket income since his cash registers calculate this for him. He wants to check to see how his receipts compare to the number of people watching the movies. There are three theatres. Absolutely no one can get into a movie for free — not even the workers there — all must pay full-price for the movie. There is one matinee showing in each theatre each day. Two of the theatres have two regular showings of older movies. The other theatre shows this week's most popular movie. All matinees cost $3.00. The regular showings of the older movies cost $5.50. For the "feature" movie, the theatre has the audacity to charge $7.50 per person. Mr. Droneon has opted to close and lock all doors to each theatre once a movie starts (what is the chance of a fire anyway huh?) and send in his most trusted employee Shirly Turtleneck to count the number of viewers seated in each theatre — which she will rigorously double check. From this information, Droneon wants a program that can calculate how many people attended matinees, how many attended regular shows and how many saw the feature that day. But most importantly, he wants to know how much money he lost that day from people sneaking into shows they have not paid for.

So how can we go about calculating this? Actually, the program is rather straightforward. Let us give it a stab.

First off, what information will be given to the program? There is the amount of money the ticket registers tallied that day, the number of people who attended matinees in each theatre, the number of people who attended each showing of the regular movies and finally the number of people who attended the two showings of the feature movie.

So let us pick some variable names.

```
Days_Receipts         The amount of money taken in at the ticket registers.
Matinee1              The number of people who were seated in the first matinee.
Matinee2              The number of people who were seated in the second matinee.
Matinee3              The number of people who were seated in the third matinee.
Theatre1Show1         The number of people sitting in theatre one for showing one.
Theatre1Show2         The number of people sitting in theatre one for showing two.
Theatre2Show1         The number of people sitting in theatre two for showing one.
Theatre2Show2         The number of people sitting in theatre two for showing two.
Feature1              The number of people who saw the first showing of the feature.
Feature2              The number of people who saw the second showing of the feature.
```

All these values should be gotten from INPUT statements.

We also know of some constants that have been built into the program. To see a matinee costs $3.00, a regular show $5.50 and a feature $7.50. These values can either be built directly into the program, or you can anticipate that some day this program might have to be reused with different ticket prices. This being the case, you may want to make these prices variables, and set them to their current value early in the program. Let us do this. We will call the variables:

```
Matinee_Cost          Cost to get in the matinee
Regular_Cost          Cost to see a regular show
Feature_Cost          Cost to see a feature movie
```

For output, we know that the count of people who saw matinees, regular shows and the feature should be printed. And, the amount of money lost by the theatre. These variables might be called:

```
Matinee_Crowd         Number of people that saw any matinee
Regular_Crowd         Number of people who saw a regular movie
Feature_Crowd         Number of people who saw a feature
Daily_Loss            The amount of money lost that day from movie sneaks.
```

Though, these might not be necessary, you may want to calculate some temporary values that are not going to be printed but may come in handy. These values will be calculated from the input variables and used to generate the outputed results. In particular, you may want to calculate the total amount of money that should have been made from each type of movie showing (Matinee, Regular and Feature) and the grand total that should have been made based on the audience count. Such variables might be:

```
ExpectedMatineeIncome   Amount of money that should have been made in matinees.
ExpectedRegularIncome   Amount of money that should have been made in reg. shows.
ExpectedFeatureIncome   Amount of money that should have been made in features.
ExpectedIncome          Total amount of money expected based on audience count.
```

And now we see most of the variables we might want to use. Let us see how all these temporary values can be calculated, and finally, how the output values might be calculated. The equations might be:

```
*Matinee_Crowd = Matinee1 + Matinee2 + Matinee3
*Regular_Crowd = Theatre1Show1 + Theatre1Show2 + Theatre2Show1 + Theatre2Show2
*Feature_Crowd = Feature1 + Feature2
ExpectedMatineeIncome =  Matinee_Crowd * Matinee_Cost
ExpectedRegularIncome =  Regular_Crowd * Regular_Cost
ExpectedFeatureIncome =  Feature_Crowd * Feature_Cost
ExpectedIncome = ExpectedMatineeIncome + ExpectedRegularIncome + ExpectedFeatureIncome
Daily_Loss = ExpectedIncome - Days_Reciepts
```

When writing the actual program, you will have to notice that there are some constraints on the actual ordering that must be used here. The starred statements (*) only refer to variables that have been input in the righthand side equations. This means two things. These equations CAN NOT be calculated until those values are input. Secondly, as soon as those values are supplied then immediately it becomes possible to calculate these new values. (Though, this doesn't mean you must calculate them immediately, only that you can if you want.)

The various expected incomes refer to the different crowd amounts in the righthand side equations. Therefore, you can not calculate these various incomes until those crowd figures are arrived at. This means you must calculate the crowds first, and then the expected income. But even with this constraint, you still have a little flexibility as to how these six statements are ordered. You can, for instance, calculate the crowd size for matinees and then immediately calculate the expected income for matinees before going on to the crowd size for regular shows and features, OR alternatively, you can calculate all crowd sizes first (in any order) and then calculate all expected income (in any order for those three statements also).

The overall expected income (that is, the variable ExpectedIncome itself) depends on the three other expected incomes, so it can not be calculated until those other three are. Finally, the Daily_Loss can not be calculated except as the very last equation. This may seem odd at first, since it uses Days_Receipts which you get right away from the input — so you might think you could calulate Daily_loss quickly. However, Daily_Loss also uses ExpectedIncome so we must wait until this is calculated — and we already said that this must come after all the abovementioned equations. That means, the Daily_Loss equations must be the very last one.

This discussion on the ordering might seem pointless. Especially since the order I immediately used is perfectly okay. We'll use this one in our program. I only go into such detail here to let you know that other orders are possible. You should see if from what I have discussed here you can find a different ordering that will also work and give the correct answer.

Even though I discussed input and output variables first, I ultimately jumped right into the calculation section without really finishing off the whole input and output section of the code. As I have stressed before, you may feel more confortable working on these easy sections of the code before you move on to the harder sections — here the calculations.

I am not going to discuss the making of all of the input and output sections here — as this is way too much detail.

The general idea for these sections is as follows.

For each value that needs to be supplied as input (see our input variables), you must decide what question to ask the user to get these values. Questions like "How much money did the cash register record today?" and "How many people saw the showing of the matinee in theatre 1?" are good here. Then to finish the input section, you need to only attach each of these questions to the correct input variable in properly formed INPUT PROMPT statements. The output is similar. For each variable that must be printed out as a result (output variable), you must decide how you are going to present that value on the screen (that is, how do you label it). Statements like "The number of people who saw matinees today is " and "The theatre lost —- dollars today from sneaks" are appropriate here. Then you create the PRINT statements by making sure the strings you have picked for labels are in quotes and any values for output variables are not in quotes and are separated in the print list by commas or semicolons from the previous item in the list. You can also decide if any titles, column headers or final messages are going to be displayed by the program.

    With all this presented, now we can see the whole program. Here is one based on what we have so far designed above.

```
REM Jt
REM July 1990
REM Another new program for the fall
REM The Theatre Ripoff Probe Program

READ Matinee_Cost, Regular_Cost, Feature_Cost
DATA 3,5.5,7.5

INPUT PROMPT "How much money did the cash register record today?":Days_Receipts
INPUT PROMPT "How many people saw the showing of the matinee in theatre 1?":Matinee1
INPUT PROMPT "How many people saw the showing of the matinee in theatre 2?":Matinee2
INPUT PROMPT "How many people saw the showing of the matinee in theatre 3?":Matinee3
INPUT PROMPT "How many people saw show 1 in theatre 1?":Theatre1Show1
INPUT PROMPT "How many people saw show 2 in theatre 1?":Theatre1Show2
INPUT PROMPT "How many people saw show 1 in theatre 2?":Theatre2Show1
INPUT PROMPT "How many people saw show 2 in theatre 2?":Theatre2Show2
INPUT PROMPT "How many people saw the first showing of the feature?":Feature1
INPUT PROMPT "How many people saw the second showing of the feature?":Feature2

LET Matinee_Crowd = Matinee1 + Matinee2 + Matinee3
LET Regular_Crowd = Theatre1Show1 + Theatre1Show2 + Theatre2Show1 + Theatre2Show2
LET Feature_Crowd = Feature1 + Feature2
LET ExpectedMatineeIncome =  Matinee_Crowd * Matinee_Cost
LET ExpectedRegularIncome =  Regular_Crowd * Regular_Cost
LET ExpectedFeatureIncome =  Feature_Crowd * Feature_Cost
LET ExpectedIncome = ExpectedMatineeIncome + ExpectedRegularIncome + ExpectedFeatureIncome
LET Daily_Loss = ExpectedIncome - Days_Receipts

PRINT
PRINT
PRINT "Today matinees were attended by ";Matinee_Crowd;" people."
PRINT "Also, ";Regular_Crowd;" customers saw the regular shows."
PRINT "And most importantly, ";Feature_Crowd;" people saw the feature movie."
PRINT "Unfortunately, people cheated us out of $";Daily_Loss
PRINT
PRINT
PRINT "Hope you can deal with this loss. Have fun!"

END
```

Chapter 4

IF Statements

4.1 Making Decisions

Oh. hello.

So, by now you are getting a bit used to BASIC. Having mastered structural statements (such as REM and END) and input and output during the first week, you then acquired some knowledge on assignment statements. So now you can in fact write some simple, in fact VERY simple programs. But there is a lot you can not do. Do you care? Why yes, you certainly do. One thing — something VERY important to continue our coverage of the main programming constructs — is needed. You need to know about IF statements.

If you think about what you already know, there is still something very important that you can't get your BASIC programs to do. They can't yet make decisions. They can trudge along on their merry way, but they will always do the same operations no matter what. You can't have them make decisions as to what statements they should do and what statements they shouldn't do during this execution of the program.

Take the following simple problem. Let's say you wanted to write a program to calculate someone's yearly income tax. Let's also say the rule is very simple. They get taxed at 15% if they make under 10,000 dollars. They get taxed at 25% if they make 10,000 dollars or more. (This example, of course, has no basis in reality. Any New Jerseyite knows that the current trend is for the government to attempt to get the full 100% share of your income — no matter what your social status may be.)

Knowing the BASIC you know, is it possible for you to write this very simple program?

What you need is a way for BASIC to make a decision. In this program it has to decide if the person is making more than or less than 10,000 dollars. Based on that decision it calculates the tax one way or another.

So how do you make a decision in a program.......**use an if statement.**

4.2   IF statement

This statement comes in four different varieties. (And one special type we will get to later.)

SYNTAX

IF *condition* **THEN** *statement*

or

IF *condition* **THEN**
statement(s)
END IF
or

IF *condition* **THEN** *statement* **ELSE** *statement*

or

IF *condition* **THEN**
statement(s)
ELSE
statement(s)
END IF

Meaning

Evaluate the condition, if it is **true** then do the statements after the THEN and before the ELSE. (Or, if there is no ELSE then the rest of the statements before the end of the IF).

If the condition is **false** then do the statements after the ELSE and before the END IF. In an IF statement that takes up only one line, there will be no END IF so just do the rest of the statements on the line after the ELSE.

If the condition evaluates as **false** and there is no ELSE, just jump to the next statement in the program after the IF statement. (Either the next line if there is no END IF, or the statement after the END IF.)

Possible Errors

1. Forgetting your END IF in a multiple line If statement.

2. Misplacing the word THEN. It must be the last word on the first line of a multiple line IF statement.

3. Misplacing your ELSE. It has to be on a line by itself in a multiple line IF statement.

4. Screwing up your condition. (We will learn about conditions in a second. But why don't we list some of the errors here so they will be easy to find later.)

   (a) Remember in a condition symbol that has two parts, there must be no space between them... like IF X < > Y THEN ...should be IF X <> Y THEN ...

   (b) Be careful when you use ANDs and ORs. All subparts of a condition must be conditions also. Like IF X > 23 and < 45 THEN ...should be IF X > 23 and X < 45 THEN ...

   (c) Maybe putting the wrong condition in. What happens in this case is that the THEN part is done when you want the ELSE part to happen. And vice versa. Look at your condition carefully, especially if you use ANDs and ORs.

5. Many others ...

4.3 Conditions

A condition is part of a statement that does a comparison of values. Conditions are used inside of IF statements. Conditions will also be used in DO WHILE and LOOP UNTIL statements that we will learn in another chapter.

A condition compares two values. These values can be in the program directly (constants) or they can be determined from variables and/or equations. The comparison can check to see if two values are the same or if one is larger than the other. A condition will generate either **true** or **false** depending on the values and the condition. Using AND, OR and NOT will allow you to combine **true** and **false** together into larger conditions.

The condition operators are:

Symbol	Meaning
=	Equal
>	Greater than
<	Less than
<=	Less than or equal
OR	
=<	Less than or equal
>=	Greater than or equal
OR	
=>	Greater than or equal
<>	Unequal
OR	
><	Unequal

In the conditions that require two symbols, those symbols must be right next to each other with no space in between

Examples of conditions: (Keep in mind, these are only parts of other statements.)

- X = 35

  true if x is currently 35. **false** for any other value

- A_Var < 72

  true if the value of A_Var is less than 72. Else **false**.

- Numm <= X + Y

  true if the value of Numm is less than or equal to the sum of X and Y. Otherwise **false**.

- X$ = "Money"

  true only if the current value of X$ is exactly "Money". When writing a BASIC program, strings in quotes have to be very precise. Small letters are different than caps. So here, if X$ was "MONEY", then this condition would be **false**.

- Nam$<>" Sally"

  Will check to see if the the current value is equal to " Sally" (Note the space). If it is unequal the condition is **true**. Otherwise it is equal and the condition is **false**. The equal and not equal condition can be used with strings, along with numbers.

Hold on people, this will all make sense when we get to some examples.

4.3.1   Comparison of Strings

It turns out that besides using the comparisons "equal to" and "not equal" with strings, you can in fact use all the comparisons.

For instance, a condition like Name\$ $<=$ "LARRY", is perfectly valid. What does it mean? After all, we are used to using "greater than" and "less than" with numbers but not alphabetic strings. Well, to say that one string is less than another means that that string precedes it alphabetically. For the most part, you can think of the strings as listed alphabetically in a phone book or dictionary. (Most of you probably know the rules for ordering words in such alphabetical listings!) The strings that are earlier in the listing are "less than" those that appear later. (Likewise, those that appear later are said to be "greater than" the earlier ones.)

Some examples are:

- "TOT" $>$ "BABY" ("T" comes after "B")

- "BASEBALL" $<$ "BASEMENT" ("B" $<$ "M" at first letter in which the two words differ.)

- "TIM" $<$ "TIMMY" (Short words come before longer words when all characters match.)

Things are actually more complicated than this. Strings can have any character in them, not just letters, but also punctuation and digits. We aren't used to this in our normal orderings. Is "?" $<$ ":"? We don't normally consider this type of question. Fortunately, computers already use a built in ordering for all characters. It is called ASCII code. Each character can be associated with a number. The characters that are associated with the smaller numbers are said to be "less than" those characters that have higher ASCII codes. (See Chapter 2 in these Lecture Notes.) We don't expect you to memorize this ordering, so it is not even presented here. If we ever compare strings in our programs, we will just assume they are alphabetic strings, like names or words, which you already how to know how order from past experience.

Just as a reminder though, you might want to remember that small letters and capital letters are represented by different ASCII codes in a computer. That is "A" $<>$ "a". If they are not equal, what is their ordering? Just in case you are interested, it turns out that in ASCII, all the capital letters come before the small letters. That is capital letters "are less than" small letters. (Isn't this just so very nice and confusing?) Another way to say this is:

"A" $<$ "B" $<$ ... $<$ "Z" $<$ "a" $<$ "b" $<$ ... $<$ "z"

(Don't worry about this too much. I do not think we would be so nasty as to include a question on an exam in which we ask you to order strings which had both small and large letters in them. Though you may not need to memorize this ordering, you had better know for sure that small letters "ARE NOT EQUAL" to the equivalent capital letters.)

4.3.2   Using NOT, AND, OR.

ANDs, ORs and NOTs can be used to combine complete small conditions into much larger, more complicated conditions. All components of these big conditions must be conditions by themselves strung together with these logicial operators, AND, OR and NOT.

A NOT in front of a condition will turn **true** into **false** and a **false** condition into **true**.

ORs can be used to combine a lot of conditions together. If any one of the conditions is **true**, the whole complicated condition is **true**. Otherwise the complicated condition is **false**.

AND's can be used to combine conditions together. If any one of the small embedded conditions is **false** the whole complicated condition is **false**. Otherwise the whole condition is **true**.

When working with conditions that use NOTs, ANDs and ORs you should note there is an order to how things are calculated. First of all subconditions are calculated to arrive at **true** or **false** for these components. Then all NOTs are done to reverse the condition they precede. Next, any ANDs are performed to their two surrounding conditions. Do all the ANDs starting on the lefthand side and working all the way to the right. Finally, all the ORs are done to their surrounding conditions. Again work left to right. Following these rules, all valid complex conditions will evalaute down to one answer — either **true** or **false**.

All of the above assumes that parentheses have not been used to change the order around. Just like with regular mathematical expressions you can cause a condition to be calculated in a different order by using parentheses to group various parts of the expression together.

In short, remember that NOT is done first, then AND, then OR always left to right. (As we just mentioned, this is lacking any parentheses to change the order.)

NOT/AND/OR examples:

Say that X has the value 34, Y is 73 and Zoo$="Gorilla"

```
(X < 45)   AND    ( Y = 73)
    T                  T
            T
```

This whole condition is **true** since: **true** and **true** is **true**

```
(X <> 34) OR (Zoo$="Chimp")
    F              F
        F
```

This whole condition is **false** since: **false** OR **false** is **false**

```
NOT( x < 100)
        T
    F
```

NOT **true** is **false**

```
NOT( X = 34) AND (X + Y = 107) OR (Zoo$="GORILLA")
     T                T                  F    .evaluate each expression
 F                                            . NOT(TRUE) is FALSE
              F                               . FALSE AND TRUE is FALSE
                               F              . FALSE OR FALSE is FALSE
         FALSE                                . The answer is FALSE
```

4.3.3   Possible Errors With Conditions

- `MYNAME = "jt"`   Values must be same type. Here we have a numeric variable on left and a string on right. No good.

- `X > 34 AND < 55`   Each condition of a complex condition needs to be a whole condition. In English this seems to make sense when you read it "X is greater than 34 or less than 55". But the computer doesn't understand it as written. You must have `X > 34 AND X < 55`   .

- `The_Ans = 34 OR 93` Ditto above. Makes good English but lousy BASIC. Should be:
  `The_Ans = 34 OR The_Ans = 93` .

Now that we know about conditions, we can look at some IF statements.

4.4   Examples of Complete IF statements

-

```
IF Name$ = "Samantha" THEN PRINT "Found her"
```

-

```
INPUT PROMPT "What is your guess?" : Guess
IF Value < Guess THEN PRINT "You guessed high" ELSE  PRINT Value-Guess " away"
```

-

```
IF Record>Hr THEN
        LET Need = Record-Hr
        PRINT "You need "; Need; " HR's to tie the record"
        ELSE
        LET Over= Hr - Record
        PRINT "You went over the record by ";Over; " homeruns."
        PRINT "You have the new record"
END IF
```

-

```
IF Salary - Tax > Poverty_Level * 2 THEN PRINT "You are lucky"
```

-

```
IF (UsualDinner$ = "Donuts" OR UsualDinner$ = "Big Mac") AND Age<35 THEN
   LET LifeExpectancy =  58
   LET InsuranceRate = 400
   PRINT "Do you know Mark Vandewettering?"
END IF
```

4.5 Programs

4.5.1 The TAX problem

Remember the tax problem I mentioned at the beginning of this chapter? Well this program will solve it.

Let's say you wanted to write a program to calculate someone's yearly income tax. Let's also say the rule is very simple. They get taxed at 15% if they make under 10,000 dollars. They get taxed at 25% if they make 10,000 dollars or more.

```
INPUT PROMPT "How much money did you earn?":Amount
IF Amount>=10000 THEN
     LET Taxrate=25
  ELSE
     LET Taxrate=15
END IF

LET Tax=Taxrate/100 * Amount

PRINT "You got taxed at a rate of ";Taxrate;" %.  You paid $";Tax


END
```

A run of this program might look like:

```
RUN

How much money did you earn?20000

You got taxed at a rate of  25%.  You paid $5000
```

In this run, the IF-statement did the THEN part.

Let us do one more run of this program. In this one, the ELSE part of the IF statement is executed.

```
RUN

How much money did you earn?5000

You got taxed at a rate of  15%.  You paid $750
```

[By the way, note that when the user entered $20,000, the $ and the , were left out. Why? Because a number is made up of all digits. $ and , are obviously not digits. The program would die if the user tried to type these characters in. It is possible to change the program and allow the user to type a string in here (with $ and , in it) but then you couldn't do math with the value in that string (like in the LET statement.) So we stick with the method we used here. That is, the program is very simple, but the user doesn't have much flexibility with how s/he can enter the values. Generally, a real programmer will write a much more complicated program which creates a nice "user-interface". This will allow the user of the program much flexibility. It will also catch many potential "data-entry" errors a user might make. If we used more complicated features of TRUE BASIC, we could use other statements to help us out of this dilemma.]

The structure of this program is very straightforward. It has an INPUT section, a calculation section and a PRINT section. The INPUT and PRINT sections are very easy to follow. If you don't understand these parts of this program, go back to the previous chapters.

If you assume that we wrote the INPUT and OUTPUT section first you can see exactly what our task is in the calculation section. We are going to be given a value called Amount and from this we want to calculate two other values, called Taxrate and Tax.

The calculation section is simple. There are two statements. In English, you can think of these statements as being "Calculate tax rate." and "Use tax rate to calculate yearly tax".

This second task is straightforward. If you have a tax rate, no matter what it is, you just multiply this rate times the yearly income (here Amount) and get the tax that must be paid. Here, we had to make sure we adjusted the tax rate so it is really a decimal less than 1. (After all, you only pay a portion of your income as taxes.) So we turned the percentage that was given for the tax rate into a decimal by dividing by 100.

The first task is the only thing new here. We use an IF statement to decide what the tax rate is. It is either 25% or 15% — the computer must make a decision as to which of the two LET statements should be executed in order to set the proper tax rate. IF statements are perfect for making decisions. Here we basically say "If the amount is equal to or more than 10,000, then set the tax rate to 25% otherwise it should be 15%." Of course, the IF statement in the program shows exactly how you do this in a BASIC IF statement — assuming that you've picked your variables for the yearly income (Amount) and the tax rate (Taxrate).

If you look back at the beginning of this section to see what exactly this program was supposed to do, all it said was to have it print out the tax that must be paid. Here, we have printed out the tax rate percentage also — and had to use a variable to store this. The program is better than what was asked for. There is really no problem with doing this, but just to show that programs can be done in other ways let us rewrite this program so it does what it is supposed to, but in less lines and without the extra variable. Here is a new version of it:

```
INPUT PROMPT "How much money did you earn?":Amount
IF Amount>=10000 THEN
      LET Tax = .25 * Amount
   ELSE
      LET Tax = .15 * Amount
END IF
PRINT You paid $";Tax
END
```

The calculation section is now one line long — a single multi-line IF statement in which we just directly figure out the tax based on the income. Hey, this program is so simple, you can directly do away with the calculation section and just do the equations right in the print section. Like this:

```
INPUT PROMPT "How much money did you earn?":Amount
IF Amount>=10000 THEN
      PRINT You paid $"; .25 * Amount
   ELSE
      PRINT You paid $"; .15 * Amount
END IF
END
```

This program generates the exact same output as the previous version. But now there is neither a variable for tax rate or even tax and there is no caclulation section. Instead there is just an INPUT and PRINT section. The PRINT section consists of one IF statement in which a choice is made to execute either one or another PRINT statement. (IF statements can be used in any part of the program, Input, Calulations, Print or any other possible section.)

This is a nice concise program but I don't recommend you writing programs like this. It is better, especially for beginners, not to try to do too much at one time. It just becomes that much easier to goof up. I will stick with the advice to not include calculations inside of your PRINT statements. This last version is presented here to just demonstrate the fact that programs can be written in many different ways — I don't intend my ending with this version to be equivalent to my saying "this is the way you should write this program!". So don't think this. Okay?

4.5.2 Amusement Ride Program

As another example of IF statements, consider the following simply-stated problem. A new amusement park named Pending Disaster has just opened up in Hoboken. It has a number of very entertaining and enjoyable rides for thrill-seekers. Besides the new roller coaster ride Thundering Horror in which you lie face down, blind folded and shackled into place as the car maneuvers through numerous sudden turns and tight loops culminating in a series of 90 degree drops, the big ride of the season is the Guillotine. A description of this ride need not be given here as it has no bearing on the program that needs to be written. Due to a number of accidents that have happened on this ride recently, some new restrictions are being enacted. In particular, only people under 63 inches in height are normally allowed on the ride. Taller people can however take an excursion, if they present a court-approved document certifying that neither they, nor their family, will sue Pending Disaster Inc., in the case of accidental decapitations.

We want to computerize admission to this ride. A program needs to be written to decide who may or may not take this ride. Essentially, after asking a few pertinent questions, the program should print out a message okaying the person to board or not.

A few moment's thought will arrive at the following outline for a program. The program should check the person's height. If they are short enough they can enter. If they are too tall, the program should check to see if they have the proper documentation — if so, they can ride. All other people are sent away. One method that can be used to formulate this program is to use a special temporary variable called a "flag". This variable will be used to keep track of whether or not the current person can board the ride. Different values will indicate the various possibilities. To be precise, let us call this flag variable CanBoard$. If this variable has the value "NO" the person can not board. When it has the value "YES" the person can get on the ride. Why don't we start out assuming this variable has the value "NO" and only change it to "YES" when we know the person can be a valid passenger. With this design in mind, we can now write the program:

```
REM Pending Disaster Amusement Ride Program
REM Jt
REM New Program for Fall 1990

LET CanBoard$ = "NO"

INPUT PROMPT "How tall is this person (in inches)?": Height

IF Height < 63 THEN
    LET CanBoard$ = "YES"
    ELSE
       INPUT PROMPT "Does this person have the proper documentation (Yes or No)":ProperDoc$
       IF ProperDoc$ = "Yes" THEN LET CanBoard$="YES"
END IF


IF CanBoard$ = "YES" THEN
    PRINT "This person may become a passenger.  Good Luck Pal."
   ELSE
    PRINT "Send this person away."
END IF
END
```

This is an interesting program in that it uses two multi-line IF statements. The first IF statement is used to attempt to give the flag variable CanBoard$ the value "YES". The second multi-line IF statement is used to print out the proper message based on the value of that flag variable.

The first multi-line IF statement demonstrates the flexibility of BASIC. This statement decides whether the person is short enough or not. If the person is, the CanBoard$ variable is set to the proper value. But look at the ELSE part. There are two statements embedded in this part. They will only be executed if the person was too tall. The two statements in the ELSE part are rather interesting statements to have embedded inside of an IF statement. The first one is a INPUT PROMPT statement. Because this is inside of the ELSE part of the IF statement, this question is only asked when the person is too tall. Otherwise this question will not be asked at all (because the THEN part was done.) And the second statement in the ELSE part is most amazing. It is another IF statement. That is, the big IF statement has a little IF statement inside of it. This is perfectly legal. You can place any valid IF statement inside of an IF, even another IF statement. Here, the purpose of the small IF statement embedded in the ELSE part is to set the flag variable to "YES" if the question from the INPUT PROMPT was answered appropriately.

If you are very very clever, you might be tempted to make this program a bit shorter. In particular, the first multi-line IF statement could become:

```
IF Height < 63 THEN
      LET CanBoard$ = "YES"
    ELSE
      INPUT PROMPT "Does this person have the proper documentation (YES or NO)":CanBoard$
END IF
```

What is different here? Well, we got rid of the small embedded IF statement. How did we do that? Well, we placed the answer to their question directly into the variable CanBoard$. If they answered "YES" that they did have the proper documentation than CanBoard$ gets this "YES" they entered. And of course, this is proper for this program. They can indeed board if they have the proper identification. Notice, we also make sure they know they are supposed to type in capital "YES". This is because the final IF statement that is used for printing checks to see if CanBoard\$ is precisely capital "YES" — only if it got set to these three letters will the person be allowed on the ride.

Using CanBoard\$ in the INPUT PROMPT was rather tricky. And if we didn't have the previous version of this IF statement to look at, it would probably confuse us to see it lying there in the INPUT PROMPT statement. Most of us would naturally choose a different variable for this question — like we did in the first version. We wouldn't think of using CanBoard\$ in this tricky manner. It is not necessarily desirable to use tricks like this to make your program shorter — if it is also going to make them more confusing. If such a tricky technique does come to you — well, then feel free to use it at your own risk. If on the otherhand, you are not quite clever enough to think up these tricks, don't worry. You can still program well, even if you are unable of discovering such short cuts. Stick to the main techniques we are trying to teach you and you will be able to solve most problems.

There is another strategy you might have chosen for this program. Consider the following version.

```
REM Pending Disaster Amusement Ride Program
REM Jt
REM New Program for Fall 1990

LET CanBoard$ = "NO"

INPUT PROMPT "How tall is this person (in inches)?": Height
INPUT PROMPT "Does this person have the proper documentation (Yes or No)":ProperDoc$

IF( Height < 63) OR (ProperDoc$ = "Yes")THEN
    PRINT "This person may become a passenger.  Good Luck Pal."
  ELSE
    PRINT "Send this person away."
END IF

END
```

See how we used OR here. If either one of the conditions is true, that is, the person is shorter enough or the person has the right documentation, then that person can get on.

What is good about this version? Well, for one thing, we didn't need a flag variable. Plus, we just stuck the PRINT statements right in that original IF statement. We didn't need another IF statement later. What is bad about this program? Well, it always asks whether the person has the proper documentation. If if this is a short enough person, it will ask this question. That might be too annoying. We have simplified the code a lot in this version. But we have made it harder for the person using the program. That person must always answer TWO questions. There is often a trade off between how complicated the code of the program is, and how complicated the program is for the user. You will have to decide exactly what you care most about when you write your programs. Do you want to make them simple? Or do you want to make them easy to use? Unless instructed otherwise, this is one of the many choices you get to make when you create a program.

4.6   Nested If Statements

Riddle me this: If an IF statement can have any statement in its THEN and ELSE parts, then can an IF statement have an IF statement in it? (Brings to mind: "How much wood would a woodchuck chuck if a woodchuck could chuck wood?")

Well, if you read the previous program you know the answer to this. Yes, an IF statement can have an IF statement embedded in it. Sometimes, you can use a special format when you have IF statements inside of IF statements. This is called a nested-IF statement.

Suppose you have a numeric test score in a variable called GRADE and you want to print out the letter grade. We will use the typical grading scheme of 90 and above A, 80-89 B and so forth. We can use a nested If statement:

```
IF Grade>=90 THEN
    PRINT "You got an A"
  ELSEIF Grade>=80 THEN
    PRINT "You got a B"
  ELSEIF Grade>=70 THEN
    PRINT "You got a C"
  ELSEIF Grade>=60 THEN
    PRINT "you got a D"
  ELSE
    PRINT "You got an F"
END IF
```

When you trace this single multi-line statement you do the following. Start at the first condition. If it is **true** do the THEN otherwise jump to the condition in the first ELSEIF part. Keep evaluating conditions until one is **true** and you can do the THEN. Once you have done one of the THEN parts then that is all you have to do for the statement — you need not go further in it. As long as conditions are **false** you keep jumping to the next condition. If there are no more conditions, you do the final ELSE (if there is one.)

When you do come to a **true** or you do the final ELSE you are expected to do all statements in that section. That is, do all statements up to the next ELSEIF, ELSE or END IF line. Just execute the statement normally (you can even forget you are inside an IF if this will make you more at ease) and stop doing this immediately upon hitting the next line starting with an ELSEIF, ELSE or END IF. Once you are done executing the statements in that "section" of the nested-if, then proceed on with the program by starting at the first statement after the IF (that is, the line after the END IF).

Try the program above with some different grades. Let's say the grade is 75. At the first condition it sees that 75 is not greater than or equal to 90. Since the condition is **false** it moves to the next condition. Here it sees that 75 is not greater than or equal to 80 so it is on to the next condition. Now we see that $75 >= 70$ is **true** and so the then part is done. Thus, the program would print "You got a C" at this point.

Notice:

1. Instead of ELSE we have ELSEIf statements. Each one has some condition. Each one of these lines starts with ELSEIF and ends with THEN.

2. The last thing is an ELSE statement with no condition rather than an ELSEIF. Thus, this print statement is executed if all else fails.

3. The condition is of the form **grade>= 80** rather than something more complicated like **grade>= 80 and grade< 90**. The reason for this is that the only way the program will get to the second condition is if the first condition was false causing the first ELSEIF to be done. You therefore already are sure that the grade is less than 90.

4. This is one (rather large) statement.

5. Either one of the prints after a THEN will be executed or the final print after the last ELSE is done. It is impossible for more than one to be done by this statement.

Note:

You use a nested if statement when you want the computer to take one of a number of possible actions.

Some quick words on the syntax of this special form of the IF statement.

- The first line of a nested-if statement is IF *condition* THEN

- The nested-IF ends in an END IF

- There can be many subsections to this IF statement. These sections can consist of a number of statements. In fact any legal BASIC statements can go into these sections. Subsections appear after the original THEN, after any of the ELSEIF lines and also after the final ELSE.

- All but the first condition appear on lines of the form ELSEIF *condition* THEN

- All ELSEIF sections appear after the original THEN section and before any final ELSE section.

- The last section of the nested-if can be an ELSE section. This section does not have to be in the statement. But, if you decide you want an ELSE section, it must be the very last section. The keyword ELSE must appear on a line by itself, after which will follow the BASIC statements (one per line) that belong to the ELSE section. An END IF will end the ELSE section (and thus the whole nested-IF).

4.7 Nested versus non-nested If Statements

Let's see what happens if we don't use nested IF statements. Let's look at the grading program using sequential IF statements.

```
IF Grade>=90 THEN PRINT "You got an A"

IF Grade>=80 THEN PRINT "You got a B"

IF Grade>=70 THEN PRINT "You got a C"

IF Grade>=60 THEN PRINT "You got a D"  ELSE PRINT "You got an F"
```

Notice, this code consists of four different IF statements. (Each line starts with the word IF.) The previous version of this program had one IF statement, a large nested-IF statement.

What exactly will this program do? Well if grade was 67 it would print "you got a D". This is because the conditions in lines 1 and 2 and 3 are false and thus the THEN parts aren't done. In line 4 the condition is true so the THEN part is finally done.

Now what happens if the grade is something like 55? Well all the IF conditions in lines 1,2 and 3 are false. So as soon as the IF statements recognize that the condition is false, the program will immediately go to the next line. Finally this forces the program to line 4. Here the condition is again false (grade >= 60 is false because 55 < 60 ah ha). But here on line 4 there is an ELSE statement to handle the false conditions so the program will print "You got an F".

Fine, so this program does what the other one does, right? It is perfect! Right? Nope. Let us say the grade is 85. The program should print out "You got a B". What does it do?

Well in line 1 it sees that 85 < 90 so nothing is printed. The program then goes to line 2 (when an IF fails, the program goes to the next line). Here it sees that 85 >= 80 so it prints "You got a B". So far so good. But now the program goes to line 3. (It does this because a program ALWAYS goes to the next statement and this IS the next statement; it happens to be another If statement.) Here it sees that

85 >= 70 so it prints "You got a C" and then on to line 4 where it prints "You got a D". So three different grades will be printed. Not what we want. Is it?

So, when there is a list of separate IF statements on separate lines, it is possible for more than one of them to be true and, thus, several actions to take place.

This program can be fixed as follows.

```
IF Grade>=90 THEN PRINT "You got an A"

IF (Grade>=80) AND (Grade<90) THEN PRINT "You got a B"

IF (Grade>=70) AND (Grade<80) THEN PRINT "You got a C"

IF (Grade>=60) AND (Grade<70) THEN PRINT "You got a D"

IF Grade<60 THEN PRINT "You got a F"
```

By using the AND, I was able to fix the program so that only one condition can be true. Thus only one print is done. Trace this program portion and understand what happens. Try it for different grades. Note:

1. There are five separate IF statements. Each one is capable of generating a print.

2. Why did I use AND in my conditions. Well think about it. In order to get a grade of B (for instance), you score has to be greater or equal to 80 and it also has to be less than 90. Therefore you have the condition $(grade >= 80)$ and $(grade < 90)$.

3. When I used AND I put parentheses around the small expressions that are connected by the AND. This is not strictly necessary, but makes it easier to read. Also, in all my examples whenever I have used two symbols for a conditions (like $<=$), I don't put any space in between them.

4. Both small conditions that are connected by the ANDs are conditions by themselves. We don't put something like:

   IF $Grade >= 80$ AND < 90 THEN PRINT "You got a B"

   since < 90 is not a condition by itself.

5. I didn't use an ELSE in line 4 like the previous programs. WHY? This is important! Lets say the line looked like

   IF $(Grade >= 60)$ AND $(Grade < 70)$ THEN PRINT "You got a D" ELSE PRINT "You got an F"

   Let's say the grade was 95. Line 1 would print out "You got an A". Fine. But what happens when the program got line 4 as I have rewritten it here. Well the condition would be false since 95 is not between 60 and 70 thus the ELSE will be done causing "You got an F" to be printed. So rather than have this happen, we just kinda forget about the ELSE and make a new IF statement.

6. Because of the way I picked my conditions, only one of the print statements will take place.

Great! I have shown you a number of ways you might attempt to do this problem. I have also shown you a number of possible errors that can happen. Two of the versions I showed do the job. The first one used a nested If and one large statement. The last way used five IF statements and conditions that had ANDs in them. Obviously, the nested-if statement was the easiest way to do the problem.

So why did I bother explaining the other ways? The reason is because I have thoroughly covered the subject of IF statements in the above discussion. If you understand all the subtle differences and the results of the above various IF statements, then you understand IF statements. Those statements may all look very similar but a computer is very, very picky and as a result, using slightly different IF statements causes major consequences in your programs.

Try to remember:

1. Use a nested IF statement if your program is supposed to choose one of a number of different possibilities.

2. Use separate IF statements on separate lines when the program has to do a number of different tasks, and some times it may have to do more than one of those tasks.

4.8 Nested-IF Program: Magazine Subscriptions

Consider the following problem. You are the sales representative for a men's monthly magazine named Trout, Porsche and Quarterback which deals with important world events. (Well, rather than mislead you — the truth is, it isn't exactly like Time or Newsweek.) Anyway, mail has been sent out offering the magazine to customers at the following rates. One Year — $35. Two Years — $65. Three, Four or Five Years — $30 per year. Six to Ten Years — $25 per year. If you opt for the last plan, you get to take advantage of a special offer; you'll also get two free special issues per year. One issue is the Automatic Weapon Review which rates the current models of a variety of weapons from around the world. The other free issue is the widely sought after Suit Of Armor Issue which features the latest in medieval warrior garb.

Customers are expected to return a reply card indicating how many years they would like. You want to write a program that will send them back an acknowledgement verifying their name, address and the number of years they desire. They should also be told exactly how many issues they will get, the per issue cost and the total cost. If the customer has made an error, such as trying to order the magazine for too many years, they are told of this error.

This is typical of the type of program for which it is wise to use a nested-IF statement. (Or later, in the next chapter we will see you can alternatively use a SELECT CASE statement.) A decision is made according to how many years have been ordered. This is not a two-way decision. Instead, it can be thought of as a five-way decision — one of four different rates (or "plans") will be selected based on the number of years that have been chosen. Plus, there is a chance a mistake has been made so there should be some type of ELSE clause to handle this fifth possibility. Because only one of the five possibilities can be chosen — it is wise to use a nested-if statement. We know that this type of statement selects one choice from a wide selection of choices. If it was possible that more than one choice could indeed take place, then a nested-IF would not be appropriate.

The person's name and address should be input to this program. So should the number of years this person desires. Calculations must be made to figure out a number of the other values that we want to print — namely, the total number of issues, the per issue cost and the total cost.

Let us pick Name$, Address$, Years, TotalIssues, CostPerIssue and TotalCost as the variable names. The INPUT and PRINT sections of this program are simple and need not be discussed.

For the calculation section, we can use the nested-IF to make a decision based on the Years in order to allow us to calculate TotalCost and TotalIssues. We could calculate CostPerIssue within this nested-IF, but the same formula is always used in all cases. That is, CostPerIssue equals TotalCost divided by TotalIssues. This is always true, it does not depend on the particular number of years. So rather than include this equation in all the various sections of the nested-IF, we will just include this equation as a separate statement after the nested-IF. In this way, no matter what route is taken through the nested-IF, we know all of them will eventually leave the nested-IF and go to the statement after the nested-IF. Here is found the calculation for CostPerIssues and it will be calculated correctly.

Let us just look at the program now and see what has been discussed above.

```
REM Jt
REM Another New Program for Fall 90 --- Magazine Subscriptions --- Nested IFs
REM July 1990

INPUT PROMPT "What is the customer's name?":Name$
INPUT PROMPT "Enter the address: ":Address$
INPUT PROMPT "How many years does customer want this magazine for?": Years

LET Errormade$ = "NO"

IF Years = 1 THEN
     LET TotalIssues = 12
     LET TotalCost = 35
   ELSEIF Years = 2 THEN
     LET TotalIssues = 24
     LET TotalCost = 65
   ELSEIF (Years >= 3) AND (Years <= 5) THEN
     LET TotalIssues = 12 * Years
     LET TotalCost = 30 * Years
   ELSEIF (Years >= 6) AND (Years <= 10) THEN
     LET TotalIssues = 14 * Years
     LET TotalCost = 25 * Years
   ELSE
     PRINT "Customer Name: ";Name$
     PRINT "Given Address: ";Address$
     PRINT "Regarding your request for Trout,Porsche and Quarterback."
     PRINT "Your order was not processed as you made a mistake on the order form."
     PRINT "Please Try Again."
     LET ErrorMade$ = "YES"
END IF

IF ErrorMade$ = "NO" THEN
     LET CostPerIssue = TotalCost / TotalIssues

     PRINT "Customer Name: ";Name$
     PRINT "Given Address: ";Address$

     PRINT "We have received your request for ";Years;" years of Trout,Porsche and Quarterback"
     PRINT "You will receive a total of ";TotalIssues;" issues"
     PRINT "Your cost will be $";TotalCost
     PRINT "This is a cost of $";CostPerIssue;" per issue."
     PRINT
     PRINT "Thank you for doing business with us. Hope you enjoy the magazine."
END IF

END
```

First of all, notice that there is a flag variable. ErrorMade$ is used to keep track of whether or not there was a mistake on the order form. If there was, then it doesn't make sense to try to calculate CostPerIssue and execute the print section. So we put this final calculation and the complete (normal) PRINT section inside of a regular IF statement. These final parts of the program are only done if that IF statement is true — that is, no mistake was made on the order form! Notice we initialize ErrorMade$ to "NO" at the beginning of the program and only set it to "YES" if an error has indeed been made.

We have been very careful writing this program to look out for a potential user mistake. Using this flag complicated the program a little but made the program better. You might not want to worry about such tiny issues in your own programs. But please note one thing here. If we did not use a flag, and the person had said they wanted some strange number of years — like 15 — what would happen? Well, the program would still do the ELSE in the nested-IF and then get out of the nested-IF statement. The next statement would have been the assignment statement in which we attempt to calculate CostPerIssue. And the computer would try to divide TotalCost by TotalIssues. But what would the values of these variables be? Well, since we would have done the ELSE part and no values are given to these variables in those parts, they would have the value of all new variables in TRUE BASIC — that is zero. In fact, it turns out that when the program tried to do this calculation, it would be attempting to divide by zero. Neither man, nor computer can divide by zero, there is no such thing. The computer would sense this error, and stop — complaining. In other words, the program would bomb for certain bad input. In the way we have written it here, the program itself complains about the error — but it ends normally — it does not just drop dead in the middle with some strange error message like "Division By Zero Attempted" – which would not be at all meaningful to the person using the program. (We as programmers would understand what this means — but not the average user of this program.)

The main part of this program is clearly the nested-IF statement. Notice that it has five separate sections, only one of which will be done during any execution of the program. In this nested-IF we calculate the TotalCost and TotalIssues. These are easy to calculate for the cases of one year and two years. We just use straight assignment statements — plugging in the correct value. For larger number of years, we have to multiply the yearly rates by the number of years, so we can't just supply the actual values while writing the program. Instead we have to use the number of years that is in the variable Years to help us calculate the correct values. Hey, did you notice that for the case of six to 10 years we multiplied by 14 to get the number of issues?

By the way, did you wonder why ANDs were used in some of the nested-IF conditions. Like the clause:

ELSEIF (Years >= 3) AND (Years<= 5) THEN

Why do we connect the first condition by using an AND — is it necessary? At first you might not think so. Because we are using a nested-IF we know only one part of the whole IF statement will be done. So, for instance, if Years=2, then the first ELSEIF is done and why should we check in the second ELSE to see if Years is at least three. If we had only checked to see if Years was less than or equal to 5, it still would not process 2 years in this part of the code because the previous part of the nested-IF caught it. So it might seem we are making things complicated by using an AND clause. Except for one thing. The user might type in other numbers besides 1, 2 etc. For instance, what if the user typed in zero, or a negative number for the number of years? Well, then certainly we don't want to process these other numbers as if they were the same as 3,4 or 5. If we had written the code with only the clause ELSEIF Years <= 5 THEN the program would handle zero, and any negative amount of years in this part of the code. That would be wrong.

Now that you see the whole program, it probably makes sense to you. It is a simple program. One complication was the flag we used to help us deal with bad user input. This is an embellishment that you probably should not worry about in the first version of your own programs. Only add such features later after you get the main part of your program working and feel like improving the code. The other complicated part to this program is the nested-IF. Actually, it is not bad at all, if you concentrate on each subsection individually and don't let the overall length of this statement scare you.

Bye for now.

Have fun,

-Jt

4.9   Problems

Syntax Errors

1.

```
IF 2 + 3 = 5
  THEN PRINT "of course it does ninny"
  ELSE PRINT "Something is wrong with this computer."
END IF
END
```

2.

```
READ TruthValue$
IF TruthValue$ THEN PRINT "This chapter is easy!"
DATA "TRUE"
END
```

3.

```
INPUT Age
IF Age>2000 THEN LET Status$ = "Old" ELSE LET Status$="Young" END IF
PRINT Status$
END
```

4.

```
INPUT Something
INPUT Orother
LET Answer = 200
LET Answer = Something * 2 IF Orother < 100
PRINT Answer
END
```

5.

```
READ A,B,C
LET PrintThis = 0
IF A > 10 THEN LET PrintThis = 1
IF B > 100 THEN
   LET PrintThis = PrintThis * 2
END IF
IF C > 1000 THEN
   LET PrintThis = PrintThis - 50
 ELSE
   LET PrintThis = PrintThis + 50
IF A + B + C = 1200 THEN PRINT "What Luck"
PRINT PrintThis
DATA 20, 75,1119
END
```

6.

```
INPUT Island$
IF Island$="Manhattan" THEN
  PRINT "Go farther away"
 ELSE
  PRINT "Island might be in the Bahamas"
 ELSE
  PRINT "It is a deserted island."
END IF
END
```

7.

```
PRINT "Store Manager Helper"
INPUT Aisle
IF Aisle = 1 THEN
   PRINT "Fresh Veggies"
 ELSEIF Aisle < 4 THEN
   PRINT "Canned Goods"
 ELSEIF Aisle = 5 OR 6
   PRINT "Frozen Food"
 ELSE
   PRINT "Boxed Items"
END IF
END
```

Tracing

1. Input to this program is: 7

```
INPUT Amount
LET Quality$="Good"
IF Amount < 5 THEN LET Amount = Amount/2 ELSE LET Amount = Amount + 10
IF Amount > 12 THEN PRINT "More than a dozen." ELSE LET Quality$="Bad"
PRINT "Quality is ";Quality$
END
```

2. Trace four times — once for each number here: 75, 3, 519, 46

```
INPUT Pages
IF Pages < 5 THEN PRINT "Quick reading"
IF Pages > 50 THEN PRINT "A long night"
IF Pages > 200 THEN PRINT "Give me a week" ELSE PRINT "Not too long"
IF Pages > 1000 THEN PRINT "I aint gonna open it."
END
```

3. Trace four times — once for each number here: 75, 3, 519, 46

```
INPUT Pages
IF Pages < 5 THEN
    PRINT "Quick reading"
  ELSEIF Pages > 50 THEN
    PRINT "A long night"
  ELSEIF Pages > 1000 THEN
    PRINT "I aint gonna open it."
  ELSEIF Pages > 200 THEN
    PRINT "Give me a week"
  ELSE
    PRINT "Not too long"
END IF
END
```

Programs

1. Write a program to calculate how many calories a person should consume in a day to maintain their weight. Ask for the sex and weight of a person. For females the calory count should be their weight times 13; for males it is their weight times 16. Find out if the person exercises daily — if so, make the calory count be 20% higher. Also find out if the person works behind a desk in an office. If so, make the calory count be 20% lower.

2. Mark VandeWettering is moving from NJ. He owns a bed, a VCR, a TV, a Yamaha Keyboard and a lot of books which are worth about $15 each. Write him a program to determine if it is worth it to move his junk with him or just toss it out. The program should ask what is the amount it will cost him to move, how many books he has and what each of his poccessions is worth. (That is, the bed, TV, VCR, and keyboard.) The program should tell him to take his stuff with him or throw it all out depending on which course of action is cheaper.

3. Write a program to rate a movie to see how many stars it should get. The acting in the movie can be "good" or "bad". The plot can be "interesting" or "boring". The filming/editing can be "superb" or "average". The directing can be "excellent" or "lacking" and the music can be "inspiring" or "grating". A movie can earn one star each for getting the ratings "good", "interesting", "superb", "excellent" and "inspiring". Tell how many stars a particular movie should get.

4. Write a program that will recalculate America's population based on supplied statistics. The program should start out by asking how many people lived in the country at the beginning of the year. Then it should ask 1) how many people were born here this year 2) how many people died of natural causes like disease or old age and 3) how many people died from accidents or crime. Then the program should ask whether the country is currently going through good times or bad times. Given that the country is going through good times, the program should ask what is the net amount of people that immigrated into the country. On the other hand, if the country is going through bad times, the program should ask 1) how many people died in battles (wars) 2) how many people died from starvation and 3) what is the net amount of people that emigrated. Before the program ends, it should tell what America's new population is and print out a message saying that the population increased or decreased compared to the value at the beginning of the year.

5. Write a program to determine how much you have to pay for a visit to Dr. Donothing's office. Everyone who visits this particular doctor has to get a complete physical ($75) and a blood test ($50). If you haven't had a tetanus shot in over 5 years you will be given one (and have to pay another $30). For seasons in which there is a flu epidemic, you must get the latest flu shot (another $30). People who live in the woods have to get a special test for Lyme's Disease (there goes another $50). And if you are on Medicaid, your bill automatically doubles. The program should ask the necessary questions and figure out the bill based on the answers to these questions. A proper bill should be printed out.

6. Two people are playing poker. Write a program to ask what each player has been dealt and from this information prints out who wins this particular hand. It turns out these players are playing a simplified game. In particular, they can (and will always) only end up with "Four of a Kind", "Straight" or "Flush". No other possibilities will result. The actual cards they have does not matter. For instance, in their game, 4 Kings doesn't beat 4 Sevens. Have the program ask the user to type in one of these strings for each player (either "Four of a Kind", "Straight" or "Flush"). The program should print out who won, or print "Tie" if they both got the same hand. Assume "Four of a Kind" beats "Straight" which beats "Flush". HINT: You can use a nested-IF statement for this program and it is possible to handle all the different ties with one (large) decision in one segment of this IF.

7. Write a program to help do date calculations. Ask the user to type in a starting date. The format should be month followed by day — the month should be a number. (The user should enter a 10 and then a 4 for "October 4") Then ask the user to enter a number from 1 to 25 — this will be the number of days after the supplied date that the user wants to calculate. Have the program calculate what the date will be that many days later. This program will have to use IF statements — it would be wise to use conditions containing AND/OR. The key thing is to add the number of days on to the day of the date. Then, check using an IF statement if you have passed the last day of the current month. For those times when you did pass the end of the month, you will have to change the month number to the next month and correct the calculated day. You can assume it is not a leap year. Also, don't forget to handle December properly — there is no 13th month! (Example: say the date supplied is December 29 and the user types in the number 4. The program should come back with the date 1-2. If you want to get a little fancier, you can have it print January 2.)

8. Write a program to determine if you should take a hit in a game of blackjack, assuming you know all the cards that have been dealt to you and the dealer so far. Say that each of you have gotten two cards. The input for this program should be two numbers between 1 and 13 for both you and the dealer. (Four numbers input in all.) 1 stands for "Ace" , 11 for "Jack", 12 for "Queen" and 13 for "King". For this program just let an Ace be worth 11 points. (That is, if the number 1 is input, this should be worth 11 points.) Jack, Queen and King should be worth ten points. Calculate the total points for both you and the dealer. Have the program type "You got Blackjack" if your score is 21 or if not, then type "Dealer got Blackjack" if the dealer has 21 points or if not, "Hit" if your score is less than the dealer or "Stay" if your score is the same or higher than the dealer.

9. Help a farmer calculate how much wheat he can expect from his land. The input should be the number of acres of land the farmer grows wheat on and some data on various conditions that existed that year. The output should be how many bushels of wheat can be expected. In a normal year say that the farmer can grow 750 bushels per acre of land. Rainfall, temperature, pests and disease affect how much yield the farmer can expect. Use the following criteria. If the mean temperature is 10 degrees below normal, yield will go down to 75% of normal. If the mean temperature is down by less than 10 degrees, expected yield is 90%. If temperature is up slightly — by 3 to 7 degrees — yield will be up 25% but if it is too high — more than 7 degrees — yield will fall significantly, to 80% normal. Rainfall below 20 inches in the growing season will cut the crop in half. 20 to 30 inches will generate 75% yield. 45 to 50 inches will increase yield by 35%. Above 65 inches of rain will also cut the yield in half. Rat infestations will eat 100 bushels per acre. Locust infestation will eat 150 bushels per acre. Both rat and locust infestation can occur in the same season. It is also possible that severe wheat blight will cause a 25% decrease in yield. Finally, a late season hail storm will devastate a crop — crops of more than 250 bushels per acre will go down by 30% but smaller crops will be wiped out. The program should allow the farmer to enter the mean temperature and amount of rainfall, tell whether there was rat and/or locust infestations, and notify that severe wheat blight or a late season hail storm has occurred. From this information, the program will calculate how many bushels of wheat the farmer can expect per acre and print "declare bankruptcy" if the amount is less than 200 bushels per acre – otherwise, it will print the total amount of bushels from all the farmer's acres.

Chapter 5

The SELECT statement

In the last chapter, Batman and Robin were just about to be disposed of by the Joker ...

No, No, wait a second, these are the notes for 110 ...

In the last chapter, we learned about IF statements. So you should be able to handle something simple like IF - THEN. And hopefully you can do ELSEs. At the very most, you are fluent with complicated IF structures such as nested-IF statements.

This time, we will learn a new statement that is very similar to nested-If statements. TRUE BASIC is one of the few BASICs to have this advanced statement. It is very useful and powerful.

This lecture will review nested-Ifs, teach about SELECTs and compare the two statements.

5.1   SELECT statements

SYNTAX

> **SELECT CASE** *expression*
>
> **CASE** *list-of-options-separated-by-commas*
>
> *statements*
>
> **CASE** *list-of-options-separated-by-commas*
>
> *statements*
>
> ⋮
>
> **CASE ELSE**
>
> *statements*
>
> **END SELECT**

Options

> -where an **option** is:
>
> - *value*
> - *number* **TO** *number*
> - **IS** *relational-operator number*

An **expression** is any valid TRUE BASIC mathematical expression. (That is, what is usually on the right-hand side of a LET statement.) Most of the time when you use the SELECT statement, the expression you use will be a single variable.

A **statement** is any BASIC statement.

A **value** is either a string or a number.

A **number** is any valid number.

A **relational-operator** is =   <>   <   >   <=   >=

All words here in **CAPITAL BOLDFACE** must be typed into your program if you use this statement or portions of it. (Remember: while those keywords are required, TRUE BASIC doesn't care if you use capital or small letters when you type them in. Though inside of quotes (in strings) there is a difference between capital and small letters.) The rest of the items (ie expression, statements ...) are information that you supply. You have to think up the particular numbers, string, operators, expressions and statements to complete each CASE.

You need not have the CASE ELSE if you don't have a use for it.

Okay okay, that is a precise explanation of what is needed but, of course, it is extremely confusing to understand. Us computer people always have to deal with this junk. Look at some examples below and see how it meets the syntax explained above. Then I will explain what the statement means and how you use it. Just look at the structure of these statements, don't try to understand what they mean yet. See why the structure is allowed according to the above rules.

EXAMPLES   (I have left out actual statements here ... any would suffice)

1.
```
SELECT CASE X
   CASE 4
     some statements
   CASE 5
     some statements
END SELECT
```
This is a very simple example

2.
```
SELECT CASE Z
   CASE 7
     some statements
   CASE 3
     some statements
END SELECT
```

This is the same as above, but just note that values need not be increasing. (7 comes before 3 in this example.)

3.
```
SELECT CASE (X-23)*4
   CASE 10
     some statements
   CASE 20
     some statements
   CASE 35
     some statements
   CASE ELSE
     some statements
END SELECT
```

Two things to note here. Rather than having a simple variable after the SELECT CASE on the first line, there is a whole equation. Also, here there is a CASE ELSE clause.

4.
```
        SELECT Something
          CASE 1,2,4,5
            some statements
          CASE 6,9,11
            some statements
          CASE ELSE
        END SELECT
```

Cases can have more than one value as long as you separate them by commas. There need not be any statements between CASE ELSE and END SELECT.

5.
```
        SELECT CASE Letters$
          CASE "word"
            some statements
          CASE "mess","other"
            some statements
        END SELECT
```

For strings, you can either have cases consisting of one value (string) or a list of values (separated by commas). Note that since the expression on the SELECT CASE line is a string variable, all CASEs consist of string constants (in quotes). I could have a CASE ELSE here if I wanted.

6.
```
        SELECT CASE Boxes
          CASE 5 TO 15
            some statements
          CASE 17 TO 20
            some statements
          CASE ELSE
            some statements
        END SELECT
```

See how the TO can be used for ranges of numbers? TRUE BASIC will let you pick overlapping ranges but this would be stupid considering the meaning of the statement. (See below for the meaning of this statement.)

7.
```
        SELECT CASE instruments
          CASE IS < 0
            some statements
          CASE IS < 25
            some statements
          CASE IS <= 100
            some statements
          CASE ELSE
        END SELECT
```

Notice how the IS clause is used. A relational-operator follows and then a numeric value.

```
8.          SELECT CASE Whoknows
              CASE 1,3
                some statements
              CASE 4 TO 10
                some statements
              CASE IS > 1000
                some statements
              CASE ELSE
                some statements
            END SELECT
```
Notice how types of options (tests) can be combined into one select statement.

Okay, hopefully you understand the different possibilities allowed. This statement is very flexible in structure. I have tried to demonstrate all of the possible themes. Chances are if you try something drastically different than these, you are gonna get some strange errors. Oh maybe not ... who knows. Try to stick to things close to what I have shown here ... unless you really know what you are doing.

POSSIBLE ERRORS

1. Forgetting your **END SELECT** statement.

2. Trying to put a statement on the same line as the **CASE**. The **CASE** *whatever* must be on a line by itself.

3. Using improper **CASE**
   examples:

   - **CASE < 50**
     -forgot to use IS.
   - **CASE X**
     -can't use variables (ie X) in a **CASE**.
   - **CASE 23-T**
     -can't use equations in **CASE**.
   - **CASE 23 45 15 8**
     -more than one choice should be separated by commas.

4. Value of **CASE** doesn't match type of variable in **SELECT CASE**.
   Example:

   ```
   SELECT CASE Name
   ```
   ⋮
   ```
   CASE "Jt"
   ```
   ⋮

   Name is numeric variable. (There is no $.) "Jt" is a string.

5. Having a **CASE ELSE** but it isn't the last case. (Bad, very bad.)

6. Many many many other errors ... oh so many.

MEANING

Oh man, all this talk and I still haven't explained what a **SELECT** means. It is simple. Evaluate the expression (usually look up the value of a variable) in the **SELECT CASE** line. Using this value, find the first CASE that passes. Do all statements AFTER the line this CASE is on and BEFORE the line of the next case; then jump to the line after the END SELECT. That is, only do one CASE even if more seem to pass. If no CASE is applicable, then do the CASE ELSE, if there is one.

Remember: Only the first good (matching) case will be used, even if ones further down are also good.

What does it mean "to pass" a CASE? Well it means if any of the choices on the CASE line is a TRUE one, then that CASE passes. There are three types of tests.

- **Straight value**

  Do it if the value of the expression (in the SELECT CASE line) is listed on the CASE line. Like:

  ```
  SELECT CASE X
     CASE 1,3,5
        do this
     CASE 2,4
        do that
     CASE ELSE
        do other
  END SELECT
  ```

  If at this time in the program, X=3, then *do-this* would be done. Or if X=1 then *do-this* is also done. How about if X is equal to 4? Ah, then *do-that* is done instead. How about if X is 19? Well since it isn't 1 or 3 or 5 and it also isn't 2 or 4 then none of the tests are true and so *do-other*, the ELSE statements are done.

- **Ranges**

  Do it if the expression's value (on the SELECT CASE line) falls in the range on the CASE line Like:

  ```
  SELECT CASE Zonk
     CASE 10 To 20
        statements-some
     CASE 22 TO 30
        statements-fun
     CASE ELSE
        statements-more
  END SELECT
  ```

  If the program got to here and Zonk was 19 , then *statements-some* would be done because Zonk is between 10 and 20 (or equal to 10 or 20) If Zonk=25, then *statements-fun* would be done. If Zonk=21, it wouldn't fall in either range and the *statements-more* would be done since they are the ELSE part.

- **Relations (IS)**

  Use the value of the expression (in the SELECT CASE line) as a left-hand side of the relation that follows IS. If the relation is true, do the statements after this CASE.
  Like:

  ```
  SELECT CASE  People
     CASE IS <= 0
        PRINT "dummy"
     CASE IS < 101
        PRINT "a lot"
     CASE IS >= 101
        PRINT "too many"
  END SELECT
  ```

  Say People = 22. The first case is not true since 22<=0 is false. But the second CASE is TRUE, 22<101, and so "a lot" is printed and the SELECT statement finishes. If People equaled 150, "too many" would be printed.

CASEs can be all mixed up. Look at the following example and try to figure out why the values in the table below are printed:

```
SELECT CASE Eggs
   CASE 12
      PRINT "That is normal"
   CASE IS < 0
      PRINT "give me a real number, dummy"
   CASE 0 To 11
      PRINT "time for more eggs"
   CASE 13 To 144
      PRINT "You are crazy"
   CASE ELSE
      PRINT "save some for other people"
END SELECT
```

value of eggs:	printed:
2	time for more eggs
55	You are crazy
11	time for more eggs
−5	give me a real number, dummy
200	save some for other people
12	That is normal

Okay, so are you getting any of this yet? Hopefully you are.

More things to worry about.

Sometimes, you don't think a CASE ELSE is necessary. You might believe you have handled all the possible cases. You may be right. But if you are wrong you could run into an error. If none of the cases pass and there is no CASE ELSE, your program will die! Bomb! Generate big errors. So, to be safe, always put in a CASE ELSE part even if there are no statements after it and you just place END SELECT on the next line. (Better yet, if

you think the program should never get to the CASE ELSE, put one in anyway and stick a statement like Print "Something is wrong" there so that if the program ever does go there, you will realize there is some problem and can try to fix it.)

5.2   Reason For Using A Select Statement

A SELECT statement is used for precisely the same reason you use a nested-IF. In fact, you often can use them interchangeably in your program. The SELECT statement is supposed to be easier to read and follow. You can use a SELECT statement when you have a bunch of possible options you want to take and you only want one of those options to be done.

For instance, in the previous chapter we saw a nested-IF statement that could print out grades based on some numeric score. You can do the same thing with a SELECT statement:

```
SELECT CASE Score
   CASE 90 to 100
      PRINT "You got an A"
   CASE 80 TO 89
      PRINT "You got a B"
   CASE 70 TO 79
      PRINT "You got a C"
   CASE 60 to 69
      PRINT "You got a D"
   CASE ELSE
      PRINT "You got an F"
END SELECT
```

In most of the examples given so far there are PRINT statements inside of the various cases. As was mentioned however, any type of statement can appear inside of the case sections. For instance, we can rewrite the program above if we store the grade inside of a variable by using a LET inside of the case section and then after the END SELECT use a PRINT statement to display the value of that variable. To further demonstrate the fact that any statement can be placed inside of a SELECT CASE statement let us add a little complexity to this grading scheme. Let's say that students who earned a D can get their grade improved to a C if they have done some extra credit work. So, if a student has a score between 60 and 69, the program should ask if extra credit work was done and if so, make the grade be C. To accomplish this, we can include an INPUT PROMPT statement along with an IF statement inside of the D case. Yes, you heard right. You can place an IF statement inside of a SELECT CASE statement. In fact, there are various times when this is highly desirable. Here is what the program looks like if we add these changes.

```
INPUT PROMPT "What score did the student get?" : Score
   SELECT CASE Score
      CASE 90 to 100
         LET Grade$ = "A"
      CASE 80 TO 89
         LET Grade$ = "B"
      CASE 70 TO 79
         LET Grade$ = "C"
      CASE 60 to 69
         INPUT PROMPT "Did this student do extra credit work (Y/N)?": Answer$
         IF Answer$ = "Y" THEN LET Grade$ = "C" ELSE LET Grade$ = "D"
      CASE ELSE
         LET Grade$ = "F"
   END SELECT
PRINT "This student gets a grade of ";Grade$
END
```

Many programs that use nested-IFs can be changed to use SELECT CASE instead. Remember the program that did magazine subscriptions? Here is how its calculation section could be rewritten using a SELECT CASE statement instead of the nested-IF. We will use the Years as the selection variable.

```
SELECT CASE Years
   CASE 1
      LET TotalIssues = 12
      LET TotalCost = 35
   CASE 2
      LET TotalIssues = 24
      LET TotalCost = 65
   CASE 3 TO 5
      LET TotalIssues = 12 * Years
      LET TotalCost = 30 * Years
   CASE 6 TO 10
      LET TotalIssues = 14 * Years
      LET TotalCost = 25 * Years
   CASE ELSE
      PRINT "Customer Name: ";Name$
      PRINT "Given Address: ";Address$
      PRINT "Regarding your request for Trout,Porsche and Quarterback."
      PRINT "Your order was not processed as you made a mistake on the order form."
      PRINT "Please Try Again."
      LET ErrorMade$ = "YES"
END SELECT
```

There are some nested-IF statements that can't be changed into SELECT statements. Consider:

```
IF X<Y THEN
    PRINT "yes"
  ELSEIF A<B
    PRINT "no"
  ELSE
    PRINT "stuff"
ENDIF
```

There is no way to turn this into a CASE statement. Anything you could try would need to have variables in the CASE part and you aren't allowed to put variables into CASE parts. Just believe me.

Now for some programs:

5.3 SELECT CASE Programs

5.3.1 Dog Food Program

Here is a simple program. Given the age of a dog, decide which type of Cyclone Dog Food the pet should receive for a meal. I seem to remember there are four different types. I ain't about to go look them up — after all, I really detest this advertising stuff. So let me just make up four different types for different age groups. [1]

We'll say that Fido gets Cyclone For Toddlers if he is less than 2 years old. Cyclone For Adolescents if one is between 2 and 5 years old. Cyclone For Yuppies when between the ages of 6 and 10. Cyclone Mush for dogs older than this who are probably losing their teeth. (Ohhhh, such a clever double-usage of the term Mush eh?)

Here is a program that asks for a dog's age and prints out the proper food to feed that dog. Let us assume that the age will only be a whole number. (No ages like 2.7312 years expected!)

```
REM The Not Meant To Be A Real Dog Food Program
REM Jt    July 1990    New Program for Fall 90
INPUT PROMPT "What is your doggie's name?": Pet$
PRINT "How old is ";Pet$;
INPUT Age

SELECT CASE Age
 CASE IS < 0
   PRINT "Yo, why don't you wait till the little guy is born before you try to feed him ok?"
 CASE 0,1
   PRINT "Give ";Pet$;" Cyclone For Toddlers"
 CASE 2 TO  5
   PRINT "Give ";Pet$;" Cyclone For Adolescents"
 CASE 5 to 10
   PRINT "Give ";Pet$;" Cyclone For Yuppies"
 CASE ELSE
   PRINT "Give ";Pet$;" Cyclone Mush"
END SELECT
END
```

---

[1] The name of this dog food is not really meant to be similar to any real dog food. And even if it is — this is all in fun. If any dog food company executives are reading this — please don't sue me.

Hey, did you notice how we asked the age? Instead of using an INPUT PROMPT, we used a PRINT statement that ended in a semicolon, to print a question which included the dog's name (which was supplied by the INPUT PROMPT above). Then, in the next line we used a regular INPUT statement. The question mark from this regular INPUT statement will print at the end of the question from the PRINT statement since we had that semicolon at the end.

Nothing amazing with this SELECT CASE statement. Note our first case used an IS relation. If the age entered was a bad number (here a negative number) we complained! The last case was a CASE ELSE. We could have had something like CASE IS > 10 if we wanted to be precise. Because we are only writing this program to deal with whole numbers, and since we can easily see that all the previous cases take care of all ages less than and including 10, we can just use an ELSE case here since it is clear that any other possible case must be an age greater than 10.

SELECT CASE statements are certainly easy to read, if not to use, when writing your own programs. Here is another program that has multiple choice decisions to make:

5.3.2 A Program: Corrupt TA grading scheme

PROBLEM: At a certain University (not Rutgers since stuff like this doesn't happen at Rutgers), a certain TA was easily influenced when grading. Most students in the class got the grade they deserved. For the others, it was discovered that they had been receiving questionable extra credit points. No, no nothing like that. Rather, extra points were doled out based on certain aspects of these students that seem to catch the TA's interest. The TA was discovered several years ago when a certain strange looking program written in BASIC on a pdp11/44 (a small minicomputer) was found hiding on a computer account. (By the way, this TA since went on to become a lecturer in a course very, very similar to 110, in fact so similar, it might even be 110 ... and no, this lecturer's name is **not** Jt ... [hey look people, believe what you want but give me a break] ... and there have only been a few other lecturers for this course ... so use your imagination. This is meant to be a humorous example. Hopefully it doesn't disturb you too much.[2]) After asking various questions this program would suggest how many points to give the student for extra credit. The rules for giving out extra credit went something like this:

```
      Hair color:
          Blonde        3pts
          Brown         2pts
          Black         2pts
          any other     1pts
      Age
          16-22         5pts
          23-30         3pts
          other         0pts

      Weight
          below 100     2pts
          100-120       4pts
          121-140       2pts
          141-150       1pts
          above 150     -3pts
```

---

[2] "Cecilia Jackson, the TA in question, who admittedly liked young, vivacious, thin, blond men, was later sued by Ted and Larry Bitstream, twin middle-aged, bald, shy, overweight students who complained about discrimination." Does this sentence go against your expectations? People in the past have claimed this programming example is sexist in nature and should be excluded from the book. If you attributed some sex to any of the participants in this example — it came out of your own imagination. This example does not mention sex at all. Also, this example in no way supports any kind of discrimination. Notice, the TA is labeled as being "corrupt", not as being a kind of role model. If anything, this example only reminds us that discrimination exists in the world — which it does — but in no way endorses discrimination.

```
        Number times came to office hours:
                0          0pts
                1          1pt
                2-5        3pts
                6-10       5pts
                more       10pts
```

So let's consider what this program might look like. Here it is using nested-IF statements. (Refer to the previous chapter for more info on nested-IFs.)

```
REM The corrupt TA problem.
INPUT PROMPT "Give me a name?":Nam$
INPUT PROMPT "What is student's hair color?":Hair$
INPUT PROMPT "What is student's age?":Age
INPUT PROMPT "What is student's weight?":Weight
INPUT PROMPT "How many times did student come to the office?":Office_Visits
LET Points=0

IF Hair$="Blonde" THEN
    LET Points=Points+3
  ELSEIF (Hair$="Brown") OR (Hair$="Black") THEN
    LET Points=Points+2
  ELSE
    LET Points=Points+1
END IF

IF (Age >= 16) AND (Age <= 22) THEN
    LET Points=Points+5
  ELSEIF (Age >=23) AND (Age <=30) THEN
    LET POINTS=POINTS+3
END IF

IF Weight<100 THEN
    LET Points=Points+2
  ELSEIF Weight<=120 THEN
    LET Points=Points+4
  ELSEIF Weight<=140 THEN
    LET Points=Points+2
  ELSEIF Weight<=150 THEN
    LET Points=Points+1
  ELSE
    LET Points=Points-3
END IF
```

```
IF Office_Visits = 1 THEN
    LET Points=Points + 1
  ELSEIF (Office_Visits>1) AND (Office_Visits<=5) THEN
    LET Points=Points + 3
  ELSEIF (Office_Visits>5) AND (Office_Visits<=10) THEN
    LET Points=Points+5
  ELSEIF (Office_Visits>10)
    LET Points=Points+10
END IF

PRINT "Give ";Nam$;" ";Points;" extra points."
PRINT "Bye Bye"
END
```

There are a number of things that you might want to notice:

1. The structure (syntax) is: IF condition THEN on the first line of every nested-if statement. A number of lines that look like ELSEIF *condition* THEN. (Maybe zero of these.) After every line that ends in a THEN is a block of statements. There might also be a line that says ELSE. If so, it must be after all the ELSEIF lines. It is also followed by a block of statements. Finally, there is an END IF statement. These rules must be followed precisely. For instance, you can't freely place a THEN on the next line after where it belongs. You can't forget the END IF line. Each ELSEIF statement must have THEN at the end. And so on.

2. Conditions may have NOTs/ ANDs /ORs in them.

3. An ELSE may or may not be present. For instance, for hair color they get points even if they don't match one of the choices. So there is an ELSE. For office visits, it is possible that they visited zero (or less?) times, in which case, the IF statement has to do nothing and so there is no ELSE.

4. Sometimes you can take short cuts in conditions. For instance, the person should get 4 points for having a weight from 100 to 120. But the condition weight<=120 was used instead of (weight>=100) AND (weight<=120). The reason for this is in order for the program to get this far into the nested-IF statement, it was already decided on the previous condition in the IF, that weight<100 was false. That is, it must already know that weight is greater than or equal to 100.

5. With Office_visits, you can't take this type of short cut and thus have to use the AND conditions. The reason for this is because while the program might make it to the second condition, it does so for any number not equal to one. Thus, if you only checked for office_visits<=5, then numbers such as -3 or 0 would now pass the second condition. (They aren't equal to 1.) So, we use the AND to make sure it is in the right range.

6. Notice how the program accumulates the point total. Essentially, there are a number of statements of the form **LET Points = Points + Number**. This says "let the new number of points become the old number of points plus this number". This is the standard way of accumulating a sum, as mentioned in the chapter on assignment statements.

Look at the four nested-IF statements carefully. Look at the conditions. Notice that some of the statements don't have a final ELSE. Each IF statement handles the points for a particular attribute. There are four separate attributes (hair color, age, weight and office visits) that must be evaluated. You use four totally unconnected IF statements since you always want all four of these things evaluated. If you somehow tried to combine two or more of these attributes (for instance age and weight) into one complicated IF statement, it is very likely that you might end up handling only one of the attributes when the IF statement is executed. This is due to the fact that a nested-IF statement is used when you want to do only one of a number of different options. In this case we always want to handle four things, so it makes sense to have four statements.

Each one of these IFs is a nested-IF since only one of a number of options can be taken. For instance, for any one person, for hair color, you either want to handle the case for blonde hair or brown hair or ...Obviously any one person only has one hair color (assume a perfect world, not the USA in the 1990's). Since we want to do only one of a number of things each time, the nested-IF is used.

Again: **Use separate IF statements when you have a number of tasks that can be done and at any one time, you can have one, all, some or none of those tasks to be done. On the other hand, use a big nested-IF, if you want to be sure that at most one task (option) will be done.**

(For here, there are four things that MUST be done. Handle hair color, age, weight and office visits. And since 4 is more than one, we can't do those four things in one big statement. However, for any one of those things, such as *hair color*, you either want to add 2 points or 3 points or however many. You want to do at most ONE of those point additions, no more than that. Thus a nested-IF statement is used to choose between them.)

All this stuff may seem confusing. But if you can understand a part of this, then you are in good shape. If you understand all of this, you might as well become a compsci major now. (No, no don't do this ...you may end up a rich yuppie, but you probably will learn to really hate computers.)

The program above uses stuff you should have known prior to this chapter. (Yeah right!) Now let's use the new stuff.

You can do the same program by using the SELECT CASE statement instead. Compare the program on the next page with the previous version of this program. It does exactly the same thing.

This program was designed to demonstrate quite a variety of features regarding SELECT CASE statements. There is actually a lot embedded here. I could list a whole lot of things to notice but your best bet is to look at the two versions of this program and understand precisely why I have picked things the way I have. This includes analyzing the placement of each and every comma. Look at the CASE ELSEs if they exist. Understand why I go to a new line and so on.

Bye for now.

Have fun,

-Jt

```
REM The corrupt TA problem.
INPUT PROMPT "Give me a name?":Nam$
INPUT PROMPT "What is student's hair color?":Hair$
INPUT PROMPT "What is student's age?":Age
INPUT PROMPT "What is student's weight?":Weight
INPUT PROMPT "How many times did student come to the office?":Office_Visits
LET Points=0

SELECT CASE Hair$
   CASE "Blonde"
     LET Points=Points+3
   CASE "Brown","Black"
     LET Points=Points+2
   CASE ELSE
     LET Points=Points+1
END SELECT
SELECT CASE Age
   CASE 16 TO 22
     LET Points=Points+5
   CASE 23 TO 30
     LET Points=Points+3
   CASE ELSE
END SELECT
SELECT CASE Weight
  CASE IS < 100
    LET Points=Points+2
  CASE IS <= 120
    LET Points=Points+4
  CASE IS <= 140
    LET Points=Points+2
  CASE IS <= 150
    LET Points=Points+1
  CASE ELSE
    LET Points=Points-3
END SELECT
SELECT CASE Office_Visits
  CASE  1
    LET Points=Points + 1
  CASE 2 TO 5
    LET Points=Points + 3
  CASE 6 TO 10
    LET Points=Points+5
  CASE IS > 10
    LET Points=Points+10
  CASE ELSE
END SELECT

PRINT "Give ";Nam$;" ";Points;" extra points."
PRINT "Bye Bye"
END
```

5.4 Problems

Syntax Errors

1.

```
LET Picker= 7
SELECT CASE Picker*22
 CASE <50
    LET Chosen=1
 CASE <100
    LET Chosen=2
 CASE <200
    LET Chosen=3
 CASE ELSE
    LET Chosen=4
 END SELECT
PRINT Chosen
END
```

2.

```
READ Highway
SELECT CASE IF Highway = 18
 CASE Trucks IS > 200
    PRINT "Slightly annoying to drive here."
 CASE Trucks IS > 1000
    PRINT "Too dangerous on the road.''
 CASE ELSE
    PRINT "its okay"
END SELECT
DATA 18
END
```

3.

```
SELECT CASE 20+30/5
CASE IS < 10
  PRINT "Try again"
CASE IS < 20 OR > 50
  PRINT "Must be close"
CASE ELSE
END SELECT
END
```

4.

```
INPUT Year
INPUT GasMileage
IF Year < 1973 THEN
   SELECT CASE GasMileage
     CASE 0 TO 15
       PRINT "Bad gas mileage"
     CASE IS > 15
       PRINT "Good Gas mileage"
     CASE ELSE
       PRINT "Bad Data"
  ELSE
   SELECT CASE GasMileage
     CASE 0 TO 30
       PRINT "Bad gas mileage"
     CASE IS > 30
       PRINT "Good Gas mileage"
     CASE ELSE
       PRINT "Bad Data"
END SELECT
END IF
END
```

5.

```
READ Insults
SELECT CASE Insults
  CASE 1 TO 10
    PRINT "Just an average day"
  CASE 20 TO 50
    PRINT "A bit too much"
  CASE IS > 50
    PRINT "You poor slob."
END SELECT
DATA 15
END
```

Tracing

1.

```
READ SmallNumber
DATA 2
SELECT CASE SmallNumber*4
  CASE 1 TO 5
    LET SmallNumber = SmallNumber + 3
  CASE 5 TO 10
    LET SmallNumber = SmallNumber + 10
  CASE ELSE
    LET SmallNumber = SmallNumber - 5
END SELECT
SELECT CASE SmallNumber
  CASE 1 TO 5
    LET SmallNumber = SmallNumber + 3
  CASE 5 TO 10
    LET SmallNumber = SmallNumber + 10
  CASE ELSE
    LET SmallNumber = SmallNumber - 5
END SELECT
PRINT SmallNumber
END
```

2. Run the following program three times with the following sets of input:

```
3,1650
0,1700
5,1800
```

```
INPUT Accidents
INPUT  Insurance
LET Surcharge = 200
SELECT CASE Accidents
  CASE IS < 2
    IF Insurance > 1500 THEN LET Surcharge = Surcharge - 100
  CASE 2 TO 4
    IF Insurance < 1500 THEN LET Surcharge = Surcharge + 200
  CASE ELSE
    IF Insurance < 2000 THEN LET Surcharge = Surcharge * 2
END SELECT
PRINT Surcharge
END
```

3.

```
LET Answer = 0
READ Accumulator
DATA 10
LET Accumulator = Accumulator * 5
IF Accumulator < 20 THEN
  SELECT CASE Accumulator
  CASE 50
    LET Answer = 27
  CASE ELSE
    LET Answer = 45
  END SELECT
END IF
PRINT "The Answer is ": Answer
END
```

4.

```
READ PrintAll
DATA 5
SELECT CASE PrintAll
  CASE 1 TO 100
    PRINT "This program ";
  CASE 5,10,15,20
    PRINT "seems to print an ";
  CASE IS < 40
    PRINT "awful lot doesn't it?"
  CASE ELSE
    PRINT
END SELECT
END
```

5. The input to this program is: 45,72

```
INPUT Russian, American
LET Satellites = Russian + American
SELECT CASE Satellites
  CASE 0 TO 100
    IF American < 100 THEN PRINT "Not enough American satellites."
    IF Russian < 100 THEN PRINT "Not enough Russian satellites."
  CASE IS < 1000
    PRINT "There are too many satellites."
    SELECT CASE American - Russian
      CASE IS > 0
        PRINT "But at least there are more American than Russian satellites."
      CASE ELSE
        PRINT "Too bad there are more Russian than American satellites."
    END SELECT
  CASE ELSE
END SELECT
END
```

Programs

1. Write a program that helps a judge determine how long a particular criminal should be sentenced to jail. The program should start out by asking what a typical sentence for this crime would be (in years). Then the program should ask the judge if it was a "violent", "greedy" or "ignorant" crime. (It can only be classified as one of those three.) The sentences for violent crimes should be three times as long. Greedy crimes should be punished twice as long. An ignorant crime needs no further punishment than what is normal. The program should ask how many offenses this person has commited prior to this crime. If 0 other crimes, this person should get a 50% reduction. If there has been 1 other crime — no change in the sentencing. Two to five crimes should be punished twice as severly. Six or more should be punished three times as severly. The judge should also consider the crowdedness of the jail — either they are "very full", "full", "normal" or "empty". If they are very full, the criminal's sentence should be reduced in half. If they are full, the criminal should get 75% of the amount of time she/he would otherwise get. If they are normal, or empty, no change should be made in the sentence. Finally, the mood of the judge should be considered: either the judge is "mad", "ok" or "pleasant". A mad judge will add two years on to a sentence. A pleasant judge will subtract a year. The program should print out how long the sentence for a criminal should be. (Answers like 6.235 years are ok.)

2. Write a program to decide if a worker should get promoted or not. The following scale will be used to grade the employee. A mark of 60 or more means the person should be promoted. Print out a message telling whether to promote the worker or not. Find out how many times during the last year the employee worked over time. 0 times earns 0 points. 1-10 times earns 10 points. 11-30 earns 15 points. Over 30 earns 25 points. Find out how many times the worker arrived to work late. The worker should get 20 points if they were always on time. If they were late 1 to 5 times, they should get 10 points. More than 5 times late earns them 0 points. Ask whether the quality of their work is "excellent", "good", "average" or "bad". An Excellent worker gets 35 points, Good earns 10, Average gets 0. If a worker is Bad subtract 15 points from their total. Also inquire about the quantity of their work. If the amount is "Above average" give 15 points, "Normal" gets no bonus, but "Below Average" has 10 points subtracted from the total. Finally ask if the worker gets along with the other employees. If this is true, add on 15 points, otherwise give no points.

3. Write a program to print out a message classifying how expensive a particular university is. Ask for what the tuition to that school is. If the school costs $20,000 or more print out "One of the Most Expensive". For a school more than $12,000 but less than $20,000 print "Expensive". For $8,000 up to $12,000 print "Average" unless the school is a state university then print "Expensive". In the range $3000 to $8,000 print "Not Bad" if the school is not a state university but "A Bit High" if it is. For schools under $3000 print "Cheap".

4. Write a program that is capable of categorizing various movies. In particular, the program should ask how much the movie cost to film, how much the movie made in theatre ticket sales, how much the movie made in rentals and how much the movie made when its viewing rights were sold (to HBO and the like). From this information, the program should figure out how much in profit the movie made or how much was loss because production costs were larger than income. A message should be printed out according to this calculated amount. Movies that make over $200 million are considered to be "Blockbusters", those over $100 million are "Big Hits", more than $40 million is considered to be a "Hit" and over $20 million is "Average" unless they starred Sylvester Stalone, in which case they are considered to be a "Bomb" (you'll have to ask if he was the star for movies in this range. Movies that lose up to $10 million are considered to be "losers" and movies that loss more than $20 million are "Big Bombs". Besides printing this message, the program shoudl print exactly how much was made or lost by the movie. Demonstrate this program by running it on various data.

5. Write a program to calculate the price a book store should charge for a book. Starting with the cost that the store had to pay to get this book the price should automatically be increased by 25%. Based on this new value, certain increases and deductions can be made depending on what type of book is being sold. Computer Books should then be doubled in price. $5 is immediately tacked on to Best Sellers. Nursing Books get a 15% discount. Due to the Science Fiction sale, all Science Fiction Books are $1 cheaper. Cook Books can be reduced by $5 only if they are Albanian cookbooks and over $17 in price to begin with (after the 25% markup!). (Assume that at most a book can only fall into one of the categories "Computer", "Best Seller", "Nursing", "Science Fiction" or "Cookbook" — no books with topics like "Medication To Prevent Spoiled Microprocessor Salads".) The program should notify the user how much profit the store is making on this book that is being sold. Then it should print up a receipt for the customer, with the book's name, type and cost displayed. Tax (7%) should also be calculated and placed on the receipt with the final line containing the overall cost to the customer — with the tax included.

6. Write a program to determine if a candidate for Graduate School should be admitted to a particular university. There are six critieria that come into play. The most important consideration is that if the candidate is a friend of someone important, they will automatically be admitted. For those who don't have connections, the student's grades, GREs, recommendations and extracurriculum activities are important. Also, the rating of the candidate's undergraduate college is considered. To rate these things, the college has a point system that ranges up to 25 points. Candidates that get over 15 points are admitted. For grades, students get five points if their grade point average is 3.5 or more. They get three points for a GPA of 3 or more. Otherwise they get no points. A GRE total of more than 2100 earns them 5 points. A total more than 1800 earns them 4. Students with higher than 1500 get 2. Recommendations are judged by a panel and can fall into five categories. They can be rated "Superior", "Highly Rated", "Good", "Average" and "Poor". Students whose recommendations claim they are "Superior" or "Highly Rated" will get 5 points. "Good" earns them 4 points. "Average" gets them 2 points. If they are judged "Poor" this hurts them — they lose 3 points. Extracurriculum activities are also rated — either "Active" "Average" or "None". Those people who are rated "Active" will get five points. The other categories get nothing. Finally, a student's undergraduate school is rated on a scale from one to five; with 5 belonging to the most desirable schools. The program should calculate one candidate's rating and print out whether this student is accepted or not. If the candidate gets all 25 points, a message should be printed saying "get this student at all costs!"

7. Write a program to calculate how long a person can stay in the sun before they start burning. Let us simplify things a bit. There are four considerations — the sun bather's skin type, what latitude they are at, what the current "tanning index" is, and what SPF (Sun Protection Factor) their sun tan lotion has. Let us start out by assuming the person is at the NY latitude. There a three skin types — light skin people start burning in 20 minutes, medium skin people start burning in 40 minutes and dark skin people start burning in 70 minutes. Besides NY, there are 4 other latitudes a person can be at: Seattle, Los Angeles, San Diago and Brownsville. If they are at the Seattle latitude multiple their time in the sun by 1.2. For Los Angeles the multiplier is .8 — for San Diago it is .7 — for Brownsville it is .6. The "tanning index" tells how intense the sun is. If it is a very sunny day — an index of 8 to 10 — people burn faster, so multiple the time in the sun by .8 to get a better estimate. If the index is 4 to 6, multiply by 2 since it is less sunny. If the index is 3, mutliple by 4 since you can stay in the sun considerably longer. Finally, the SPF can be a number between 2 and 32. All you need to do is multiply the time in the sun by the SPF to get a new estimate of how long a person can stay in the sun. (For instance, if a person could stay in the sun for 25 minutes with no lotion on, then if they put a lotion with a SPF of 10 on, they can now stay in the sun for 250 minutes.)

8. You want to buy a new car but find it very confusing picking out a reasonable choice in a consistent manner from the many models available. Write a program that will help you rate these cars on a consistent scale. The program should ask for some information about the car you want to judge and then print out a number representing the rating of that car. You will rate the car on styling, handling, safety and cost. To make this program more useful, you should add your own rating categories that more accurately reflect what you are looking for in a car. For this assignment, you must add at least one more category — but are encouraged to add more. However, for the built-in categories listed above, you should use the following criteria. Styling: a car gets 300 points for being "sleek", 200 points for "average" and 50 points for "ugly". Handling: "sporty" gets 250 points, "responsive" gets 150 points, "sluggish" gets 50 points. Safety: "excellent" gets 400 points, "average" gets 150, and "unsafe" gets 100 points *taken away*. However, a car otherwise "average" in safety will get another 100 points if it also has air bags and antilock brakes. For Cost: under $15000 gets 500 points, $15001 to $25000 gets 300 points, $25001 to $35000 gets 150 points, over $35000 gets 50 points.

9. A forensic anthropologist is often called upon to determine characteristics of an individual who has died from undetermined causes and has become skeletonized. This often involves trying to determine the age, sex and race of the individual. Through extensive studies, it has been determined that on average certain characteristics in the bones are more likely to show up in individuals of one race when compared with another. But since there is extensive variation, singular characteristics by themselves do not tell you much. Rather, it is the accumulative evidence of many characteristics which can be used by the forensic anthropologist to infer the likely racial affiliation of a particular individual. Write a program to help a forensic anthropologist guess the likely race from a particular skull. Assign ratings based on characteristics of the nose, eye, palate and cheek. If the total points is -4 to -2, have the program state "this skull tends towards caucasoid characteristics", for a total rating of -1 to 1 state "mongoloid" and for 2 to 4 state "negroid". A skull gets 1 point for a broad nose, -1 for a narrow nose and zero for moderate. The skull gets one point for a rectangular eye socket, zero for a circular eye and 1 point for in between. For palate, it is -1 for narrow, 1 for wide and 0 for moderate. Finally, for cheek it is 1 point for "no projection", 0 for "forward projection" and -1 for "recessive". (This program will be far from perfect but it will give you an idea of how a computer could be utilized in a useful manner to assist in this process.)

Special Chapter 2

Now that we know two statements for making decisions when writing TRUE BASIC programs, let us go through a whole example and see when, why and how we use the IF and SELECT statements, and their many options, to help us in our program writing.

The following program deals with the rules at a condominium development. As you may know, when you own a condo, you own your own building, but you share the grounds with other people. Because of this, committees are created to form the Condo Rules and Regulations — which set up guidelines informing you how you should live your life — at least that aspect of it which involves your coexistence with your neighbors. As with any good bureaucratic system, these rules are generally pretty lousy. (You know, I really don't enjoy sticking with these mild adjectives — but then again, I don't want to disturb any of my readers. So those of you with more creative imaginations, plug in any adjective you feel is appropriate.)

Let us say you live in Anxiety Hill, a development of dirt cheap condos for yuppies-to-be. A committee here has come up with an extensive list of rules which tenants should follow. Due to time and space constraints, I will not itemize this whole list. Rather, I will just present several of the rule categories, and the associated warnings and fines involved. Several members of this committee have been concerned with the fact that too many owners have moved out of their condos and are leasing them out to less-well-to-do tenants. In particular, these tenants seem to have less of a desire to upkeep the condo grounds. Because of this, it was decided that rules for renters should be somewhat more severe than rules for owners.

A partial list of the rules is as follows:

Rules for Owners:

Rule Name	Description	Warnings	Fine
Doggie Law	Pets must be well behaved	2	$25
Parking Law	No parking in fire zones	2	$25
Garbage Law	Garbage and recyclables must be sorted	2	$25
Noise Law	Parties should not disturb the neighbors	1	$50

Rules for Renters:

Rule Name	Description	Warnings	Fine
Doggie Law	Pets must be leashed and waste properly disposed	1	$50
Parking Law	No parking allowed anywhere	2	$75
Garbage Law	Thou shall never create any garbage	1	$125
Visitor Law	All visitors must be of high intellect and beauty	0	$250
Noise Law	Never never make noise after 10pm or before 8am	0	Automatic Dismisal

You'll notice you get two warnings concerning parking. That seems kind, but then you have to realize how easily those warnings are usually used up. First, by your moving truck when you originally move in, and later by your moving truck when you soon move out.

Notice that at least one rule calls for automatic dismissal from the condo development. Also, there is a further rule that specifies that as soon as the total amount of fines you have paid out to the committee over the years goes over $500, you must leave the development.

Well, say that the input to this program is your name, condo number, the amount of fines you have already paid out and whether you are a *renter* or an *owner*. A fifth item of input will be the current rule you have broken. Finally, the program will ask how many times the person has been warned. The program's purpose is to print out a message informing the violator of a warning, a fine that must be paid or an eviction notice.

Let us think up some variables.

For input, we will have Criminal$ for the person's name, CondoNum for the address of the condominium, TotalFines for the fines this person has paid so far, and Status$ for the status of the person, be it "renter" or "owner". For the rule that has been broken we will use the variable Rule. (In a moment, we will discuss why a numeric variable, rather than a string variable, has been chosen here.) Lastly, the variable Warnings is used to hold the number of previous warnings this person has had regarding this rule.

As we are creating the program, we are not sure of the exact nature of the message we are going to print out at the end; it may be a warning or a notice of a fine. We will use the variable Message$ to hold onto the message we want to print.

To help us decide if the person should get an eviction notice or not, we will also use a flag variable, called Evict$. This variable will be initialized to "no" but if it is switched to "yes", the person should be evicted.

Let us think about the main structure of the program. As has already been implied, we plan to make this a typical three part program. There will be an INPUT section to ask questions, a "calculation" section to determine the fine and choose the appropriate message and a PRINT section in which an appropriate message is created. There also may be some variables initialized towards the beginning of the program. For the most part, the INPUT and PRINT sections will be rather straightforward. We will discuss them in a moment. The CALCULATION section will be a little more involved.

This last section need not be anything fancy, as there aren't any difficult equations to solve, but we do plan to use the decision making statements we have learned in the last couple of chapters.

We won't go into detail about the calculation section yet, but let us start planning some general ideas for it. We know right off that there are two different set of rules, depending on whether the person is a renter or an owner. That is, we immediately should see that the program has to make a decision as to which set of rules to use, either one or the other. Whenever a decision must be made by a program, we should start thinking about using IF or SELECT statements. Here, it is only a two-way decision, either the person is a renter or an owner. Two-way decisions can be handled by simple IF statements. So the main statement of the calculation section should be an IF statement. In the THEN part we can deal with the owner rules, in the ELSE part we can deal with the renter rules.

To plan a little deeper, let us just consider the renter rules. There are five different rules. The program must make a decision as to which of these rules must be handled at this time. This is a five-way decision. That means, we want to use a nested-IF or a SELECT. Since SELECT is probably easier, let us plan to use the SELECT statement. You can see that a similar type of SELECT statement can be used for the owner rules too. So the structure of the calculation section will be something like:

```
IF person is owner THEN
     SELECT CASE whichever owner rule was broken
      CASE First Rule
         Handle first rule
      CASE ...
     END SELECT
  ELSE
     SELECT CASE whichever renter rule was broken
      CASE First Rule
         Handle first rule
      CASE ...
     END SELECT
END IF
```

Check this out. We want to have a large multi-line IF statement in which both the THEN and ELSE section has a SELECT CASE statement in it.

We'll get back to this shortly. First, let us design the input section. Shouldn't be too hard. We just want to ask six questions and make sure the answers get placed in the variables we chose. Questions like "Who broke a law?" and "In what condo does this person live?" would be appropriate. That will lead to INPUT PROMPT statements like:

```
INPUT PROMPT "How much has this person paid in fines previously?":TotalFines
INPUT PROMPT "Is this person a renter or an owner?":Status$
```

For one of the questions we may want to do things differently. Consider the question of which law was broken. It may look like:

```
INPUT PROMPT "Which law was broken?":Rule$
```

Later in the program when we get to the select statement we may have:

```
SELECT CASE Rule$
 CASE "Doggie Law"
   handle the doggie law ...
 CASE "Parking Law"
   ...
END SELECT
```

This would be fine. It is syntactically and logically correct. In fact, if you designed your program this way, and got it to work and turned it in, the chances are you would get full credit for it. But there is a bothersome problem with this method. In particular, the person using the program has to be very precise when they type in the rule's name. As long as they typed in exactly "Doggie Law" when the program was run, it would handle the case correctly. But if they typed in anything else, such as "The Dog Law", "The Pet Rule" or closer, even "DOGGIE LAW" or "Doggie Law" (there is an extra space between the two words) the program would not find a perfect match with the string built into the SELECT CASE statement which is "Doggie Law" and so it will not do this case, even though this is where the code that handles the rule broken by the tenant is located. At best, if there is a CASE ELSE, that is where the above-mentioned flawed input will be handled. At worst, there is no CASE ELSE and the program will stop dead with a bomb. (As we pointed out in the chapter on SELECT CASE, if no case matches, not even a CASE ELSE, the program stops dead!)

How can we make it easier for the person who has to enter the rule's name? Well, we can just have them enter a number instead. 1 might stand for "Doggie Law", 2 for Parking Law etc. If we want to do this, then we should print out a menu, ask the person to choose an item off that menu by typing in a number, and store this answer in a numeric variable. How do you print a menu? Use a PRINT statement of course. Like:

```
PRINT "Enter 1 for Doggie Law"
...
```

And after this, use a regular INPUT PROMPT to get their choice into the variable Rule (no dollar sign!).

Of course, doing things this way will mean that there will be a number of PRINT statements in our INPUT section. However, there is nothing wrong with that. They are just there to help the person who is going to be typing in the input.

Ok, one more thing before we get back to the Calculation Section. Let us design the output. Oh, we could start out by printing the person's name, and their condo number. Maybe we want to add some general message like "We don't like your type", or "You've been caught sucka." Then, you probably want a line telling exactly what law was broken. Eventually we want to print some specific message like "This is a warning to never do it again." Or, "You owe $25". These types of messages will handle fines and warnings. The variable Message$ will hold this specific message — it will get its value in the Calculation Section. Why don't we initialize the Message$ variable to some common message, such as the warning message, at the beginning of the program and only reset its value if we discover that some other message should be printed. Whatever the final message, at the end of the program all we will have to do is print out this variable.

Another message like "Because of your extreme abuse of the Condo Rules and Regulations, let this be your notice that you have 30 days to move out." can handle evictions. How does the program know whether or not to print this statement? Well, it has to make a choice either to print it or not, by looking at the flag variable Evict$ which is expected to indicate this. It will be "no" if the person is not to be evicted, and "yes" if the person should be evicted. A decision. Two choices. A simple IF statement would be wise here. The eviction notice is only printed within the IF statement. That is, our PRINT section will end with an IF statement. (By now you should know that IF statements can appear in any part of the program including the INPUT, Calculation or PRINT sections.) Something like:

```
IF Evict$ = "yes" THEN PRINT "You have been evicted."
```

One thing to notice here is that we have chosen to print out the name of the law that was broken. But wait a second, we won't have this name in a variable, because the user of the program is typing in a number. We have already decided that. So we had better create a variable, let us call it RuleName$ and make sure it gets the right value. We can set its value in any SELECT CASE statement which uses the number Rule as a selection variable. Why don't we have a small SELECT CASE statement directly after the INPUT section for this purpose.

Like:

```
SELECT CASE Rule
 CASE 1
   LET RuleName$ = "Doggie Law"
 CASE 2
   LET RuleName$ = "Parking Law"
 ...


END SELECT
```

Ok, time to get specific about the Calculation Section. The one part we will have to work on is the big outside IF statement. But before doing that, we can work on the last statement of this section. In particular, besides setting the Message$ that must be printed, and adjusting the amount of the TotalFines, the Calculation Section is supposed to check to see if the person has accumulated over $500 in fines. If so, this person is to be evicted. How can the program check this? Well, it has to make a decision — has this person been fined over $500 or not? Decision! Two choices – "yes" or "no". Think IF statement here. In BASIC this can be done with a simple IF statement once you realize that the fine total is in the variable TotalFines and the flag variable Evict$ should be set to the value "yes" if the person should be evicted. The statement is:

```
IF TotalFines > 500 THEN LET Evict$ = "yes"
```

Ok, everything is done except for that one large IF statement in the calculation section that is going to handle the various broken rules. We have already seen how this IF statement will have two SELECT statements embedded in it — one to deal with owners, and one to deal with renters. Let us see more precisely what this will look like in BASIC.

```
IF Status$ = "owner" THEN
    SELECT CASE Rule
      CASE 1
          Handle Doggie Rule for owner
      CASE 2
          Handle Parking Rule for owner
      . . . .
      CASE ELSE
          Handle bad numbered inputted for the variable Rule
    END SELECT
  ELSE
    SELECT CASE Rule
      CASE 1
          Handle Doggie Rule for renter
      CASE 2
          Handle Parking Rule for renter
      . . . .
      CASE ELSE
          Handle bad numbered inputted for the variable Rule
    END SELECT
END IF
```

Notice that both SELECT CASE statements have a CASE ELSE. This is to catch the cases when the user of the program enters a number that is not between one and five. There is no law to match up with these numbers, so some type of error message should be printed. A simple PRINT statement can be placed in the CASE ELSE section to complain about the error. The same message can be printed in both SELECT CASE statements. Nothing else has to be done in the case of bad data.

There is one strange case. The owners don't have to worry about the Visitor Law. So we will just set the variable Message$ to say this in that particular case. Like:

```
LET Message$ = "But this is okay, since owners are allowed to."
```

So at the end something like the following will be printed:

```
You have broken the Visitor Law
But this is okay, since owners are allowed to.
```

What should be done in the rest of the cases? Well, for each rule, we need to pick an appropriate message to be printed and adjust the total amount of fines this person has accumulated, if indeed they have been fined. Thus, in each case, we will set out to give Message$ and TotalFines new values.

Some cases are simple. For instance, for the Visitor Law for renters there is no check to see how many previous warnings they have had. They automatically get fined 250 dollars. So the message should express this, and their total fine should be increased by $250. This can be done as follows:

```
CASE 4
    LET Message$ = "You are being fined $250"
    LET TotalFines = TotalFines + 250
```

The case for renters when they break the Noise Law is they are automatically evicted. The message should reflect this, and the flag variable Evict$ should be set. Like:

```
CASE 5
    LET Message$ = "You've made a big mistake."
    LET Evict$ = "yes"
```

All the rest of the cases have the same pattern. In particular, for the rest of the rules, the program must decide if the violator has used up all his warnings. If so, then that person should be fined the necessary amount. The message should reflect this and the tenant's total fines should be adjusted. Also note that the first three rules for renters have exactly the same warning counts and fines — this means these three rules can be collapsed into one case.

Let us consider one of the remaining cases. How about the Parking Law for owners? Here they get 2 warnings but after this they pay a $75 fine. How can the computer decide whether to give a fine or not? Well, it is a two-choice decision — either give the fine or don't. So we want to use an IF statement to make this decision. In particular, in English we would say "if the person has used up all their warnings then fine them." How can we make the proper condition for the TRUE BASIC IF statement here? Well, note we have a variable called Warnings which has the exact number of warnings this person has been given already. So we just check to see if this number is 2 or more. We end up with a complete IF statement like:

```
CASE 2
    IF Warnings >= 2 THEN
        LET Message$ = "You are being fined $75."
        LET TotalFines = TotalFines + 75
    END IF
```

Why did we use a multi-line IF statement here and not just a single-line one? Well, we had two things we had to do, both set the message, and adjust the total of the fines. The syntax of the single-line IF statement only allows one statement after the THEN. Since we have two things here, we need the multi-line form which allows for more statements between the THEN and END IF. Why don't we have an ELSE? Well, here an ELSE would handle the case where the person just needs to be warned. For this case, the total fines need not be adjusted, because the person is not fined. (The amount stays what it was before this violation.) The message should say something like "This is a warning, do not break this rule again." But wait a second, the message does say that already because we initialized Message$ to that at the beginning of the program. So we certainly do not have to regive it this value. (It is stupid to assign a value to a variable if it already has that value at this time!) So there is really nothing to do here for the "give a warning" ELSE part. So we just drop the ELSE part and stick with a simple multi-line IF — THEN statement.

Well, did you catch what we ended up with? For each case where we have to worry about giving a warning or not, we end up with an IF statment inside of one of the CASEs of a SELECT CASE statement. Well, we know any statement can go in these parts — so certainly an IF statement is valid.

So, we have spent a lot of time discussing this program. In fact, we have talked about every aspect of the program. There should be no surprises in what follows. Though, it may seem a bit shocking to see it all at once. This turns out to be our biggest program so far.

Putting it all together, we get the program you see on the following three pages.

```
REM Condo Rule Program
REM Jt
REM July 1990

LET Evict$ = "no"
LET Message$ = "This is a warning, do not break this rule again."

INPUT PROMPT "What is the lawbreaker's name?":Criminal$
INPUT PROMPT "What condo does this person live in?":CondoNum
INPUT PROMPT "How much has this person paid in fines previously?":TotalFines
INPUT PROMPT "Is this person a renter or an owner?":Status$

PRINT "Type in a choice from the following menu:"
PRINT "----------------------------------------"
PRINT "Doggie Law ---- Enter 1"
PRINT "Parking Law --- Enter 2"
PRINT "Garbage Law --- Enter 3"
PRINT "Visitor Law --- Enter 4"
PRINT "Noise Law ----- Enter 5"
PRINT "----------------------------------------"
INPUT PROMPT "Enter the number of the rule that was broken:":Rule
INPUT PROMPT "How many  times has this person been warnned about this rule?":Warnings

! Set the name of the rule based on the number the person entered.
SELECT CASE Rule
   CASE 1
     LET RuleName$ = "Doggie Law"
   CASE 2
     LET RuleName$ = "Parking Law"
   CASE 3
     LET RuleName$ = "Garbage Law"
   CASE 4
     LET RuleName$ = "Visitor Law"
   CASE 5
     LET RuleName$ = "Noise Law"
   CASE ELSE
END SELECT
```

```
! Create the message and adjust total fines based on which law
! was broken and who broke it.
IF Status$ = "owner" THEN
        SELECT CASE Rule
        CASE 1 to 3
            IF Warnings >= 2 THEN
                LET Message$ = "You are being fined $25."
                LET TotalFines = TotalFines + 25
            END IF
        CASE 4
            LET Message$ = "But this is okay, since owners are allowed to."
        CASE 5
            IF Warnings >= 1 THEN
                LET Message$ = "You are being fined $50."
                LET TotalFines = TotalFines + 50
            END IF
        CASE ELSE
            PRINT "There is no such law, output from this program will be nonsense."
        END SELECT
    ELSE
        SELECT CASE Rule
        CASE 1
            IF Warnings >= 1 THEN
                LET Message$ = "You are being fined $50."
                LET TotalFines = TotalFines + 50
            END IF
        CASE 2
            IF Warnings >= 2 THEN
                LET Message$ = "You are being fined $75."
                LET TotalFines = TotalFines + 75
            END IF
        CASE 3
            IF Warnings >= 1 THEN
                LET Message$ = "You are being fined $125."
                LET TotalFines = TotalFines + 125
            END IF
        CASE 4
            LET Message$ = "You are being fined $250"
            LET TotalFines = TotalFines + 250
        CASE 5
            LET Message$ = "You've made a big mistake."
            LET Evict$ = "yes"
        CASE ELSE
            PRINT "There is no such law, output from this program will be nonsense."
        END SELECT
END IF
```

```
! If the person has too much in total fines, this person should be evicted
IF TotalFines>500 THEN LET Evict$ = "yes"

! Print out the notice.
PRINT
PRINT
PRINT Criminal$,
PRINT "Condo Number:";CondoNum
PRINT "This notice is being sent to you regarding a recent violation"
PRINT "of one of the Condo Rules and Regulations."
PRINT "You broke the ";RuleName$;"."
PRINT Message$
PRINT
PRINT "You have accumulated ";TotalFines;" so far."
PRINT
IF Evict$ = "yes" THEN
    PRINT "Because  of your extreme  abuse of the  Condo Rules and Regulations"
    PRINT "let  this be your  notice that  you have  30 days  to  move out."
END IF
END
```

This program not only demonstrates various aspects about IF and SELECT but amazingly, it shows that you can have a SELECT statement embedded inside of an IF. And likewise, you can also have an IF statement embedded in a SELECT. Both are legal. Here, we see that the smaller IF statements are embedded inside of CASEs of a SELECT which itself is embedded in a large outside IF statement. Whoa! We don't expect the structures of your own programs to be this convoluted. It is only demonstrated here, to show a wide variety of uses and locations for these decision-making statements. The final program may look impressive, even scary, but if you were following the discussion all along, you realize that the program really is not that complex at all.

Good luck on your own programs.

Have fun,

Jt

Chapter 6

FOR Loops

Ok, now, sure you can write programs that use input to generate output after doing various calculations. And yes, you can indeed make decisions with your programs by using IF - THEN -ELSE statements and SELECT CASE statements, but your programs still aren't flexible enough.

6.1 Loops

If you think to yourself for a while you might realize that there is definitely something important missing. For instance, if the computer can do millions of instructions per second, does this mean that some programmer who wants to use the full power of the computer has to type in programs that are millions of instructions long? (Or BASIC programs that are thousands of lines long and translated into millions of machine instructions!) Can't be.

Consider the following program. A programmer writes a program to ask 10 people for their names and scores on a test. The average score is then calculated and finally the program prints out each person's name, his score and how much he was above or below the average.

Great. So you need 20 INPUT PROMPT statements (10 for names and 10 for numbers), some calculations and then at least 10 PRINT statements. You know enough to do the problem yourself, right? Ok, then this guy comes to Rutgers and finds out that a particular class has 500 students. Now what does he do? He has to rewrite his program so it has 1000 INPUTS and 500 PRINTS. Oh, man. There has to be a better way. And there is. He can use a loop. A loop allows certain actions to be repeated over and over again.

Later we will do a specific program that uses loops. But first let's understand exactly how to use and interpret a loop.

There are two types of loops. FOR loops and DO - LOOPS. DO - LOOPS are used when you are not sure exactly how many times the loop should "go around". FOR loops, or counted loops, are used when you are sure how many times that the loop should cycle. This number can be placed in the actual statement or it can be held in a variable that is used in that statement.

Today we will concentrate on FOR loops:

6.2 The FOR statement

SYNTAX

> **FOR** *variable=expression* **TO** *expression* **STEP** *expression*
>
> *Statements (that make up the body of the loop).*
>
> **NEXT** *variable*

Note:

1. The STEP expression part is not necessary
2. The variable in the FOR statement and the NEXT statement are the same.

EXAMPLES

- FOR X = 1 TO 10
  $\vdots$
  NEXT X

- FOR Y= A To A+10 STEP 2
  $\vdots$
  NEXT Y

- FOR I=10 TO 1 STEP -1
  $\vdots$
  NEXT I

POSSIBLE ERRORS

1. Forgetting to place the variable name after the NEXT.
2. Having the WRONG variable name after the NEXT. It must match what is on the FOR statement.
3. Forgetting the NEXT statement totally.
4. Having the NEXT statement in the wrong place.

MEANING

1. The variable in the FOR statement is called the "counting variable". It will be used to keep track of how many times we have gone through the loop.
2. When the program finishes the statement prior to the FOR and thus goes on to the next line and encounters this FOR loop, the variable is assigned the value after the equals. (This is the first of the two expressions.) Often, the first expression is a value, such as 1.
3. The program then proceeds thru the loop executing all statements exactly as they are normally executed.
4. When a NEXT is encountered, the program "jumps" back to the FOR statement.
5. The variable is incremented by the default value of 1 **or** if there is a STEP, the variable is incremented by the step expression which often is a value. (If the expression is a negative value, the variable is essentially decremented or made smaller.)
6. If the variable's new value is greater than the value of the second expression of the FOR loop, then the loop stops and the program goes to the statement after the NEXT. (If the step expression is negative then it does this jump when the variable's new value is LESS than the second expression)

USE

1. Allows statements to be executed over and over again a set amount of times.
2. Allows a variable to be incremented (or decremented) in an orderly fashion. Generally, the variable's values are used in the algorithm enclosed in the loop.

6.3   Some Traces Of FOR Loops

What do the following programs print?

```
FOR X=1 TO 10
  PRINT X
NEXT X
END
```
                              prints->   1
                                                  2
                                                  3
                                                  4
                                                  5
                                                  6
                                                  7
                                                  8
                                                  9
                                                  10

```
FOR I= -2 TO 4
  PRINT I
NEXT I
END
```
                              prints ->   -2
                                                 -1
                                                  0
                                                  1
                                                  2
                                                  3
                                                  4

```
FOR I=5 TO 7
  PRINT I
NEXT I
END
```
                              prints ->   5
                                                  6
                                                  7

```
FOR J=5 TO 5
  PRINT J
NEXT J
END
```
                              prints ->   5

```
FOR K=1 TO 5 STEP 2
  PRINT K
NEXT K
END
```

              prints ->   1
                               3
                               5

```
FOR H=4 TO 9 STEP 3
  PRINT H
NEXT H
END
```

              prints ->   4
                               7

```
FOR KK=5 TO 2 STEP -1
  PRINT KK
NEXT KK
END
```

              prints ->   5
                               4
                               3
                               2

```
FOR P=5 TO -3 STEP -2
  PRINT P
NEXT P
END
```

              prints ->   5
                               3
                               1
                              -1
                              -3

```
FOR I=6 TO 3
  PRINT I
NEXT I
END
```

        Doesn't print anything since I will start out at 6, which
        is greater than the ending value, 3. (The step here is
        the default value, which is 1, a positive number.)

```
    LET A=3
    LET B=7
    LET C=9
    LET D=3
    FOR I=A TO B STEP C/D
      PRINT I
    NEXT I
    END
```

```
              prints ->    3
                           6
```

Here is a more meaningful example, with several statements in the loop along with statement before and after the loop.

```
    PRINT "**********"
    FOR I=1 TO 3
      PRINT "i is ";I
      LET S= I^2
      PRINT "i squared is";S
      PRINT "----------"
    NEXT I
    PRINT "ALL DONE"
    END
```

```
              prints ->   **********
                          i is 1
                          i squared is 1
                          ----------
                          i is 2
                          i squared is 4
                          ----------
                          i is 3
                          i squared is 9
                          ----------
                          ALL DONE
```

Notice how statements *before* the loop are done once. Statements *after* the loop are done once. All the statements *in* the loop are done in a regular order. The loop "loops around" when the NEXT statement is reached. Statements in a loop may be done many times.

When tracing a program that has a loop, don't let this complication distract you. Just precede in a normal way, doing one line at a time. Do exactly what that line says to do. Only worry about the loop itself when you hit the FOR or NEXT statements. For all other statements, you should just forget you are in a loop and just use your knowledge of BASIC exactly as you have before.

Statements that are not in a loop, (they are either before or after it) will only be done once. When tracing, you should not do the actions in these statements more than once. It is only the statements in the loop, between the FOR and NEXT that may happen more than once.

6.4   Tracing and Debugging Loops

You may have noticed some strange examples, some loops only executed once, others never allowed the statements within them to be executed at all, and still others didn't stop at the value they claimed to be the ending number. Why would you write such strange things? Well, unless it was for the purpose of writing a tricky test question, you might not write statements which such strange values included in them. On the other hand, many times as you write the FOR loop, you will use variables within them. This is especially true for the "ending" expression. Now, once you start including the variables in these expressions, there is no telling as you write the program exactly how many times they will execute. This will not be known until the person using the program supplies the necessary input and these variables get their values. Depending on what values are supplied, it then becomes possible that the loop might go around ten times, once or none at all.

In short, if you use actual values (numbers) as you write the FOR statement, then it becomes easier to spot some of the strangeness that we refer to above. You'd be able to guard for this. But if you use variables, and many programs work better if you do use variables, then it is no longer easy to spot all the strange things a loop might do. Now, when you run your program, if something strange happens, you will have to look at the loop very carefully and see what values the variables (or expressions) eventually turned into when that loop was executed. By changing these variables into their values, it will then become apparent why the loop did what it did.

Suppose you write a program in which there where some PRINT statements in a loop. When the program was run, for some reason the PRINTs do not come out on the screen. What could this mean? Well, you should think to yourself — "Hmmmm, those statements didn't seem to execute and those statements were in a loop. Maybe the loop never went around." You should then look at the loop and try to figure out what was wrong. Let us say the particular loop started with the following:

```
FOR I = 5 TO Count
```

There is only one thing that could have stopped this loop from going around. That is, the variable COUNT was less than 5.

Sure enough, if you look previously in the program you may find the error. It may be something like.

```
INPUT PROMPT "How many times do you want to print?":Kount
```

Look at that, you used the variable Kount up there ... with a "K". No wonder the value of the variable Count (with a "C") is less than 5. It has the value 0, since we never gave this different variable a value. It is the first time we have used a variable named Count (with this "C" spelling) in this program and as we know, TRUE BASIC will start a numeric variable off with the value 0, if you don't initialize its value in some way yourself.

Likewise maybe you have a statement at the end of your program like:

```
PRINT "The sum of all your numbers is ";TotalSum
```

This is in a program that is supposed to add up nine numbers. You run the program, type in a bunch of numbers and it at the end it prints out:

```
The sum of all your numbers is 0
```

You scream something like "Stupid computer, the sum of all those numbers I typed in is not 0", and you run into the consulting room claiming "I think my computer is broken!"

Of course, the problem is probably with your program, not the computer. Reflecting on what you have done, you remember that you used a loop to add up your numbers. Maybe something happened and that loop never went around.

You look at your program and you see something like:

```
LET TotalSum = 0
FOR I = 10 to 9
      .
      .
      .
   LET TotalSum = TotalSum + AnotherNumber
      .
      .
      .
NEXT I
```

You now should smack your head and say "No wonder the TotalSum is zero. The body of this loop never executed. I accidently typed in the number 10 instead of 1, to start the loop." And you'd then fix it.

These problems presented here are not meant to discourage you. Nor is this meant to itemize all the possible errors you might make when you use loops. Believe me, you'll think up your own ingenious ways to make mistakes. Fortunately, and this should please you, most of the times when you use loops, especially FOR loops, you'll get it right the first time. These examples are discussed to show you a methodology to use when trying to track down problems with programs that use loops. Often, a problem with a loop may not materialize until later in the program. You need to be aware that you may have to backtrack thru the program in order to pinpoint your problem.

6.5 Some Programs

So now that you have seen most of the possibilities, you should be able to trace and debug loops.

But how do you know when to use a FOR loop when writing a program?

Let's look at two uses for FOR loops by working thru a couple of programming examples.

6.5.1 Physics Problem

Suppose you wanted to investigate some physics problems. You know the equation F=ma, or Force equals Mass times Acceleration. What you want to do is supply a bunch of numbers for mass and acceleration to the computer and it will tell you the force. You want to do this a number of times, so that you can see the various changes in force that result when you play around with the acceleration and mass values. Let us say you want to use about 100 sets of values.

Well how do you go about writing this program? First of all, forget about the fact that the program is supposed to allow you to do 100 problems. Instead, just concentrate on designing the program without a loop. How can you write a program to ask for the mass and the acceleration, calculate the force and print this answer out? Come on, this is a simple one. Use two INPUT PROMPTS to allow the user to enter the required values, use a LET to calculate the force and then finally end with a PRINT to print out the result. Four lines. Not very hard.

So, now how do you make this happen 100 times? Guess what, it is again very simple. You want to enclose these four lines in the body of a loop. That loop should be one that executes 100 times. What is the easiest loop that goes around 100 times?

Here is a valid program, with a small elaboration, to do the task:

```
REM Program to study a physics equation.
  FOR I=1 TO 100
    INPUT PROMPT  "What is the mass?":Mass
    INPUT PROMPT  "What is the acceleration?":Accel
    LET Force=Mass*Accel
    PRINT "With a mass of ";Mass
    PRINT " and an acceleration of";Accel
    PRINT "  you get a force of ";Force
  NEXT I
  END
```

If you look at this program carefully, you see that you are causing some process to happen 100 times. That is what the loop is for. The FOR i=1 to 100 is exactly what we need for this process to happen 100 times.

What process is happening 100 times? Simple. A cycle of a process consists of an input stage, calculation stage and finally an output stage.

Without using a loop, it would have been necessary to write out

```
INPUT PROMPT ...
LET ...
PRINT ...
```

at least 100 times.

Something else good about using a FOR loop is that if we later decide we want to do our process (here it is calculating force) 1000 times, all we have to do is modify the loop. This is very nice since we need not touch the other parts of the program at all.

One last thing to notice about this program is that the counting variable, I, is used solely for the purpose of counting the loop. We do not use this variable any place else in the program. It has no secondary purpose.

The presents the simplest way in which to use a FOR loop. Use a FOR loop to surround a collection of statements which you want to execute a certain amount of times. This is extremely easy to do as we have seen here.

6.5.2   Gas Mileage (Again) Program

Remember the gas mileage program? Let us do the same thing again. But this time, let us say we want to figure out the gas mileage for a number of months. The person using the program will know exactly how many months and will have the amount of gas used, and the miles traveled for each month. We want the program to print out the monthly gas mileage, and in the end, the total gas mileage.

We are going to need a number of variables. GasUsed can be the amount of gas used in one month. MilesGone can be the number of miles traveled in that month. TotalGas will be the amount of gas used in all months, and TotalMiles the total number of miles traveled during the whole time period.

What do we do for one particular month? Essentially, we want to ask how much gas was used in the month, how many miles traveled, add these figures on to the totals, figure out the monthly gas mileage and print it. Something like the following would do:

```
INPUT PROMPT "How many miles did you go in this month?":MilesGone
INPUT PROMPT "How much gas was used?":GasUsed
LET TotalMiles = TotalMiles + MilesGone
LET TotalGas = TotalGas + GasUsed
LET MPG = MilesGone / GasUsed
PRINT "Your gas mileage in this month was ";MPG
```

Of course, we want to do this a number of times. So a loop is necessary. Each time around the loop we will handle the figures for one month. But wait, how many times do we want the loop to go around? Well, that is a tough one. We just don't know as we write the program exactly how many times. The person using the program will make that decision. What can we do? Well, we can ask the person using the program by using an INPUT PROMPT. We should do this once, at the beginning of the program, some time prior to the loop. Let us say we ask the person how many months of data they have, and store the answer to this question in the variable Months. With this being done, we can now design our loop statement. It should look like:

```
FOR J = 1 to Months
  ...
NEXT J
```

What else needs to be done? Well, we know we should do some initialization at the beginning. In particular, besides asking the question about Months, we should set our total counters to zero. Should these be set to zero in the loop, or before the loop? Well certainly we do not want to do this in the loop. If we put it here, then every single time we handled a new month, the totals would go back to zero and we lose the sum of all the previous months' values. So, we set these to zero, once before the loop.

And what do we do at the very end of the program? Well, we want to calculate and print the overall gas mileage. We can do this from using our total counters. Should this be in the loop or after it? Well, we only want to calculate and print the overall gas mileage once after we have handled all the months individually. Since this is something we want to do once, we place it outside of the loop — or in this case after the loop.

Now we have thought about it enough and can present the whole program.

```
REM Gas Mileage program Revisited
REM Jt    July 1990
REM  New example for Fall 90
LET TotalGas = 0
LET TotalMiles = 0
INPUT PROMPT "How many months of gas data do you have?":Months

FOR J = 1 to Months
  INPUT PROMPT "How many miles did you go in this month?":MilesGone
  INPUT PROMPT "How much gas was used?":GasUsed
  LET TotalMiles = TotalMiles + MilesGone
  LET TotalGas = TotalGas + GasUsed
  LET MPG = MilesGone / GasUsed
  PRINT "Your gas mileage in this month was ";MPG
NEXT J

LET MPG = TotalMiles / TotalGas
PRINT
PRINT "During this ";Months;" month period of time,"
PRINT "your overall gas mileage was ";MPG
END
```

6.5.3 Summation Problem

Another way you can use a FOR loop is to actually utilize the value of the loop counter variable in the loop's body to perform some task.

How can you write a program to ask for a number and then print out the sum of all numbers from 1 to that number?

For instance, if the number is 6 the program should print 21. $(1 + 2 + 3 + 4 + 5 + 6 = 21)$

Well let us look at this systematically. Here is one way you can go about this. Let us say that we have a variable called Summ which should be the sum of all the numbers. Why don't we slowly accumulate the sum into this variable Summ? For instance, first start Summ at zero. Then add the number 1 on making Summ be 1. Then add the number 2 on making Summ grow to 3. Continue adding to Summ, the numbers 4,5, 6 ... and so on. Why don't we create a variable to hold on to the current number we should be adding on — let us call it Numm.

Before we even do this, why don't we trace an example and see what we intend to happen. Let us say we want to add together all numbers up to six. Start Summ at zero, and Numm at 1.

```
                    Summ
    Numm             0
     1
```

Now add the current number on to the sum.

```
                    Summ
    Numm            *-*
     1               1
```

And increment the number to the next value.

```
                    Summ
    Numm            *-*
    *-*              1
     2
```

Ok, add this new number on to the sum and increment the number again.

```
                    Summ
    Numm            *-*
    *-*             *-*
    *-*              3
     3
```

And again:

```
                    Summ
    Numm            *-*
    *-*             *-*
    *-*             *-*
    *-*              6
     4
```

Until we get all the way up to the number 6. Here we see all the numbers uncovered so we can see what happened.

	Summ
Numm	0
1	1
2	3
3	6
4	10
5	15
6	21

What does a BASIC program to do this look like?

Well, first of all, note that we want to initialize the sum to zero. Also, we need to ask the person using the program which numbers they want to add up. That is, what is the last number in the sequence. The main part of the program will involve working through all the numbers and adjusting the sum as needed. Finally, we want to print out the answer.

The initialization, inputing and printing should all be straightforward to you now. The part of the program to work through all the numbers, adjusting the sum is something new.

In particular, to cycle through a series of numbers we have the ideal statement. A FOR loop does precisely this. The catch here is not only do we want to use the counting variable to make sure we go through the loop the correct amount of time, but we also want to use this counting variable in our calculation. That is, this variable will hold the number we need to add on to the sum. So this program will be the first example in which we actually use the counting variable within the loop's body for some purpose.

Ok, so here is the whole program:

```
LET Summ=0
INPUT PROMPT "What number do you want to sum up to?":N
FOR Numm=1 TO N
    LET Summ=Summ + Numm
NEXT Numm
PRINT "The sum of all numbers up to ";N;" is ";Summ
END
```

Things to note:

1. In line 1 we give Summ an initial value. This is BEFORE the loop. This process is called initialization. In our version of BASIC, variables are automatically initialized to zero, so we didn't have to do this. It is a good idea to do this simple step, however.

2. Line 2 asks the user for a number. This number, N, is used in the loop statement in line 3 as the terminating expression. Thus this program is general. The value isn't built in. It will work for any value supplied.

3. In line 4 Summ is on both sides of the equal sign. You can read this line as follows. "The new value of summ is equal to the old value of summ plus k". Thus Summ is modified depending on its old value. In this way, the Summ accumulates the answer we want.

4. In line 4 Numm is used. THIS IS THE POINT OF THIS EXAMPLE. Numm happens to be the variable used in the FOR statement. That is, Numm is the loop counter. But we aren't just using

it here to calculate how many times the loop will circle around (like we did in the last example). Rather, we are actually using that value of Numm in our calculations to add on to Summ making a new subtotal.

5. What is the value of Numm before the program ends? Would you believe it is one bigger than the number N that the person supplies. That is, if they want to add up all the numbers from 1 to 6, Numm will end up with 7. This 7 is never added on to Summ, because the FOR loop will realize 7 is too big and will not enter the loop body at this time where the summing is done — but the FOR loop did increment this variable as its very last step.

6.5.4 Multiplication Table Problem

As has been explained, the body of a loop can contain any legal BASIC statements. Well, we know that FOR and NEXT statements are legal in BASIC. So, a FOR statement can be one of the statements inside of the body of a loop. That is, one loop can be inside of another loop. This program demonstrates a use for such a program structure.

Let us say we want to write a program to print out a multiplication table. To make it easy, we will work with a small table — using the numbers from 1 to 5. But you'll be able to see easily how to expand this program. We want the table to look as follows:

```
1   2   3   4   5
2   4   6   8   10
3   6   9   12  15
4   8   12  16  20
5   10  15  20  25
```

Well, you could attempt to break down this problem by thinking of the table as consisting of five rows. Let us deal with each row one at a time. The first row you can get by using a loop. Like:

```
FOR I = 1 TO 5
  PRINT I
NEXT I
```

Well, that is close but not quite. This would print:

```
1
2
3
4
5
```

A column, not a row, is printed. This is true since each time through the loop a new PRINT statement is executed causing each new number to appear on a new line. We can fix this program by remembering that there is a way from keeping a PRINT from going to a new line. That is, end the PRINT with a comma or semicolon. Here we want numbers to line up in columns, so we use a comma to get over to the next tab stop. We also have to put in an extra — regular — PRINT after the loop to make sure the computer goes to a new line before the next line of the table is printed. Also, instead of using the variable name I, let us use something more meaningful to remind us that we are moving from one column to the next within this row. Thus, to print out the one line we do.

```
FOR Column = 1 TO 5
  PRINT Column,
NEXT Column
PRINT
```

So how can we print the second line of the table? How about:

```
FOR Column = 1 TO 5
  PRINT Column*2,
NEXT Column
PRINT
```

Which prints:

```
2   4   6   8   10
```

Try tracing it and make sure you understand how that works. The third line can be printed with.

```
FOR Column = 1 TO 5
  PRINT Column*3,
NEXT Column
PRINT
```

Notice that when we do the second row, we multiply by 2, and when we do the 3rd row we multiply by 3. This suggests we can do the whole table by using a variable (like Row) which we multiply by Column in the PRINT statement. The whole table can in fact be printed by a program that uses this form. Such as:

```
LET Row=1
FOR Column = 1 TO 5
  PRINT Column*Row,
NEXT Column
PRINT
LET Row=2
FOR Column = 1 TO 5
  PRINT Column*Row,
NEXT Column
PRINT
LET Row=3
FOR Column = 1 TO 5
  PRINT Column*Row,
NEXT Column
PRINT
LET Row=4
FOR Column = 1 TO 5
  PRINT Column*Row,
NEXT Column
PRINT
LET Row=5
FOR Column = 1 TO 5
  PRINT Column*Row,
NEXT Column
PRINT
END
```

But wait a second. Here we see the same code repeated five times with a slight change each time. First Row=1, then the next time we let Row=2, the third time Row=3 and so on. Whenever you see code repeated a number of times, especially when you see a variable taking on an orderly sequence of values, you should think "loop". Row is taking on all the values from 1 to 5. So that brings to mind a loop with a structure such as:

```
FOR Row = 1 TO 5
  print out the whole row
NEXT Row
END
```

Well, how do you print out a whole row of numbers? Well, we already saw that. We used a FOR loop to do that also. So the whole table can be written by a very simple program. It is:

```
FOR Row = 1 TO 5
   FOR Column = 1 TO 5
     PRINT Column*Row,
   NEXT Column
   PRINT
NEXT Row
END
```

Hey, here we have ended up with a FOR loop inside of a FOR loop. The main structure of the program is "print five lines". We use the FOR Row loop to do that. How do we print a line? Well, we use a FOR Column loop to print the numbers in all five columns. Not too tough is it?

One thing to be careful about. When tracing programs that have loops inside of loops, always be careful to jump back to the matching FOR statement whenever you get to a NEXT statement. If it says "NEXT X" then go back to the statement "FOR X=". The variable tells you which FOR and NEXT statements match up. Also keep in mind that when tracing FOR loops which have loops inside of them, the "inner" loop will be started over many times. Here Row gets set to 1. Then the inner loop causes the value of Column to go from 1 all the way up to 5. Then this inner loop ends causing the program to pass by the Next Column and hit the Next Row for the first time. This jumps the program back to the For Row statement causing Row to get the value 2. Then it is back into the For Row loop where we find the For Column loop AGAIN! This starts Column back to the value 1, and this inner loop cycles around for a second time causing Column to go through all the values up to 5 again. And so on. Of course, this whole process continues until Row eventually makes it all the way up to 5.

When writing or debugging programs that have loops inside of loops look out for a very common syntax error. In particular, you must end an "inner" loop before you end an "outer" loop. That is, the NEXT statement must have a variable on it that matches up with the closest FOR statement that does not have a NEXT yet. It is an error to "overlap" loops. For instance, it would be an error in this program to mix up our NEXT statements like:

```
FOR Row = 1 TO 5
   FOR Column = 1 TO 5
     PRINT Column*Row,
   NEXT Row
   PRINT
NEXT Column
END
```

This not only makes no sense and wouldn't print out what we want; this is a syntax error so if we tried to run this program an error message like "Ending Does Not Match Beginning" would immediately be displayed at the bottom of the screen. The computer wouldn't even try to start running the program since it knows you goofed up.

6.6   Summary

We have seen that FOR loops can be used in two ways. One use is to execute a certain process over and over again a set number of times. This is a main theme in programming; having loops greatly reduces the amount of code that otherwise would have to be generated. Secondly, FOR loops should be used when a particular variable is supposed to take on values in a systematic, mathematical manner. (For instance going up by 1 number at a time or creating all the odd numbers.)

You can expect to use some type of loop in many of the programs during the rest of this course.

Next time we will learn about another form of loop, DO - LOOP, which allows you to use conditional clauses with the WHILE or UNTIL attachment.

Have fun,

-Jt

6.7 Problems

Syntax Errors

1.

```
LET Answer = 15
FOR I = 1 to 20
  LET Answer = Answer + I
NEXT Answer
PRINT Answer
END
```

2.

```
LET FirstResult = 25
LET SecondResult = I * Firstresult  FOR I = 100 TO 200 STEP 20
LET ThirdResult = I + FirstResult + SecondResult
END
```

3.

```
READ Value
DATA 200
IF Value = 200 THEN
  FOR Counter = 20 TO 30
    LET Value = Value + 1
  ELSE
    LET Counter = 45
END IF
PRINT Value + Counter
END
```

4.

```
LET I = 5
PRINT "First I is ";I
LET I = 15
PRINT "Next I is ";I
FOR 20 TO 100
  PRINT "Now I is ";I
NEXT I
END
```

5.

```
LET Counter = 50
FOR Bigger = 10 TO 20
  LET Counter = Counter - 1
  FOR Smaller = 1 TO 5
    IF Bigger<Smaller THEN PRINT "Smaller" ELSE LET Counter = Counter + 1
  NEXT Bigger
NEXT Smaller
PRINT "bye"
END
```

6.

```
INPUT Fix
SELECT CASE Fix
  CASE  2
    FOR J IS 1 TO 20
     PRINT "hello"
    NEXT J
  CASE IS < 100
    FOR K IS 1 TO 20
     PRINT "Good bye"
    NEXT K
  CASE ELSE
END SELECT
END
```

Tracing

1.

```
FOR I = 5 TO 9
  READ X
  READ Y
  LET Easy = X - Y
  READ X
  PRINT "The answer is ";Easy
NEXT I
DATA 67,17,33,19,4,15,41,1,12,18,2,7,42,5,3,29,12,13,44,22,11
END
```

2.

```
LET Dizzy = 100
FOR I=10 TO 20 STEP 4
  LET Dizzy = Dizzy - I
NEXT I
FOR J = 20 TO 10 STEP 5
  LET Dizzy = Dizzy + J
NEXT J
FOR L = 30 TO 30 STEP 2
  LET Dizzy = Dizzy * 2
NEXT L
FOR M = 4 TO 1 STEP -1
  LET Dizzy = Dizzy + 1
NEXT M
PRINT Dizzy
END
```

3.

```
LET Ender = 2
FOR I = 1 to Ender
  LET Ender = Ender + I
NEXT I
FOR I = 1 TO Ender
  LET Ender = Ender + I
NEXT I
FOR I = (Ender*2) TO (Ender*2)
  PRINT Ender
NEXT I
END
```

4.

```
LET Something = 0
FOR K = 1 to 5
  READ Number
  LET Something = Number * K + Something
NEXT K
PRINT Something
DATA 2,4,1,3,7
END
```

5.

```
LET Answer = 1
FOR Ring = 1 to 3
  LET Q = 100
  FOR Subtract = 40 TO 20 Step -10
    LET Q = Q - Subtract
  NEXT Subtract
  Let Answer = Answer * Ring * Q
NEXT Ring
PRINT Answer
END
```

Programs

1. A new laundry machine has been invented. It is a combination washer/dryer. There are four cycles for washing: "Quick Rinse" which last 3 minutes, "Light" which lasts about 12 minutes, "Normal" which lasts about 20 minutes and "Extreme" which lasts a full 45 minutes. There are three drying cycles: "Speedy" which is a 5 minute verison, "Normal" which is about 45 minutes and "Fry" which bakes the clothes for 90 minutes. Write a program which asks how many loads of wash you have to do and what cycle for washing and drying you want to use on each load. The program should print out the total number of minutes it will take to do the wash.

2. Write a program that can help keep the stats for a scoreboard for a 9-inning baseball game. (Forget about tie games.) For each inning, it should tell what inning it is and ask how many hits and runs each team got. At the end of the game, it should print out the total number of runs and hits for each team. Make sure the program prints out a message announcing the "7th Inning Stretch" during the middle of the 7th inning. (That is, after the visting team's stats are asked for but before the home team is inquired about. Think IF statement here people!)

3. Killinburg is a large city. There are seven separate regions in the city. In each one there are a number of murders, suicides and accidental deaths. Write a program to print out the total number of unnecessary deaths within this city and tell which of the seven regions had the largest number of these deaths. ("Unnecessary deaths" is the sum of the number of murders, suicides and accidental deaths.) Use READ/DATA. You can think up your own statistics — including coming up with the names of the seven regions.

4. Rutgers has a Frisbee golf course on the Cook/Douglass campus. There are 18 holes in all. For the pros, par on any particular hole is considered to be 3 tosses. If you get the frisbee in the cage with 2 shots, you've gotten a birdie. If you get it in four throws, you've gotten a bogey. Write a program that will keep track of the scores for two people as they play a round — 18 holes — of Frisbee golf. This program should ask for the number of throws each player made on each hole. The program should keep track of how many birdies, pars and bogeys each player got along with their total number of throws. In the end, the program should print a table comparing these four numbers for both players. The players' names should be included in this table. As the very last line, the program should print out who won this round of golf — that is, the player who completed all the holes in the least amount of throws.

5. A certain gambler has a weird system when he goes to the racetrack. He bets on all nine races during the day. As the day goes along and he warms up, he feels more and more confident about his horse-picking abilities. So, he has always bet ten times the number of the race on the horse he picks. That is, in the third race, he will bet $30. Another quirk he has is that he will only bet on horses that have 3-1 odds. If there is a horse with those odds, he bets on it — if not, he skips betting on that race. (Let us say that there are never two horse that have 3-1 odds in any one race.) To make sure you understand this — assume it is the fifth race and there is a horse with 3-1 odds. He bets on it and the horse wins. How much money does he get paid? Well, it is the fifth race – so he bet $50. Due to his 3-1 odds, he wins three times what he bet — or $150 on that race. If his horse would have lost, he would have lost his $50. Write a program to help you calculate how much money this gambler loses or wins in a day. For each race, you'll have to ask if there was a horse that had 3-1 odds of winning. If so, you'll have to ask whether or not that horse won the race. (You should never ask how much money he bet — since this is easy for you to calculate. Also, never ask the odds, since you know this information also.) For output, tell how many times this gambler picked a winner, and give the total amount of money he won or lost.

6. Write two different programs to print out the mathematical table described here. With each even number between 10 and 20 (including both 10 and 20) print out a line containing that number raised to the second, third, fourth and fifth powers. For instance, for the number 10, the line should look like:

Number	^2	^3	^4	^5
10	100	1000	10000	100000

You can use the column headers supplied here or think up something better. Write this program first using one loop. Then, rewrite it to use two loops — one loop inside of another. Hint: What should be the range of the loop that makes the rows? What should the range of the loop that makes the columns be? How can you force one number to print without going to a new line? (If you don't feel confident about this yet, read the next chapter where nested-loops are discussed.)

7. Pretend there is a new type of car race. To make it more exciting drivers can get points on each lap of the race. The winner of the race is selected from the drivers who completed all the laps — it is the driver with the most points. The scoring is as follows: the leader at the end of a lap gets the lap number times 2 added on to his/her point total. The person in second place at the end of each lap gets the lap number added on to his/her point total. (Example: if it is lap 7 and Tim leads with Joe right behind, Tim will get 14 more points and Joe will earn another 7.) Since earning points is the way to win, the race will be more exciting with a competition for first place at the end of each lap. Write a program to declare the final point totals of all the drivers in a race. To make the program easier, let us say there are 8 laps and 3 drivers. You can assume all drivers finish the race. The program should end by printing out the winner of the race. Hint: It is a good idea to start out by picking a different variable for each driver's name and point total – that is 6 variables right there. A straightforward design for each lap would be to ask who won the lap and adjust the point total for that driver and then ask who came in second and adjust the points for him/her also.

8. You decide you want to take a ten day hiking trip. There are numerous trails and camping areas at the national park you will be staying at. Between each of the camping areas you have calculated alternative trails which you can hike — one considerably longer than the other. You decide you will take the longer trail on each day that it is not raining and the temperature stays below 85, otherwise you will take the shorter trail. Write a program that calculates how far you traveled in the ten days. Use READ/DATA to list the short distance and long distance for each day. Have the program ask the user what the high temperature for that day was and what the weather conditions were ("rainy", "cloudy" or "sunny".) Print the total distance hiked in the ten days along with the average high temperature.

9. Write a program that prints out the total number of gifts given away on each day of the song "The Twelve Days of Christmas" and the overall total given away during all twelve days together. (Look, you don't need to know the actual items. On the first day, one gift was given away — does it matter that it was a Partridge in a Pear tree? On the second day, three gifts were given away — 2 + 1 —, you could think of it as "Two of these and One of those". And so on — Day 3: 6 gifts — 3+2+1.)

Chapter 7

DO - LOOP WHILE/UNTIL

7.1 A Different Type of Loop

When we last left BASIC, we had left it spinning happily within the FOR loops. We saw how these counted loops could be used to do a section of code over and over a set amount of time. We also saw how the loop variable could be used within the loop within equations, print statements, and the like, if the various values of this variable are ever needed.

Last time, I mentioned that there were other types of loops rather than just FOR loops. The term I have used for FOR loops is "counted loop", since it does the loop a set amount of times. There is also another category of loops which are called "conditional loops". In our version of BASIC, the DO - LOOP with WHILE and UNTIL clauses fits into this category of loops. Conditional loops keep circulating until some condition is met. In order to understand what that means, we need to understand what conditions are.

Refer back to the chapter on IF statements if you forgot what conditions are. Remember that conditions are expressions that evaluate as either TRUE or FALSE. (Such expressions are called "boolean" expressions.) These expressions consists of logical operators (such as $>$ $<$ $=$) and boolean operators (AND OR NOT).

7.2 DO LOOP

SYNTAX

> **DO** *clause*
>
> *statements*
>
> **LOOP** *clause*

A Clause Is:

- **UNTIL** *condition*
- **WHILE** *condition*
- nothing at all.

EXAMPLES

> 1. `DO WHILE Nam$ <> "Dorothy"`
>   `   some-statements`
>   `LOOP`

169

```
2. DO UNTIL Kount > 100
     other-statements
   LOOP

3. DO
     many-statements
   LOOP UNTIL (X=15) OR (Day$="Tuesday")

4. DO
       forever-statements
   LOOP
```

POSSIBLE ERRORS

1. Missing or misplaced LOOP

2. Having an infinite loop because you have no clause.

MEANING

1. When you get to the DO statement, if there is no clause go directly into the body of the loop.

   If there is a clause on the same line as DO, then evaluate the condition. If the condition is TRUE and the CLAUSE is a WHILE then go into the loop. (....OR.....if the condition is FALSE and the clause is an UNTIL then go into the loop). OTHERWISE jump to the statement after the LOOP statement (which marks the end of the loop.)

2. Once in the loop, do all the statements in the loop in the order they are written.

3. When you reach the LOOP statement, if there is no clause on the same line, then go directly back to the DO statement and start over at step 1.

   If there is a clause on the same line as the LOOP, then evaluate the condition. If the condition is TRUE and the clause is a WHILE (OR if the condition is FALSE and the clause is an UNTIL), then jump back to the line that has DO on it (at the top of the loop) and start over at step 1.

   Otherwise go to the next statement after the LOOP line.

In short, you keep looping around as long as a WHILE clause is true and an UNTIL clause is false.

7.3   DO LOOPS with no clause

A DO and LOOP are used to mark the beginning and ending of a body of statements that act as a loop. When the program makes it to the DO statement for the first time it will jump into the loop, that is, the next line of the program! (We are talking about DO - LOOPS with no clauses here!)

It will execute all statements in that loop one at a time in order. (A loop body can have any statements we have talked about plus those we haven't talked about. Thus there can be input, print, let, FOR loops and even DO -loops inside of other loops.) All statements do what they would normally do. That is, if you are tracing them, you can pretty much pretend they aren't even in a loop when you get to them; they will act the same as they usually do.

Upon reaching the LOOP line, jump all the way back to the DO line and start again.

An example might be

```
LET X=1
DO
  PRINT X
  LET X = X + 1
LOOP
END
```

WHICH WILL PRINT:
1
2
3
4
.
.

and so on
.
.

A normal DO - LOOP would go on forever. Loops that never stop are called **infinite loops**. (You will want to stay away from these because they take a very very long time to finish their work and I don't think any mortal would want to sit there and wait for them to end!!!!) TRUE BASIC SUPPLIES A STATEMENT CALLED AN EXIT, BUT WE WILL STAY AWAY FROM THESE AS THEY ARE NOT NECESSARY IF YOU USE THE FOLLOWING TWO FORMS OF THE DO - LOOP.

7.4 The Two Most Popular Types Of DO LOOPS

1.

```
DO WHILE condition
  statements
LOOP
```

Each time the loop comes to the DO WHILE, the condition is evaluated. IF it is TRUE, the loop is entered, otherwise the loop is completed and the program goes to the statement after the LOOP line.

If you think about it, that means that this loop might never be entered. This is because the condition might be false the very first time you get to the DO WHILE line.

2.

```
DO
  statements
LOOP UNTIL condition
```

Enter the loop. When you reach the end, evaluate the condition. If it is FALSE then go back to the beginning of the loop again (the DO Line) and enter the loop. When the condition is finally TRUE when you reach the LOOP UNTIL line, then the loop stops and you continue with the program starting at the next line after the LOOP line.

This type of DO LOOP is **always** done at least once. This is because you have to reach the end of the loop before any decision (condition) has to be made.

7.5   Steps To Follow In Programs That Use Conditional Loops

- Decide what type of loop you want to use (UNTIL or WHILE).

- Figure out the necessary condition to keep the loop executing.

- Decide what type of initialization to do before the loop. Make sure that this is done correctly so the loop is entered at least once. (See examples below.)

- Decide which statements you want executed many times. These should be placed in the loop.

- Make sure that the value of the necessary variables within the loop condition can change in the loop body. If these don't or can't change, the loop will execute forever. (See examples below).

- Decide what statements you want done once, after the loop is over. These should be placed after the loop. Often totals are printed, final calculations made etc, after the loop.

7.6   Loops That Are Never Executed

Look at the following programs carefully. You can see that these loops never get entered.

```
LET X=10
DO WHILE X < 10
  PRINT "I am here"
LOOP

PRINT "I am done"
END
```

This program prints:
I am done
REASON: X is 10, not less than 10 when it reaches the DO line for the first time. Thus the loop is never entered.

Here is another program:

```
DO WHILE Z >= 45
  PRINT "I am here"
LOOP
PRINT "bye bye"
END
```

This program prints:
bye bye
REASON: the value of Z starts off as 0 and the condition is false right off. This BASIC initializes all numeric variables to zero. It is up to you to initialize them to other values.

7.7   Loops That Never Stop

The following loops are entered but they will never end.

```
LET X=2
DO WHILE X < 10
  LET X = X-1
LOOP
END
```

This loop goes on forever because X keeps becoming one less and is always less than 10.

```
LET Myguy = 16
DO
  LET  Myguy=Myguy * 2
LOOP UNTIL Myguy = 33
END
```

Myguy will equal 32 but never 33 ... so the program goes on forever — an infinite loop.

```
LET Flag$="T"
DO
  LET Newflag$="F"
LOOP Until Flag$="F"
END
```

See, Flag\$ never gets changed. It always stays as "T". Yeah, Newflag\$ gets a value, but that doesn't effect the execution of the loop at all. Make sure that the values that determine the conditions can actually be changed in the loop. If they can't be, then you are in big trouble.

In general, you use a conditional loop when you are not sure of how many times you want a loop to go around. If you know how many times as you are writing the program, you can use a FOR loop and a constant value. Like FOR i=1 to 10. If you know you can figure out how many times you want the loop to go around from a prior part of the program, you can use a FOR loop and a variable, as in the example FOR i=1 to N ; where N has been calculated earlier in the program. If you can't do any of these things, you probably want a conditional (DO) loop.

Conditional loops are used when you are not sure how many times the loop should go around (in fact, maybe that is precisely what you want the program to calculate for you!) but you know what condition should be met for the loop to end.

7.8   WHILE or UNTIL

How do you choose between an UNTIL and a WHILE? **It doesn't matter. The two statements can be freely interchanged. Any program you write using an UNTIL can be changed into one using a WHILE by just using the reverse condition.**
LIKE:

```
LET X = 3
DO WHILE X<10
  LET X=X+2
  PRINT X
LOOP
END
```

Is the same as:

```
LET X = 3
DO UNTIL NOT(X<10)
  LET X=X+2
  PRINT X
LOOP
END
```

They both print the numbers: 5 7 9 11 on separate lines. (Trace them very slowly to see why this is so. It is so mainly because the PRINT is after the LET and must be done before the loop loops around and evaluates the terminating condition.)

By the way, there may be more than one way to "reverse" a condition. "NOT" always works, but there may be others, for instance this program could be:

```
LET X = 3
DO UNTIL X>=10
  LET X=X+2
  PRINT X
LOOP
END
```

7.9   Clause At The End Versus At The Beginning

When should the clause be at the end of the loop and when should you put it at the beginning? Most of the time it doesn't matter. The big difference is that if the clause is at the end, the loop will execute at least one time but if it is at the beginning then it might not execute at all.
Watch:

```
LET Xx=23
DO
  PRINT "Hi there"
  LET Xx=Xx+1
LOOP WHILE Xx<23
```

will print:
Hi there

But:

```
LET Xx=23
DO WHILE Xx<23
  PRINT "Hi there"
LET Xx=Xx+1
LOOP
```

will print nothing at all!

7.10 A Common Error

Loops finish up even if the condition of the loop is met in the middle of the body.

One of the most common causes of error when tracing a DO - LOOP is that people jump out of the loop at the moment the WHILE or UNTIL condition is met. But you must realize that once in the body of the loop, the program will do **all** statements in the body before it can reevaluate the condition and finally get out of the loop.

Consider:

```
LET Done = 0
DO WHILE Done <> 1
  PRINT "it's friday"
  LET Done = 1
  PRINT "And I wanna go home!"
LOOP
```

will print:
> **it's friday**
> **And I wanna go home!**

This is even though Done=1 before the second print. Like I said, once you make it into the body, you must finish it. Here the program won't decide that Done=1 and it is time to jump out of the loop until it gets back to the DO WHILE line.

Since we are human and can concentrate on the whole program at one time, there was a temptation for us to stop tracing the loop as soon as Done got the value of 1. After all, we can plainly see that the loop should stop when the value becomes 1. So we might be tempted to think this program only prints
> **its friday**

but we would be wrong. The definition of these loops, as I have already stated, is that the whole body of the loop will be executed once the program enters the loop for another spin. There is no leaving. The computer follows this rule. Thus, you should keep this rule in mind when you are tracing other programs, or writing your own.

Many of you will not have fallen for this trick here. You probably figured out what this loop did as soon as you saw it. After all I warned you of the problem right before I gave the example AND this is a simple example. In a different situation such as during a test or while writing your own program, there might be a harder example of this and you may try to rush the tracing of the program thus ending up with the wrong answer or a malfunctioning program. **So be careful when you trace and work each step out slowly!**

7.11   Loops Inside Of Loops (Nested Loops)

I said that a DO - LOOP might be one of the statements inside of the body of a loop. If you trace things carefully, you will see that this might not be so bad.

Take the example of having a while loop inside of a for loop:

```
FOR I=1 TO 2
  LET J=1
  DO WHILE J<=3
    PRINT "i is ";I
    PRINT "j is";J
    PRINT "* * *"
    LET J = J + 1
  LOOP
NEXT I
END
```

```
will print:
i is 1
j is 1
* * *
i is 1
j is 2
* * *
i is 1
j is 3
* * *
i is 2
j is 1
* * *
i is 2
j is 2
* * *
i is 2
j is 3
* * *
```

This might not be clear at first, but if you trace things carefully you should be able to get this result. If so, you understand both types of loops pretty well. In short, each time through the for loop, you will do all the statements in it. The first statement in it is the initialization for the up-coming while loop (LET J=1) and then the WHILE loop itself. How many times will that WHILE loop go around ... well, three of course! Each time around in the WHILE loop does the value of I (the FOR loop counter) change? NO!!! Why should it? We have to get to that NEXT after the end of the WHILE loop in order for this I thingee to change! Eventually the WHILE loop will end causing the NEXT to happen. When it does, we jump back to the FOR and add one on to I, then we jump into the FOR loop body and what the heck do we find there? Well, would you believe it? We find some initialization for a WHILE loop (LET J=1 again!!!!) and then a WHILE loop again. So we have to spin around that WHILE loop once again.

This is a fairly simple example of having nested loops! You should be able to follow this one. Nested loops come in all forms and styles for various interesting and not-so-interesting problems. Hopefully we will not have to use them too often in this course. But just keep in mind, if you can follow and reproduce this example without looking at these notes, you understand LOOPS very well.

7.12   Choosing Between Counted Loops And Conditional Loops

Often when writing a program, you realize that you must use a loop. However, it may not be so clear what type of loop you should use. Should you use a simple counted loop (FOR loop) or some more complicated conditional loop (DO - Loop). This is something you learn with more experience.

However, consider an example:

Last time we used a counted loop that hit us with 100 examples of the force - acceleration relationship in physics. Essentially the program was:

```
FOR I = 1 TO 100
        .get some input.
        .do some calculations.
        .print the results.
NEXT I
```

Well, what would happen if we weren't sure that we actually wanted to see 100 examples of this relationship? Can we rewrite the program to stop when we feel like stopping? Well, yes we can. But first you should realize that we can no longer use a counted loop. We have no way of knowing as we write the program how many times the user is going to want to keep seeing examples. So we must use a conditional loop. Ok fine, but what the heck condition should we use? Well, there isn't much we can work with. Obviously we want to let the user tell us when he/she wants to stop. How can we ask the user? Well the only way we have of asking the user is through INPUT statements. If you remember, we already have inputs in the program. We ask for the acceleration and the mass. We can have the program stop when the person enters some value, let's say zero for the mass. Oh, just watch:

```
    INPUT PROMPT "What is the acceleration?":Accel
    INPUT PROMPT "and mass (enter zero when done)?":Mass
    DO WHILE Mass<>0
        .Calculate.
        .print.
        INPUT PROMPT "What is the acceleration?":Accel
        INPUT PROMPT "and mass (enter zero when done)?":Mass
    LOOP
    END
```

This, as you should notice, is only a partial program. But the key point is made. I can rewrite the program using a conditional loop rather than a FOR loop. Now you can see 100 examples or more or less of this particular physics relationship. How many times this loop goes around is user-dependent rather than programmer-dependent. What did I do here? Well first of all I picked some "sentinel" value that the user can use to notify the program that he/she is done. In this case it is when mass is equal to zero. Secondly, I made sure that the program tells the user this (in case he/she doesn't already know). It notifies the user in one of the Input Prompt statements. The main portion of the program then becomes a DO - Loop that spins around as long as that sentinel value hasn't been reached. All this should seem clear so far. What may not seem clear is WHY the heck do I have input statements twice? The first time I have input statements is before the loop. These statements are only done once (they are BEFORE the loop). They ask the person the first info. If it so happens that the person enters zero for the mass right away, the program will never enter the loop body. This is what I want. I don't want any calculations and printing when the person enters the sentinel value. I just want to get the heck outta there as soon as the person asks me too. By having the INPUT before the loop, I can handle the case when a person enters zero (the sentinel) right away. There is one other problem. Each time through the loop, you want to make sure that you ask the user for more input. If you don't, what happens? Well think about it. If you only get the input before the loop and it isn't the sentinel value, then you make it into the loop. This loop stops when the sentinel value is reached. **But if you never ask for new input in the loop, you freakin' are gonna be stuck in an infinite loop for a long time, because the person has no chance to enter the new (possibly sentinel) input.** In fact, it is a very stupid infinite loop, it just keeps using the same old input that you got BEFORE the loop started. You keep seeing the same prints over and over again with no change in values. One of the things I warned you about with conditional loops is that there had better be a way that the terminating condition will eventually be met in the body of the loop. **When using sentinel loops like this, make sure there is INPUT inside of the loop!**

Ok, so why do I put it after all the other statements in the loop? Didn't I once say that statements are executed in order? What's the deal here, does the program magically know to immediately jump to the end of the loop to get some input before it proceeds through the loop normally? NO! Think about what I have before the loop. I got my first input. As soon as I get into the loop the first time, I already have my input. Thus, I don't need to ask for it. The input at the end of the loop is FOR THE NEXT TIME AROUND. The way I have it set up, as soon as you reach the top of the loop, you have your input (either from before the loop or from the previous time around the loop). Now all I have to do is calculate and print using those values. Furthermore, I know I am about to loop around again so the last thing I should do before I loop around for the next time is make sure I have the next values: that is, do some more input.

A few words should be mentioned about sentinels. First of all, the sentinel value should be some value you never expect to be used. 0 is good, possibly a negative number, or maybe something very big. If the variable is a string, you might choose some special string that isn't being used to act as the sentinel value. Here, we expect large scale objects to have mass, and so zero is unlikely to be desired as the mass for the equations being calculated. Also, usually we do not want to process the sentinel value. Once the sentinel is entered we normally don't want to include this value in our calculations, printing or whatever we are doing. For instance, here we do not want the program to print out "The force is 0" after we type in zero for the mass. We meant for the program to just end when we typed in this sentinel of zero. We no longer care about these force equation problems.

Getting back to the method we used for the sentinel loop, using this double-the-input idea seems to work. Still this may seem like a really stupid thing nevertheless. I mean I still have to put those inputs into the program twice. Yuk! Yes it rots. There are other ways to handle this problem. If you find a way that works then feel free to use it. The key is that whatever method you use, you DON'T WANT TO PROCESS THE SENTINEL VALUE.

Another way that works is like this:

```
LET Mass = 9999

DO WHILE Mass<>0
   INPUT PROMPT "What is the acceleration?":Accel
   INPUT PROMPT "and mass (enter zero when done)?":Mass
   IF Mass<>0 THEN
      .calculate.
      .print.
   END IF
LOOP
END
```

Again, the sentinel value (mass=0) will not be processed (calculated and printed). And we did it using only 1 set of INPUT. But now we had to use TWO conditions and an IF statement!

Furthermore, we had to set the Mass to some non-zero value (9999) right before the loop, just for the heck of it, just to make sure we got into the loop in the first place. Remember, TRUE BASIC initializes values to zero. If we didn't do this initialization here, the loop would have never been entered because Mass would have already had the sentinel value 0 and the WHILE condition would have been false. (There are other ways around this. For instance, we could think up some non-zero sentinel value and thus forget about this phony initialization step. Or, maybe we could have used a DO — LOOP UNTIL instead.)

Maybe you like this better. At any rate just believe me, whenever you are using a conditional loop that works with a sentinel you can use the following format:

```
.input.
DO WHILE .not sentinel.
  .do what has to be done.
  .input.
LOOP
```

That is put the input right before the do line and right before the loop line.

You will very likely be seeing this construct often in later chapters so start feeling comfortable with it. Ok, how about some program with conditional loops in them!!!

7.13 Sample Programs: Simple Conditional Loops

7.13.1 Calculating Averages

Here is a program that calculates averages and by using a sentinel. Let's say you want a program that does averaging of a set of numbers. You have no idea how many numbers there are. Obviously to figure out the average, you need the sum of all the numbers and you divide that by how many numbers there are. Thus besides summing up the numbers, you must also count them. You can't use a FOR loop since you don't know how many numbers there are. Thus you need a sentinel. So let the sentinel be zero. That is, when the user enters zero, you know that all the numbers have been entered. You don't want zero to be calculated as part of the average thus the count shouldn't increment when zero is entered:

Cake:

```
LET Count = 0
LET Sum = 0

INPUT PROMPT "Give me a number (zero if done)-":Somenum
DO WHILE Somenum<>0
  LET Sum = Sum + Somenum
  LET Count = Count + 1
  INPUT PROMPT "Give me a number (zero if done)-":Somenum
LOOP

LET Average = Sum/Count
PRINT "There were ";Count;" numbers."
PRINT "The average was"; Average
END
```

Ok, by now you should understand the **sum = sum + somenum** line. This is our standard way of accumulating a sum. I just keep adding the new numbers on to the old sum giving the new sum. You should also understand that count comes out to be the number of numbers there were. (Notice that using this set-up, that the sentinel value ZERO is not counted! We never get into the loop body when the sentinel is entered, and so the increment of the count here won't be done.) Finally, you should see that I used the standard I-am-using-a-sentinel template to make this program. One last thing that you should be clear on is that I put the PRINTs *after* the loop. Why? Well if I put them in the loop, I would get counts and averages printed out every single time I spun around the loop. I only want the average printed out once. In fact there is only one place I could print it and that is after I have calculated it. This indeed is AFTER the loop.

7.13.2   The Population Doubling Problem

You are given 4 rabbits and you are told that the population of rabbits doubles every two months. How long will it be before you have at least 1000 rabbits?

Check out this program:

```
LET Rabbits = 4 ! initialize
LET Months = 0

DO
  LET Months=Months+2
  LET Rabbits = Rabbits * 2
LOOP UNTIL Rabbits > 1000

PRINT "It took ";Months;" months."
END
```

We use a conditional loop because we know that some condition must be met in order for a loop to end: namely the condition rabbits > 1000.

Before the loop I initialize months to zero since no months have passed yet, and I start rabbits off at 4, since the problem stated this as the starting condition.

Each time through the loop represents a doubling period. Since it takes two months to double, I add two to the number of months. Also, I modify the number of rabbits by doubling it.

After the loop is when I print out the number of months. I only want this to be printed out once. If it was in the loop, it would print out every time through the loop.

Let's modify the previous program as follows. Rather than finding out how long it takes the population to reach 1000, let the program ask what population you are interested in. Also, let the program ask for the starting number of rabbits and how many months the population takes to double.

```
LET Months = 0
INPUT PROMPT "How many rabbits do you start with?":Rabbits
INPUT PROMPT "What do you want the population to grow to?":Finalrab
INPUT PROMPT "How many months for population to double?":Nummdouble

DO
   LET Months=Months+Nummdouble
   LET Rabbits = Rabbits * 2
LOOP UNTIL Rabbits > Finalrab

PRINT "It took ";Months;" months."
END
```

Note: this is the same program as above, but with the constant values replaced by variables. Rather than initializing rabbits to 4, I got the number in an input statement. Since each time through the loop represents a whole doubling period, I add on Nummdouble to months since it represents the number of months it took to double. The loop stops when the number of rabbits is more than Finalrab, the ending number for the population that I have the user input.

7.13.3 The Interest Growth Doubling Problem

Here is a a program that asks you for the initial balance in a bank account and the yearly interest rate that that balance grows by. (Say, the interest is calculated only once — at the very end of the year!) This program tells you how many years it takes the money to double.

As you can see, this is similar to the rabbit problem, but with a catch. In the rabbit problem, we knew how long it took to double. Here, this is what we are trying to calculate. Hope you all remember how to calculate interest.

Here it is:

```
INPUT PROMPT "What is the starting balance?":Orig_Bal
INPUT PROMPT "What is the interest rate?":Rate

LET Current_Bal=Orig_Bal
LET Num_Years=0

DO WHILE Orig_Bal * 2 > Current_Bal
   LET Interest_Made = Current_Bal * Rate
   LET Current_Bal = Current_Bal + Interest_Made
   LET Num_Years=Num_Years+1
LOOP

PRINT "It took ";Num_Years;" to double your money"
PRINT "You started with ";Orig_Bal
PRINT "And ended with ";Current_Bal
END
```

NOTES:

- Lines 1 and 2 supply the input for the program.

- In line 3, you see we copy the value of orig_bal into current_bal. That is because you need to keep the original balance unchanged. How else can you tell if the balance has doubled unless you have kept the original balance some place? Current_bal will be the variable that holds the balance as it is modified from year to year.

- In line 4, we initialize the number of years passed as being zero.

- Lines 5 - 9 are the loop. Each time through this loop represents another year. That is why in line 8 we add one to the number of years. What happens each year? Well first you must figure out the interest. How? Well the balance up until that year is held in the variable current_bal. This balance times the rate gives you the interest. This interest is added on to the old balance (the balance prior to that year). This generates the new balance. Well the old balance was held in current_bal and the new balance should also be held there, for the next time around the loop. So in the updating line, Current_bal is used in both the left and righthand side of the equation. The loop keeps executing while Orig_Bal * 2 > Current_Bal. Think about it. We want the loop to keep going if the balance HASN'T doubled yet. Well if two times the original balance is still more than the current balance, then you haven't doubled the balance yet have you?

- After the loop there are a few PRINT statements to tell the final results.

7.13.4   The Car Service Shop Problem

Here is a program that demonstrates using conditional loops. In particular, this program will use a sentinel loop that processes DATA.

Let us say that a particular garage has a number of customers who bring their cars in to get preventative service. This shop has a number of diagnostic checks and regular maintenance procedures that it can perform on a car. Rather than having one overall price which to charge the customers, this shop prefers to charge each item separately. Before starting work on the car, the customer is asked to choose each task that they want performed on the vehicle. The overall cost is calculated as a total of all the separate items. (There is no tax, since this shop is in Oregon — a state with no sales tax.) As an incentive, this shop has been circulating coupons for various services. For each coupon a customer brings in, they can get that particular service for free.

This garage has decided that it should computerize the billing process. Write a program to help the shop calculate how much a customer has to pay for the service done on the car AND how much the shop is giving away in free service to this customer.

There are many services at this shop. These services change from week to week, month to month. So, you'd like to make it easy for the shop to add and subtract services from their computer. Thus we should place some DATA in the program. For instance,

```
DATA "an oil change",17
DATA "the brakes checked",15
DATA "a lube job",12
...
DATA "SERVICE END",0
```

Here we use a sentinel to mark the end of the list of services. Notice that besides having a string describing the service, there is also a number which is the price for the service. If the garage wants to add a service, they merely have to add a DATA line. To change the price of a service, they just edit the number amount on the appropriate line. To get rid of a service, they can delete the unnecessary DATA line.

Now to start work on this program, we should realize that the customer is going to have to be asked if they want each of the services done on the car. Thus, a loop has to go around using up all the DATA. Thus, we should make a sentinel loop which READs data. Here is how that can be done.

```
...
READ Service$
DO WHILE Service$<>"SERVICE END"
  READ Cost
  <rest of body of the loop>
  READ Service$
LOOP
...
END
```

After the first statement in the body of the loop we have a description of the service in the variable Service$ and amount that service will cost in the variable Cost. What further work do we have to do in the body of the loop? Well, we have to ask if the customer wants that service. If so, we should ask whether the customer has a coupon for that service. So adding this on we get:

```
...
READ Service$
DO WHILE Service$<>"SERVICE END"
  READ Cost
  PRINT "Do you want ";Service$;"(Y/N)"
  INPUT Reply$
  IF Reply$="Y" THEN
     INPUT PROMPT "Do you have a coupon for this service?":Coupon$
     ...
  END IF
  READ Service$
LOOP
...
DATA <place the data lines here>
END
```

Very little is left to do. In particular, we have to keep track of the amount of the bill and the amount of money saved by the customer by using coupons. Let us use the variables Bill and Saved. These must be initialized once at the beginning of the program — this should be before the loop so that they aren't set back to zero each time the loop comes around and the next service is inquired about.

Also, if the customer has decided that they want the service, the amounts must be appropriately adjusted depending on whether a customer has a coupon for the service or not. If the customer had replied they do not want the service, then we need not adjust these values. Thus, we only have to place the adjustment of these values inside of the IF statement we already have. How do we decide whether to adjust the variable Bill or the variable Saved? Well, if the customer says they have a coupon, then Saved is adjusted; otherwise Bill is adjusted. We can use an IF statement to look at the value of Coupon$ and make this decision. How do you make an adjustment? Simple, you add the current Cost of the service on to the variable being adjusted. (If the Bill is currently $45 for previous services and the customer wants another $10 service, but has no coupon, then Bill should become $55 — not $10. Right?)

Finally, after the customer is asked about all the services — that is, the loop is over — the values of Bill and Saved should be printed as the results of our program. We don't want to do this printing in the loop — or else we would get something printing every time around the loop. This is not good for this program. We only need these amounts to print once, right before the program ends.

Incorporating these changes into our program we get:

```
Let Bill = 0
Let Saved = 0
READ Service$
DO WHILE Service$<>"SERVICE END"
  READ Cost
  PRINT "Do you want ";Service$;"(Y/N)"
  INPUT Reply$
  IF Reply$="Y" THEN
    INPUT PROMPT "Do you have a coupon for this service (Y/N)?":Coupon$
    IF Coupon$="Y" THEN
      LET Saved = Saved + Cost
    ELSE
      LET Bill = Bill + Cost
    END IF
  END IF
  READ Service$
LOOP
PRINT "The charge for these services is $";Bill
PRINT "$";Saved;" was saved by using coupons."
DATA <place the data lines here>
END
```

Makes sense eh?

A lot more could be added to this program to make it fancier. Just to pique your curiosity as to what changes could be made, imagine that the customer comes with a top price they are willing to pay. Maybe the program should start out by asking them right away what that price is and the loop should *also* stop as soon as the total cost goes over that price. The beginning of the program can be changed as follows to allow this feature:

```
INPUT PROMPT "What is the highest price you are willing to pay?":TopPrice
Let Bill = 0
Let Saved = 0
READ Service$
DO WHILE Service$<>"SERVICE END" AND Bill<TopPrice
 <Rest of program>
```

(Yes, if you understand what is going on, you may realize that one way this loop might end is when Bill gets bigger than TopPrice. Thus, the customer may end up paying slightly more than their top price — but it will be fairly close and the customer probably won't mind going a few dollars over. However, you could make the program even more complex than suggested here and make sure that the cost does not pass the highest price the customer is willing to pay. Try working on it.)

Anyway, we could go on virtually forever making improvements and refinements to this code, and in fact, ANY, program we write. If you have followed what we have been doing here, you can see that you can build up a program incrementally. Work on small pieces at a time and add statements (and features) as necessary. There is no need to try to tackle a whole program at one time. You often do not have to consider ALL details at all times as you are writing a program.

Good luck on your own programs.

7.14 Summary

We learned about DO - LOOPs, reasons for using them, problems to look out for, steps you should think about as you write programs using them, loops that never execute or never stop, loop terminating conditions that are met in the middle of the loop body, nested loops, using counted versus conditional loops and the standard I-am-using-a-sentinel template.

Today you learned about conditional loops. In TRUE BASIC the conditional loops are DO - LOOPs and have clauses like WHILE and UNTIL. We saw a number of programs that used conditional loops. If that isn't enough to confuse you, wait until next time ...

Have fun,

-Jt

7.15 Problems

Syntax Errors

1.

```
INPUT People
DO People < 5
  INPUT Population
  LET People = People + Population
LOOP
PRINT People
END
```

2.

```
LET Score = 1
DO
  READ Card
  IF Score < Card THEN LET Score = Card
UNTIL Card > 8
PRINT "Winner"
DATA 2,4,1,6,2,5,9,2,3
END
```

3.

```
LET Flag$="Go"
LET Count = 1
DO WHILE Flag$="GO"
  INPUT Direction$
  IF Direction$="PRINT" THEN PRINT Count
  INPUT Flag$
NEXT Count
PRINT "The final count was"; Count
END
```

4. Input to this program is: "Yes","Yes","Yes","Yes","No"

```
LET TotalHours=0
INPUT Word$
DO IF Word$="YES" THEN
    INPUT Hours
    LET TotalHours = TotalHours + Hours
    PRINT TotalHours
    READ Word$
LOOP
END
```

5.

```
INPUT PROMPT "How many times you wanna get on the merry-go-round?":Times
FOR I = 1 TO Times
INPUT PROMPT "Are you sick of spinning yet?": Answer$
DO WHILE Answer$<>"Yes"
PRINT "Around and around you go"
INPUT PROMPT "Are you sick of spinning yet?": Answer$
NEXT I
LOOP
END
```

Tracing

1. The input to this program is: 2,20

```
INPUT Starting
INPUT Ending
DO WHILE Starting<Ending
  READ Some
  LET Starting = Starting * 2 + Some
  PRINT "Using ";Some;" we are now up to ";Starting
LOOP
DATA 3,1,6
LET Result = Starting - Ending
PRINT "The answer is ";Result
END
```

2.

```
LET Travel=1
LET Goal=2
DO WHILE Travel=1
  SELECT CASE Goal
    CASE 1 TO 10
      LET Goal = Goal * 2
    CASE 10 TO 19
      READ Goal
    CASE ELSE
      PRINT Goal
      LET Travel=2
  END SELECT
LOOP
DATA 3,11,4,2,5,91,23,4,2,2
END
```

3.

```
LET Large = 1
DO
  LET Top= 0
  FOR I = 1 TO Large
    LET Top = Top + I
  NEXT I
  LET Large = Large + 1
LOOP UNTIL Top > 25
PRINT Large
END
```

Programs

1. Write a program that announces the score in a ping-pong game. There should be two players. For each player, it should ask who won the point and announce the score. The game ends when someone has 11 points and they have at least a two point advantage. The game will continue past 11 points until someone wins by two points. When the game ends, the name of the winner should be announced. Once you have this working, expand the program to keep track of a three game tournament. After the tournament is complete, the program should announce how many games each player won.

2. Write a program that keeps track of expenses and miles travelled during a European trip. The program should keep asking for the name of a city and the mileage of the trip there. Then the program should inquire about the plane fare to travel to that city, the cost of the hotel and how much was spent on food at restaurants. The program should assume the vacation is over once the user enters "HOME" as the name of a city. The program should end by printing out the total amount spent on the trip and the number of miles travelled.

3. There are three categories of planes. Any plane that has a wingspan longer than the length of the plane is "undignified". Any plane that has wings that are 50% or less as long as the length of the plane is classified as "dangerous". The last category, "normal", is any plane where the wings are shorter than the length of the plane but still bigger than half the length of the plane. Write a program that keeps asking for dimensions of planes — until 0 is entered for the wingspan — and tells how many of each category of plane is encountered. The program should also print out a total count of how many planes were analyzed.

4. Write a program to help determine the performance of flights arriving at an airport. There should be a number of data lines — there is no limit to the data, but your program should have at least 8 lines. Each line should be of the form:

```
DATA "Boston",10,15,10,30,300
```

This data will represent flights that have arrived at this airport. The string in the data represents where the flight originated from. The next two numbers represent the time the flight was supposed to arrive – first hour, then minute (here 10:15). Then the next two numbers are the time the flight did arrive — hour and minute (here 10:30). All times will be in military time. That is hours will be from 0 to 23. (Minutes, of course, are from 0 to 59). The last number represents the number of passengers on the flight. The last line of data will be:

```
DATA "LAST FLIGHT",0,0,0,0,0
```

Simply stated, all the program has to do is print out how many happy customers there were (because they arrived on time or sooner than expected) and how many sad passengers (because they were late). HINT: check the planned hour time to the actual arrival hour first — only if these are equal do you then use the planned and actual minute values to find out whether the flight was early (or on time) or late.

5. Write a program to sell an item at an auction. Use READ/DATA to get a description of the item and the initial asking price. When the auction begins, the audience should be told what the item is and an opening bid. The program will then take bids from the audience. When 0 is entered, this means no more bids are being offered and an announcement telling that the item is sold should be made. Whenever someone bids, a check should be made to make sure they are offering more than the last person — if not, the new bid is ignored. Each time a new bid comes in, the auctioneer will ask if anyone is willing to buy it at a ten percent increase over the last price. Thus, if someone just bid $100 — the auctioneer will say something like "Do I hear $110?" (Even though the auctioneer is trying to get $110, an offer of $105 should be accepted.)

Hint: you might find that this program can be made very simple if you use three variables — one to keep track of the current asking price (opening bid, or ten percent increase), another to keep track of the last valid bid accepted and finally a third one which contains the bid currently being made by a member of the audience. The program should cycle around telling what the current asking price is, getting an offer from the audience and finally comparing this offer to the last bid accepted to see if this current bid should be accepted. You might want to treat the very first bid of the auction separately (ie. some code before the loop.)

When you have the program working, get a printout of it. Now modify the program so that five items are auctioned off. After all the items have been sold the program should announce how much money the auction made. You'll have to add more DATA. You will need another loop. You'll also need a variable to keep track of the money made so far. Make sure you adjust the value of this variable after each item is sold.

6. Write a program that will help calculate America's foreign debt. In particular, the program should repeatedly ask the user for the name of a country, whether we owe them or they owe us, and how much is owed. The program should calculate our debt from the information supplied about a number of countries. When "NO MORE" is entered for the country's name, the program should print out our debt or (depending on the numbers you supply) the amount of money owed to us. There is one small catch, for certain countries there is some question as to whether or not we will pay off our loans to them, or they will pay off their loans to us. A separate total should be kept for these countries. The countries are "China", "Brazil", "Argentina", and "Iran". If any of these is entered as the country, their information should be calculated into this separate special figure. Besides printing these two calculated figures, the program should print out the name of the (non-special) country that we owe the most money to. (For this last piece of infomation you will want to have two variables — one which is the name of the country we owe the most to — and the other the amount of money we owe this country. If at any time a number is entered which shows we owe more than this amount to another country, both the variable that holds the name, and the variable that holds the amount should be updated.)

7. Write a program to decide if a senior can graduate or not. The program should start out by asking how many credits the senior had earned prior to this semester. Then the program should ask for the names of classes the senior had this semester, how many credits each of these classes are worth and what grade the senior got for those classes. The student does not earn the credits for that course if they got a TF, F or W. When a sentinel is entered (of your choice), the program should stop and declare whether this student can graduate or not. A student with 120 credits or more can graduate.

8. Write a program to help compute the tips of a waitress for an evening of work and determine if her customers were pleased with her performance. Have the program keep asking for the amount of a customer's bill and how much in tips was earned from that table. When 0 is entered as the amount of a customer's bill, the program should print out the total amount paid by all the customers for their food and the total the waitress earned in tips. If the tips were more than 20% of the customer's checks then the program should print "The waitress had a very good night." After you get this working, adjust the program to print out how much the waitress earned that night. The scheme is as follows: the waitress earns $2.25 an hour (ask how many hours she worked) plus her tips minus 2.5% of her customer's checks. (This deducted money is shared by the hosts and bartenders of the restaurant.)

9. As a musicologist you want to do a study of the symphonies of Mozart, Beethoven and Haydn. You have a pile of manuscripts in front of you. After determining the initial motif in each piece of work, you will count up how many times that motif reappears in one form or another within that composition. You want to use the computer to calculate the average number of times each composer revisits the main motif within these symphonies. You will calculate different numbers for each of these composers. For each symphony, you want to enter the composer and the number of times you discovered the motif. You will enter "No More" instead of name of the composer when you are done with all the manuscripts. The output will be the average number of times the motifs appeared in the work of each of the three composers. The composers name and the averages should be printed out in order – from most to least. (That is, if Beethoven used a motif on average 24 times but Haydn used his 31 times, Haydn's name should be listed first.)

Special Chapter 3

If you ever have had to go grocery shopping, you know that at some of these places you can spend your life waiting on the check-out line. So let us dream a little. Let us journey to a world in which you can check out your own items.

Shop Yuronyaown is in a galaxy far far away. Yoda is the manager of this grocery store. He has decided that too much money is being wasted paying out a salary to slow and incompetent cashiers.[1] He decides to do away with these workers. By doing so, he hopes he will not only save money for the store, but also speed up the check-out process. Of course, he needs to come up with an alternative plan. His plan is to allow the shoppers to tally up their own bills. He realizes that by doing this he increases the likelihood of the store being ripped off by the consumers — since they may lie when they total up their items. But Yoda believes in the goodness of human nature (or, is it centaurian nature) — his customers will not rip him off.

Shop Yuronyaown has the usual shopper incentives — including a wide variety of items, and numerous sales. Most importantly, they have a weekly mailing, called The Stellar Circular, in which they provide their neighborhood customers with numerous coupons.

Yoda doesn't want to purchase sophisticated holographic scanning technology. Besides, he knows that at times, these machines can actually slow down the check-out process. In particular, without a good supply of Windex, items may have to be scanned numerous times before they are registered.

So instead, Yoda buys some cheap Macintosh computers and the TRUE BASIC software package. He'd like to write a program for the customers to use at the check-out aisles.

This program should allow the customer to enter the list of prices for their items. They also should be able to enter the list of discounts they should receive from their coupons. To make it a little more flexible, he'd like the customers to be able to switch from entering item costs to entering coupon discounts as often as they like. Also, at any time, customers should be able to see the subtotal of everything they

---

[1] A student read this comment and felt it was important to set me straight. I contacted this student and made peace with her — as I didn't intend to insult all cashiers everywhere in the universe. She was glad I made this effort to listen to her concerns and gave me permission to include her letter here.

December 1, 1993

Dear Jt,

I am writing in response to your book and something I read in it (specifically special chapter 3). I took particular offense to what you said about super market checkers. As you have probably already guessed, I am one of the "slow and incompetent cashiers". Just for the record, I am neither slow nor incompetent. If Mr. Yoda wanted to speed up the checking process he should tell the lazy ungracious shoppers to bag their own groceries. I don't know how it is in the store that you shop but in my store the checkers must also bag if the customer does not. Also, Yoda could put some sort of spell on them to count their money faster. You could make money faster than these people count it. While you are at it you could have the person keep everything that is scanned rather than voiding off many items which requires an override by the office staff. Since we are dreaming of another world, could you please have those people taken away that yell and scream and (yes some do) get violent. Most of the time whatever they are upset about has nothing to do with us or our competency but the competency of him who enters everything into that one great big computer in the sky.

As you hopefully now see, there are many reasons why check out lines move so slowly. I am sure you are an intelligent man who strives to have all of his facts straight when writing so I thought I would enlighten you to the world of a cashier. PS. I forgot to tell you about all of the people who suddenly remember things they forgot to get while I am in the middle of their order and leave to go get them.

Sincerely,

Alexandria Lukowiak

have processed so far. When the customers are done, they should be able to enter a command to have their bill calculated.

In the beginning it would be nice to have some greeting message. Of course, at the end, a message should be displayed telling the customer what they owe and how many items they purchased. There should be a limited amount of error handling, in case the customer enters a bad command.

One unique feature at Shop Yuronyaown is that it is possible, thru various coupon incentive plans and sales, to end up deducting more through coupons than you have accumulated thru the item's current prices. This doesn't happen very often, but when it does the store will give you an extra $1000 added on the whatever the store already owes you from your coupon windfall. Obviously, Shop Yuronyaown advertises this incentive vigorously — and has attracted numerous customers, even many from nearby galaxies.

Because some customers travel from far away, they'd prefer to do as much shopping as possible at one time. They like to just load up their space shuttles to the bursting point, so they don't have to make this shopping journey too often. As opposed to humans, who might make weekly shopping visits, these creatures like to make millenium shopping excursions. The problem with this is that it takes an awfully long time for them to check-out their items. Part of the reason for installing this check-out system in the first place was to speed up the check-out process. So, Shop Yuronyaown has enacted a 1000 item limit on these check-out out aisles. Customers with more items than this are expected to go to the loading bays at the back of the store, where their groceries are weighed and they pay a bulk rate. The program should not allow the customer to do any more processing after they have attempted to enter more than 1000 items.

How can we write a program for the Shop Yuronyaown check-out computers? (Hmmmm, talk about "psuedo-realistic" programs.)

First of all, we can plainly see that loops will come in handy when writing this program. We want to do a certain process over and over again. Either we will be handling costs or coupons over and over again, or we will be processing requests for subtotals or the final request for the grand total.

With this in mind, there are only a few variables this program will need. We want to keep track of the running cost; let us call this Total. Every time we get the cost of a new item, we will add on to this variable. The amount of each coupon will be deducted from this Total variable. Also another variable is needed for the count of items purchased — Items. At the moment, we can see very little need for more than this.

Actually, if we think a moment we can see the need for one more variable. Consider that from time to time we will need to ask the customer what operation they want to perform. Do they want to enter the cost of items, deduct coupons, get a subtotal or just finish up and get their final bill? So we will have to ask a question of what they want to do by using an INPUT PROMPT and of course, this statement will have to place the answer in a variable. Let us allow them to enter simple commands, such as Total — to enter a list of costs, Deduct — to enter coupon amounts, Sub — to get a subtotal and Bye — when they are done and want their final bill.

So the INPUT PROMPT should be something like:

```
INPUT PROMPT "Total items, deduct coupons, subtotal or be gone? (Total,Deduct,Sub,Bye)":Choice$
```

This INPUT PROMPT will not come at the very beginning of the program. In fact, we will want to have it in several places, during the main part of the program — so we will get back to it. First there are some simple matters we can take care off.

For instance, we know the program should start off with some greeting message and maybe some directions on how to use the check-out software. So there will be a number of lines starting off the program like:

```
PRINT "             Welcome to Shop Yuronyaown."
```

We also know we have to intialize our variables. One is a counter, another is an accumulator. Both should be set to zero. Simple:

```
LET Total = 0
LET Items = 0
```

What has to be done at the end of the program is very simple, too. We want to print out the count of how many items they have purchased.

```
PRINT "You bought ";Items;" items."
```

And then after this we want to print out what they owe the store, or what the store owes them. In fact, this is a decision the program must make. Does it print the "you owe us" message or the "we owe you" message? How does a program make decisions? Well, it uses an IF statement. In particular, if the amount that has been accumulated in Total is more than zero, than the customer owes the store. Otherwise, the store owes the customer because the coupons deducted more than the items added up to be — and we got a negative number for Total. Furthermore, the store must add an extra $1000 to this amount. This is a little tricky. Since the Total will be negative, how do you arrive at the proper amount? Well, let us say the bill came out to be -23. We want the customer to get $1023. The equation for this is Total = 1000 - Total. Check it out: $1000 - (-23) = 1000 + 23 = 1023$. The whole IF statement that will do this printing will look like:

```
IF Total > 0 THEN
   PRINT "You owe us $";Total
 ELSE
   LET Total = 1000 - Total
   PRINT "Congratulations, we owe you $"; Total
END IF
```

Now for the main part of the program. What do we want to do there? Well, we want to handle the customer's requests over and over again. Do they want to add up items, deduct coupons, get the subtotal or just finish up? Essentially, we ask them what they want to do and then we do it. Over and over again, we do these two things.

Well, how do you do something over and over again? You use a loop. What type of loop? Should we use a counted loop or a condition loop? Well, as we write the program, do we know how many times they are going to be making requests? No, we don't. Can we ask the person using the program how many requests they will make and then place this number in a variable? This is not practical. The chances are, they don't know how many times they will want to switch from entering numbers to deducting coupons to getting subtotals before they've even begun to use the software. They probably will just decide what operation to perform when they get the urge as they are using it. So we can't use a counted loop because we don't have a number and we can't ask them for that number.

So we will use a conditional loop. What is the condition of when we should stop? Well, it is when the person tells us to stop. In particular, it will be when they type in "Bye" to our INPUT PROMPT. So we have a sentinel condition here. We want the loop to keep going around as long as Choice$ does not have the value "Bye". And how do we make a sentinel loop with its associated INPUT statement? Well, this is something you should know. Here it the outline of the main part of our program:

```
INPUT PROMPT "Total up items, deduct coupons or be gone? (Total,Deduct,Bye)":Choice$
DO WHILE (Choice$<>"Bye")

   ***** Process the customer's current request *****

   INPUT PROMPT "Total items, deduct coupons, subtotal or be gone? (Total,Deduct,Sub,Bye)":Choice$
LOOP
```

Actually, we should add to this. In fact, we also know we should not let the customer do anything else once they try to total up more than 1000 items. In other words, this loop should only go around if the number of items is less than or equal to 1000 items. So here we modify the WHILE condition so the loop only keeps going as long as the sentinel has not been entered and the number of items is not over 1000.

```
DO WHILE (Choice$<>"Bye") AND (Items <= 1000)
```

Well, so far so good. Nothing difficult yet. And we have one thing left to do. That is, we must process the customer's request. Well, the program must decide whether to handle costs, deduct coupons, print a subtotal, or in fact handle bad input. This is a four-way decision. How do we handle multi-way decisions? Easy. We either use a nested-IF statement or a SELECT CASE statement. We'd rather use the latter if at all possible. And here it is fine. The selection variable is Choice$ which contains the various operations the customer may want to do. So we end up with a skeleton for this statement looking like:

```
SELECT CASE Choice$
   CASE "Total"
        allow the person to enter costs
   CASE "Deduct"
        handle coupons
   CASE "Sub"
        print subtotal
   CASE ELSE
        handle error
END SELECT
```

You may be asking why the program doesn't have to handle the "Bye" request. The reason is that the way we wrote the sentinel loop, the computer will not have to deal with "Bye", since Choice$ will never have this value when it is at the SELECT statement. We make sure we got out of the loop as soon as possible, when "Bye" is entered.

The last two of these cases are very easy. To print the subtotal is straightforward:

```
PRINT "So far the total is ";Total
```

and for the CASE ELSE we want to catch all the other words the customer might have typed in. We should print out exactly what the customer typed, and show him/her what they are allowed to type.

So, now, let us handle the coupons. For every coupon, we need to get the amount of the coupon; let us place this in a variable called Deduct by using an INPUT PROMPT. Then we subtract the amount from Total to adjust the amount the customer owes. Notice, we said "for every coupon." Clearly, this process of getting a coupon amount, and subtracting it from the total is something that will happen a number of times. So, whenever we see the same process being done over and over again, we think LOOP. Should we use a counted or conditional loop? Here, we can probably get away with a counted loop. We don't know as we write the program how many coupons there are, but we do expect that the person using the program (the customer) is likely to be standing there with a small stack of coupons in their hand and can count them up easily enough. So, we can use an INPUT PROMPT to ask for how many coupons there are (NumCoupons) and then use a counted loop (FOR) to process every coupon. To make things a little easier for the customer, why don't we print out a message telling them what coupon they should be on). So, to process the coupons we end up with something like:

```
INPUT PROMPT "How many coupons do you have?":NumCoupons
FOR I = 1 To NumCoupons
   PRINT "For Coupon Number ";I
   INPUT PROMPT "What is the deduction?":Deduct
   LET Total = Total - Deduct
NEXT I
```

Of course, this processing for the coupons is done inside of the SELECT CASE statement, and we know that statement was inside of a conditional DO—WHILE loop. So this little FOR loop is nested deep inside another outside loop. Here we are seeing an example of a loop inside of a loop. As was mentioned in a prior chapter, there are indeed reasons for having such complexity. Loops inside of loops pop up often inside of computer programs.

For the Case "Total", in which we want the customer to enter the cost of various items, we again will have to use a loop so that they can keep entering costs over and over and over again. But this time we probably do not want to force them to count up how many items they have. They may have many many items all in a big pile and they may be hard to count. So instead, we should use a conditional loop. We can again use some sentinel value. Here, for instance, we can tell them to enter the value of 0 as the cost of an item when they have run out of items. Again, we have the usual sentinel loop and can write its outline quickly.

```
INPUT PROMPT "Enter the cost of the item: (0 when done)":Cost
DO WHILE Cost <> 0
    process this item
INPUT PROMPT "Enter the cost of the item: (0 when done)":Cost
LOOP
```

For processing, we want to add the cost on to our total amount and add one on to our count of the number of items the person has purchased. Oh, and this reminds us, we don't want the person to buy more than 1000 items. So this loop should only continue as long as the person has purchased less than 1000 items. We can edit our WHILE clause by adding an AND to take into account this other condition. We end up with:

```
INPUT PROMPT "Enter the cost of the item: (0 when done)":Cost
DO WHILE (Cost <> 0 )AND (Items <= 1000)
    LET Total= Total + Cost
    LET Items = Items + 1
    INPUT PROMPT "Enter the cost of the item: (0 when done)":Cost
LOOP
```

If the person does enter more than 1000 items, we probably don't want to stop without telling them what happens. So right after this loop ends, we should check to see if it did so because the person bought more than 1000 items. If it did, we should print out a message telling the person what happened. How do we make this "check"? Well, we can us an IF statement. So after the DO—LOOP we see here we should also include the following statement inside of this particular CASE:

```
IF Items > 1000 THEN PRINT "You have purchased enough. Bye now."
```

There doesn't seem to be anything left that we must discuss.

We have gone through in detail how to create this program. Hopefully, this helped you see how a large program can be broken down into little pieces that are easily attacked. As we were going along, if you only concentrated on what was currently being discussed, it probably made sense. If, on the other hand, you tried to picture the whole program at one time, it might have gotten a little confusing. When you write more complicated programs, you should concentrate on small parts of it at one time and just get them to work. By doing this, you can slowly build up larger programs.

This is still a small program, it is only one page long, but as we can now see by looking at the whole thing on the next page, there is a lot to this one program.

```
REM Jt, Jul 1990, New Program for Fall 90
REM Shop Yuronyaown Program
PRINT "                  Welcome to Shop Yuronyaown."
PRINT "Because we believe in customer relations, we have decided"
PRINT "that you can check out your own items."
PRINT "We trust you very very much, so please do not misuse this register."
PRINT "No more than 1000 items. Thank you very much."
PRINT
LET Total = 0
LET Items = 0

INPUT PROMPT "Total up items, deduct coupons or be gone? (Total,Deduct,Bye)":Choice$
DO WHILE (Choice$<>"Bye") AND (Items <= 1000)
  SELECT CASE Choice$
    CASE "Total"
      INPUT PROMPT "Enter the cost of the item: (0 when done)":Cost
      DO WHILE (Cost <> 0 )AND (Items <= 1000)
        LET Total= Total + Cost
        LET Items = Items + 1
        INPUT PROMPT "Enter the cost of the item: (0 when done)":Cost
      LOOP
      IF Items > 1000 THEN PRINT "You have purchased enough. Bye now."
    CASE "Deduct"
      INPUT PROMPT "How many coupons do you have?":NumCoupons
      FOR I = 1 To NumCoupons
        PRINT "For Coupon Number ";I
        INPUT PROMPT "What is the deduction?":Deduct
        LET Total = Total - Deduct
      NEXT I
    CASE "Sub"
      PRINT "So far the total is ";Total
    CASE ELSE
      PRINT "You typed in ";Choice$
      PRINT "This is not a legal operation at this time."
      PRINT "Only valid operations are Total, Deduct, Sub or Bye"
      PRINT "Please try again."
  END SELECT
  INPUT PROMPT "Total items, deduct coupons, subtotal or be gone? (Total,Deduct,Sub,Bye)":Choice$
LOOP

PRINT "You bought ";Items;" items."
IF Total > 0 THEN
  PRINT "You owe us $";Total
 ELSE
  LET Total = 1000 - Total
  PRINT "Congratulations, we owe you $"; Total
END IF
END
```

    Have fun, -Jt

Chapter 8

Built-In Functions

8.1 Subprograms

We have spent a couple chapters learning about loops. We saw how these loops could be used to do a section of code over and over again. Between regular sequential instructions (such as INPUT, PRINT and LET), decision statements (IF, SELECT) and loops (FOR, DO), we have most of the necessary components to write decent programs.

Now what we need is a way of making programs easier to write. Programs can get to be rather long. It would be a good idea if we can break big programs down into smaller pieces that are easier to work with. Most BASICS, and especially TRUE BASIC, allow you to write subprograms that can be grouped into larger programs.

There are two types of subprograms. There are FUNCTIONS and SUBROUTINES. The main difference is how you use them. To use a subprogram you do an action known as "calling". You generally call a subroutine on a line by itself. A FUNCTION, on the other hand ,is called from inside of a mathematical expression. That is, you will generally see calls to FUNCTIONs in the right-hand side of a LET statement. (Though they can be anywhere else expressions are allowed, such as in IF statements (logical part) and PRINT statements.) A FUNCTION call evaluates to one value which is given back as the result. Another way to say this is that the function "returns" or "passes back" a value. Thus when you are tracing a program that calls a FUNCTION, your first step is to evaluate the function and then replace the **call** to that function with the value it calculates out as. This is a lot like replacing a variable name by the value that the computer finds when it looks up that variable — we do this all the time in LET statements and have become quite used to doing it.

You will understand what I am talking about when you see some examples. Today we will talk about functions.

There are two types of FUNCTIONS that we care about. BUILT-IN and INTERNAL. BUILT-IN functions are already written for you. All you need to do is use them. Therefore, these functions are fairly easy to use and they will be discussed in this chapter. INTERNAL functions are subprograms that you write yourself. To simplify this course, we will not teach about these type of functions. However, they are mentioned here so you can think about the usefulness of being able to write your own functions. By the end of this chapter, if you reconsider this prospect you'll probably agree that being able to write INTERNAL functions might come in handy. Maybe someday you'll learn more about TRUE BASIC and how to write these types of functions.

8.2 Built-In Functions

These are functions that have already been supplied for you by the makers of TRUE BASIC. Many common mathematical and some special functions are supplied.

8.2.1 Mathematical Functions

When I discussed assignment statements, I only mentioned a few of the mathematical operations that BASIC can perform. Namely, they were addition, subtraction, multiplication, division and exponentiation. Obviously, it wouldn't make much sense if these were the only operations a computer could perform. After all, a typical calculator can perform dozens of different functions.

There are also a number of functions that BASIC can perform. I will not list them all here but I will give an example of a few of them. (You can find a list of these functions in many other books on TRUE BASIC.) In general, a mathematical function will consist of the function name and then a list of arguments in parentheses. Most mathematical functions in our BASIC only have one argument. The argument can be either a number, a variable or an equation consisting of numbers, variables and mathematical operations. When you use a mathematical function, it is termed "calling a function." Inside of LET statements, you must call a function on the right hand side of the equal sign. The function call can be by itself on the right hand side OR it can be built into an equation. By looking at some examples, you will understand this a little better.

Here are some mathematical functions:

ABS(x) This returns the absolute value of the argument.

Example

```
LET X=ABS(3)
LET Y=ABS(-5)
LET Z=ABS(4) + ABS(-2)
LET A=ABS(7-10)
LET B=17
PRINT X,Y,Z,A,ABS(B-10)*3
END
```

Output 3   5   6   3   21

INT(x) This truncates a real number to the next lowest integer. If the argument is already an integer, this function returns the value of the argument. Think of a number line. All real numbers get mapped to the left on the number line. Thus INT(4.34) is 4. and INT(-3.75) is -4

Example

```
LET One=INT(4.4)
LET Two=INT(4.6)
LET Three=INT(-6.3)
LET Four= -INT(7.8)
LET Five=INT(5.7-1.3)
LET Six=INT(2.3) + INT(4.3)
LET Seven= -7.5
PRINT One, Two, Three, Four, Five, Six, INT(Seven-.1)
END
```

Output 4   4   -7   -7   4   6   -8

MAX(x,y) This function takes two numerical arguments. It returns the larger of the two arguments.

Example

```
LET I=MAX(3,7)
LET J=MAX(6,7-5)
LET K=MAX(12,10)+MAX(7,5)*2
LET L=22
LET M=4
PRINT I,J,K,MAX(L,M*6)
END
```

Output 7   6   26   24

Likely Errors

```
LET Answer=MAX(5,10,7)
```

This is an error because MAX can take only two arguments and here we have given it three, namely 5, 10 and 7.

MIN(x,y) This function takes two numerical arguments and returns the smaller of the two arguments.

Example

```
LET I=MIN(3,7)
LET J=MIN(6,7-5)
LET K=MIN(12,10)+MIN(7,5)*2
LET L=22
LET M=4
LET P=MIN(MIN(4,8),MIN(2,7))
PRINT I,J,K,MIN(L,M*6),P
END
```

Output 3   2   20   22   2

Likely Errors

```
LET Answer=MIN(5,10,7,-3,6)
```

This is an error because MIN can take only two arguments and here we have given it five, namely 5, 10, 7, -3 and 6.

REMAINDER(x,y) This function takes two numbers as arguments. It divides the first by the second and returns the remainder from this division.

Example

```
LET A=REMAINDER(12,4)
LET B=REMAINDER(14,4)
LET C=REMAINDER(7,3) * 15 + 3
LET D=REMAINDER(10,4) + REMAINDER(10+7,4-2)
LET E=REMAINDER(12.345,10)
LET F=25
PRINT A,B,C,D,E,REMAINDER(127,F)
END
```

Output 0   2   18   3   2.345   2

ROUND(x) This function returns the integer calculated by rounding the numerical argument to the nearest integer.

Example

```
LET One=ROUND(4.4)
LET Two=ROUND(4.6)
LET Three=ROUND(-6.3)
LET Four= -ROUND(7.8)
LET Five=ROUND(5.7-1.3)
LET Six=ROUND(2.3) + ROUND(4.3)
LET Seven= -7.5
PRINT One, Two, Three, Four, Five, Six, ROUND(Seven-.1)
END
```

Output 4   5   -6   -8   4   6   -8

ROUND(x,y) This version of round takes two arguments. The first number is the number you want rounded. The second number tells what decimal place you want to round the number to. This second argument must be an integer. If it is 1, this means round to the nearest tenth, 2 means round to the nearest hundredth and so on. If you specify a negative number here you can round to higher places. -2 rounds to the tenth place, -3 rounds to the hundreds place and so on.

Example

```
LET One=ROUND(4.43784,3)
LET Two=ROUND(4.633,1)
LET Three=ROUND(-6.3466,2)
LET Four= -ROUND(7.8,1)
LET Five=ROUND(5.75-1.35,1)
LET Six=ROUND(2.378,2) + ROUND(4.314,1)
LET Seven= -7.5558
PRINT One, Two, Three, Four, Five, Six, ROUND(Seven-.5,3)
END
```

Output 4.438   4.6   -6.35   -7.8   4.4   6.68   -7.056

RND This returns a random number between zero and one. The number can be zero, but it can never be 1. When tracing a program using RND, you have no way of knowing what number will be picked. It will be picked randomly when the program is run.

Example

```
LET Ans=RND
LET Result=RND*7
LET Computation=(RND+RND*5)+13
PRINT Ans, Result, Computation, RND*10
END
```

Output (one possibility) .7233456   5.679918   16.35678   3.45618

SQR(x) This returns the squareroot of the argument.

Example

```
LET Me=SQR(16)
LET You=SQR(25)+SQR(7.84)
LET Who=SQR(30+6)
LET They=20
PRINT Me, You, Who, SQR(They*5)
END
```

Output 4   7.8   6   10

8.2.2   Special Functions

DATE This returns the current date (based on the last setting of the Mac clock) as a number in a format like YYDDD where YY is the year and DDD the day of the year (up to 365).

TIME Returns a number that represents the number of seconds that have elapsed since midnight.

DATE$ Returns a string. This string has the format "yyyymmdd" so that if the current date is October 4th 1986, you would get "19861004".

TIME$ Returns the current time as a string in a format like "hh:mm:ss". Seven thirty four and 17 seconds PM would be "19:34:17"

8.2.3   Mixed Example

```
LET X=10
LET Y= -20.2
LET Z=9
LET Ans1 = SQR(Z) + SQR(25)
LET Ans2 = INT(SQR(10))
LET Ans3 = INT(7.5 + 3)
LET Ans4 = INT(X) + INT(Y) + ABS(-3)
PRINT Ans1,Ans2,Ans3,Ans4
LET Result = MAX(INT(7.6),ROUND(7.6))
LET Result2 = REMAINDER(MIN(12,23),ABS(ROUND(-4.7)))
LET Result3 = SQR(MAX(25,13)) + INT(ROUND(3.4833,3))
PRINT Result, Result2, Result3
END
```

This program will print.

```
8    3    10    -8
8    2    8
```

8.3   Some Program Examples Using Built-In Functions

8.3.1   Comparing Values of Two Mathematical Functions

Let's write a program to compare the values generated by two equations. All we want to know is how far apart the two equations are at any given value. We don't care to know which is bigger or smaller. Let's say the two equations are $y = 1/2x^2 + 22x$ and $y = x^2 + \sqrt{x}$. Let's say we want to compare the values of these two equations from 1 to 10. How can we do it? The following program will work:

```
FOR I=1 TO 10
   LET A = 1/2 * I^2 + 22 * I
   LET B = I^2 + SQR(I)
   LET Diff = ABS(A - B)
   PRINT "When the value is ";I;" the difference between these "
   PRINT "two functions is ";Diff
NEXT I
END
```

Some things to notice here:

1. The argument to SQR is a variable. In this case I. Arguments can be constant values, variables or whole equations. (Even equations that call other functions.)

2. The call to SQR is in the right-hand side of a LET statement. When tracing it you can think in these terms: when the program sees SQR it jumps to some other code in the computer which figures out squareroots. After it figures out the squareroot of the number supplied it sends the value back to this LET statement. The **value** is thus used in the LET statement. Thus when tracing, you know all function calls will evaluate to some number.

3. A-B will be a positive or negative number. We only want the magnitude here, we don't care about if it is negative. So we use the absolute value function to get this. Notice the argument to ABS is a whole equation: A-B. We could have done this in two steps such as LET C= A - B and then LET DIFF=ABS(C). But why bother making this extra step when we can do it in one step?

4. Something to think about: What if we didn't want to worry about getting the difference between these two functions down to the smallest decimal place? (Maybe we just wanted to approximate the difference and just worry about the non-decimal part.) Then we could use something like LET DIFF = INT(ABS(A-B)). The big thing to notice here is that the argument given to INT (remember arguments are what you see in the parentheses) is ABS(A-B). That is, an argument to a function can in fact be any equation—in this case the equation is another function call.

8.3.2   Input Section To a Program That Deals with Temperatures

As we know, most programs have an input section. In many of the programs we have written, we have made the input section very simple. We just assumed that the user of the program would enter intelligent data if we presented him/her with a simple question to answer. In practice, this isn't a wise decision to make. Instead, the program should try to force the user to enter reasonable values for data. After all, many computer users, through typographical errors or just plain ignorance, enter unusual data. So we can often add statements to our input sections to cause the program to try to filter out bad data.

For instance, assume you are writing a program that records daily temperatures at some meteorological center in order that more intense statistical or predictive analysis can be performed on the data. Temperatures are almost always in the range 150 F to -150 F degrees no matter where on Earth they are taken. Therefore, we can write a program to throw out any values that are out of this range. In fact, we can have the program loop around until the person enters valid data. In this particular case, we can see that the magnitude of the value can not be bigger than 150 whether the number is positive or negative. Here would be a good case to use the ABS function. Watch:

```
DO
    INPUT PROMPT "Please enter the temperature in the range 150 to -150:":T
LOOP UNTIL ABS(T)<=150
```

$\vdots$

Looking at this loop carefully you should see that it will keep looping around if the magnitude of the number is more than 150. Thus, any number out of the range -150 to 150 will cause the program to loop around again asking for the temperature.

By the way, you would probably want to modify this program to ask about the validity of numbers out of the range and if the user confirms it, then accept those odd values. In this program, they are automatically rejected even if they turn out to be acceptable due to some extraordinary weather event.

Oh, the ABS function would not be appropriate for all data-validity loops. Here it just turned out that we could use it intelligently.

8.3.3 A Program To Find The Distance Between Two Points

You all might remember that there is a way to figure out the distance between two points on an X-Y coordinate system. It is rather simple. You can always create a right triangle using those two points. You then figure out how far apart the two points are on the X-axis and how far apart they are on the Y-axis. Simple geometry tells us that the distance between the two points is d where $d = \sqrt{\Delta x^2 + \Delta y^2}$. See:

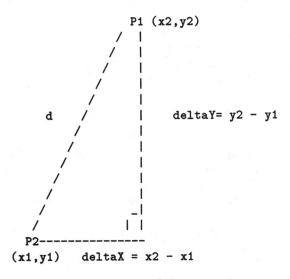

So, let's write a simple program to tell us the difference between two points. We will have to ask the user for four pieces of data (the four coordinates) and then calculate the value using the squareroot function. Finally, we can print the result. Watch:

```
INPUT PROMPT "Enter the X coordinate of the first point? ":X1
INPUT PROMPT "Enter the Y coordinate of the first point? ":Y1
INPUT PROMPT "Enter the X coordinate of the second point? ":X2
INPUT PROMPT "Enter the y coordinate of the second point? ":Y2
LET Deltax = X2 - X1
LET Deltay = Y2 - Y1
LET Sumofsquares = Deltax^2 + Deltay^2
LET Answer = SQR(Sumofsquares)
PRINT "The distance between the two points is ";Answer
END
```

The only thing new to note here is that we use a built-in function to help us calculate the answer. That function is SQR and a call to it appears in the right-hand side of a LET statement. (Remember a call to a function can not appear on a line by itself.) In this case, SQR is a function that expects one argument. We give that one argument here in the form of a variable (Sumofsquares). Having the built-in function SQR helps us a lot because it would take us a lot of programming to write code to figure out the squareroot by ourselves.

This program can be shortened if you realize that the argument to a function can be a whole equation. There is no need to use intermediate variables to store partial results. So, we can place the whole equation inside the parentheses after SQR. See:

```
INPUT PROMPT "Enter the X coordinate of the first point? ":X1
INPUT PROMPT "Enter the Y coordinate of the first point? ":Y1
INPUT PROMPT "Enter the X coordinate of the second point? ":X2
INPUT PROMPT "Enter the y coordinate of the second point? ":Y2
LET Answer = SQR((X2-X1)^2 + (Y2-Y1)^2)
PRINT "The distance between the two points is ";Answer
END
```

Or if you wanted, you can even put the whole call of SQR inside the PRINT statement and not even use a variable to store the final result. Remember, a function call is usually on the right-hand side of an equation but it can appear any place an expression is allowed. (We have learned that an expression can appear in a print statement.)

```
INPUT PROMPT "Enter the X coordinate of the first point? ":X1
INPUT PROMPT "Enter the Y coordinate of the first point? ":Y1
INPUT PROMPT "Enter the X coordinate of the second point? ":X2
INPUT PROMPT "Enter the y coordinate of the second point? ":Y2
PRINT "The distance between the two points is ";SQR((X2-X1)^2 + (Y2-Y1)^2)
END
```

While all these programs do the same thing, it is not necessarily true that the shorter program is the *better* program. It really depends on what you are trying to do. If you try to condense a program too much it becomes that much harder to debug and understand. Personally, I would say the second version of the program would be the best in this case.

8.3.4 The Crazy Architects Program

Let us say there is a new community about to be built in a very special land. Here a buyer will be able to purchase a home for a very reasonable price. Unfortunately, in order to do this they have to put up with some very strange architects. There are four architects and all of them have little quirks. Rather than giving the owners the homes they want, these architects are very insistent on designing the home based on some strange rules. Fortunately, they each only have a couple strange rules — the rest of the home they will design as the buyer wants.

Ken will only design square, blue houses. He will ask the owner how large a home they want and plan the dimensions accordingly.

Kevin only allows homes to be painted red. He also has a strange rule concerning how many bedrooms the house must have. In particular, he bases the number of bedrooms on the larger of two numbers. The first number is the number of children who will be living in the house. The second number is the owner's yearly income divided by 20,000. (So, if in a particular home there will 3 children and the owner makes $50,000 a year — there will be three bedrooms. On the other hand, if this same owner was making $200,000 a year, there would be ten bedrooms.) Kevin feels that wealthy people prefer more bedrooms even if they don't need them.

Kathi likes homes which are green. She has a rule about the garage. She bases the size of the garage on the smaller of two numbers. The first number is the number of cars belonging to that home. The second number is the number of drivers. This way if a particular driver has more than one car, they only end up with one spot in the garage. On the other hand, if some driver doesn't even own a car, they shouldn't get room in the garage.

Kris, who likes black-painted homes, insists that the cost be based on the owner's salary times 4.12345.

All these architects want to get an equal amount of business. So, the community has decided the following. The house number is the determining factor as to who gets to design the home. Kevin gets the first home, Kathi the second, Kris the home that is number 3 and Ken gets house number 4. Then it cycles around over and over again. Kevin, 5; Kathi, 6; Kris, 7; Ken, 8 and so on.

Let us write a program that notifies owners of various house numbers exactly what quirks they have to put up with.

Let us start out by assuming that when this program is run there may be a number of interested home owners who want to get information. So, we should have the main structure of the program be a sentinel loop. Also, the key question being asked is the house number of the home. We can use a special value for this to be the sentinel. How about zero? So the main structure of the program is:

```
INPUT PROMPT "What is the house number (0 when done)?":HNum
DO UNTIL HNum=0
   <Process this house number and tell about the quirks.>
   PRINT
   INPUT PROMPT "What is the house number (0 when done)?":HNum
LOOP
END
```

In order to process one particular house number it is necessary to figure out which architect is designing the house. We can use a SELECT CASE statement to handle each of the four architects. How do we figure out which architect based on the house number? This is simple. There is a built-in function to help us. In particular, if we find out the remainder when we divide the house number by 4, this will be helpful. If there is no remainder, then Ken is the architect. A remainder of 1 means it is it is Kevin. 2 means it is Kathi. And of course, 3 means it is Kris. (If you don't buy this, try an example. Take house number 5. Remainder(5,4) is equal to 1. A remainder of 1 means Kevin is the architect. And sure enough, this is what we said before!) So to process the house number we can use a SELECT CASE based on the value calculated by the REMAINDER function where 4 is the number we divide by. Here is what this SELECT CASE can look like:

```
SELECT CASE Remainder(HNum,4)
  CASE 0
    <handle Ken's quirks>
  CASE 1
    <handle Kevin's quirks>
  CASE 2
    <handle Kathi's quirks>
  CASE 3
    <handle Kris' quirks>
  CASE ELSE
END SELECT
```

Let us as look at how each case should be written.

For Ken we should tell that his homes will be blue and then ask the owner how many square feet they want their house to be. From this we can calculate how many feet one of the sides of the square house should be by using the SQR function. We should tell the owner this dimension.

```
CASE 0
  PRINT "Your architect is Ken. Your house will be blue."
  INPUT PROMPT "How many square feet should your house be?":SFeet
  LET Side = SQR(SFeet)
  PRINT "Ken says your house will be ";Side;" feet on a side."
```

If Kevin is the architect we should notify the user that the house will be red. Then we should ask how many children will be living in this house and what the owner's salary is. We can calculate the number of bedrooms by supplying the MAX function with two numbers. The first will be the number of children. The second is the salary divided by 20000. But wait! If we divide the salary by 20000, we may not end up with an exact integer. So the number of bedrooms could come out to be a strange number like 2.75. This isn't good. Let us make a decision to truncate this down to the next lowest integer by using the INT function. (We could alternatively use ROUND if we wanted to get to the closest integer.) We could divide the salary by 20000, take the INT of the result and place the answer into a temporary variable by using a LET statement. Then we could give this variable as an argument to MAX. But we know that arguments to functions can be small equations themselves. So why don't we just make this equation be the second argument to MAX and do away with having an extra variable. So we end up with:

```
CASE 1
  PRINT "Your architect is Kevin. Your house will be red."
  INPUT PROMPT "How many children do you have?":Kids
  INPUT PROMPT "How much is your salary?":Sal
  LET Bedrooms = MAX(Kids,INT(Sal/20000))
  PRINT "Kevin says your house will have";Bedrooms;" bedrooms."
```

For Kathi, who likes green houses, we need to ask for the number of cars and number of drivers. The size of the garage is just the MIN of these two numbers.

```
CASE 2
  PRINT "Your architect is Kathi. Your house will be green."
  INPUT PROMPT "How many cars do you have?":Autos
  INPUT PROMPT "How many drivers in your household?":Drivers
  LET GSize = MIN(Autos, Drivers)
  PRINT "Kathi says your house will have a ";GSize;" car garage."
```

For Kris we should tell about the black houses. Then we should ask for the owner's salary. We should multiply this number by 4.12345 and then print out the result as being the price of the house. Since we know that money amounts should only have two decimal places, why don't we use the two-argument form of the ROUND function and round the number to two decimal places. If you remember, the first argument should be the number we want to round off and the second argument is the number of decimal places. (Here it is 2.) For the first argument we could just supply the equation — the salary times 4.12345. However, just to demonstrate there are a number of ways to do things, let use use a LET statement which places the result of this equation in a variable (Temp) and give this variable as the first argument to ROUND.

```
CASE 3
   PRINT "Your architect is Kris. Your house will be black."
   INPUT PROMPT "What is your salary?":Sal
   LET Temp = Sal*4.12345
   LET Cost = ROUND(Temp,2)
   PRINT "The cost of your home will be $";Cost
```

That is all there is to this program. Let us see the whole thing all put together:

```
INPUT PROMPT "What is the house number (0 when done)?":HNum
DO UNTIL HNum=0
  SELECT CASE Remainder(HNum,4)
   CASE 0
     PRINT "Your architect is Ken. Your house will be blue."
     INPUT PROMPT "How many square feet should your house be?":SFeet
     LET Side = SQR(SFeet)
     PRINT "Ken says your house will be ";Side;" feet on a side."
   CASE 1
     PRINT "Your architect is Kevin. Your house will be red."
     INPUT PROMPT "How many children do you have?":Kids
     INPUT PROMPT "How much is your salary?":Sal
     LET Bedrooms = MAX(Kids,INT(Sal/20000))
     PRINT "Kevin says your house will have";Bedrooms;" bedrooms."
   CASE 2
     PRINT "Your architect is Kathi. Your house will be green."
     INPUT PROMPT "How many cars do you have?":Autos
     INPUT PROMPT "How many drivers in your household?":Drivers
     LET GSize = MIN(Autos, Drivers)
     PRINT "Kathi says your house will have a ";GSize;" car garage."
   CASE 3
     PRINT "Your architect is Kris. Your house will be black."
     INPUT PROMPT "What is your salary?":Sal
     LET Temp = Sal*4.12345
     LET Cost = ROUND(Temp,2)
     PRINT "The cost of your home will be $";Cost
   CASE ELSE
  END SELECT
PRINT
INPUT PROMPT "What is the house number (0 when done)?":HNum
LOOP
END
```

8.4   Random Numbers

I have already stated that RND will pick a random number between 0 and 1. However, for most purposes this is not good enough. Generally, you need a random number in a certain range. For instance, if you wanted to write a program to pick the numbers for BINGO, you want to pick numbers in the range 1-75. So how do you do it if RND only picks numbers between 0 and 1? When using RANDOM numbers in your program, there are certain rules you should follow.

8.4.1   Rules To Follow In Programs That Generate Random Numbers

1. Have the statement RANDOMIZE in your program. This insures that each time you run the program you will get different random numbers. Without this statement, you will get the same random numbers every time you run the program. (This is good for debugging.) RANDOMIZE should appear as one of the first lines of the program. In general, if you are writing a program that uses random numbers, then it would be wise to put the line

   RANDOMIZE

   as the first line in your program.

2. If you want to pick a number from 1 to some number (let's say 45 in this example) do:

   LET Numm = INT(RND * 45) + 1

   You, of course, can use any variable name other than Numm, and if your range is to some number rather than 45, use the number you need.

3. If you want to pick a number in any range from some lower bound (let's say 7 in this example) to some upper bound (let's say 17) do the following:

   LET Numm = INT(RND * 11) + 7

   Notice:

   (a) The equation is always of the same form.

   (b) The lower bound is the number after the plus sign.

   (c) The upper bound is the sum of the two arguments - 1.
       (The two arguments are the number after the * and the number after the +)

   In this example the upper bound is 11 + 7 - 1 = 17

Why This Works

Let us look at why this works:

   Numm = INT(RND * 11) + 7

The RND is done first. A number between 0 and 1, but not 1 is picked.

This is multiplied by 11. This generates a number that can be 0 up to 11 but not 11.

This is then passed as an argument to INT. Thus any decimal places are truncated. The only possible numbers at this point are

0 1 2 3 4 5 6 7 8 9 10

Then 7 is added generating one of the possible numbers:

7 8 9 10 11 12 13 14 15 16 17

So essentially, to use random numbers you have to do two things. One, you need to have RANDOMIZE at the beginning of your file. Secondly, you have to come up with the proper equation to generate random numbers in the range you want.

An equation like:

Numm= INT(RND * 45) + 1

is usually good enough. Just stick the high number you want in place of 45.

8.4.2 Program: Random Numbers. RU's TA picking program

Okay, so here is another one that is bound to get me in trouble. Let us say there is a certain university called RU (for Random University.) They need to assign TAs to a certain course. Because all these TAs are extremely nice people, they would rather not have to differentiate between them. Rather they would like to just assign TAs to courses randomly. The following program segment gives you an idea as to how this is done. This is not a completely working program but you'll get the general idea as to how random numbers can be used to meet this problem. Let us say that there are five TAs and seven sections in this particular course. This program would help:

```
RANDOMIZE
FOR Sec = 1 TO 7
    LET Ta = INT(RND * 5) + 1
    SELECT CASE Ta
    CASE 1
        PRINT "Joe is assigned to Section ";Sec
    CASE 2
        PRINT "Ping-Pong is assigned to Section ";Sec
    CASE 3
        PRINT "Patel is assigned to Section ";Sec
    CASE 4
        PRINT "Bjorn is assigned to Section ";Sec
    CASE 5
        PRINT "Zsa-Zsa is assigned to Section ";Sec
    END SELECT
NEXT Sec
END
```

Okay, so as you can see, seven sections will be given TAs. (These sections are numbered from 1 to 7.) This is the purpose of the FOR loop. We used the counting variable Sec to remind us that this variable stood for a section number. (Of course, the program would have worked just as well if we used I instead.)

There are only five TAs. Thus some TAs will have to get more than one section. One of the problems with the program is that it is possible that some TA gets ALL the sections. That isn't very good. This program can be improved. Arrays would help. We will learn about arrays soon.

It is important to realize that this loop goes around 7 times. The loop counter is used both to count how many times the loop goes around and to specify which section is getting a TA during the current pass through the loop. In the loop you pick a random number from 1 to 5. This random number is used to stand for one of the five TAs. It isn't enough to just print out this number. It is more helpful to print out the name that goes with the number. This is done here by using a SELECT CASE statement that chooses cases based on the numeric variable that gets the random number.

You can do this program differently. Rather than having the PRINT in each CASE of the SELECT CASE structure, you can instead assign some string constant to a string variable and print this string after the END SELECT. Here we can see that we replace the SELECT CASE in the loop by the following SELECT CASE and PRINT statements. (The other statements, including the LET would remain as in the previous version of this code.)

```
SELECT CASE Ta
CASE 1
    LET Taname$="Joe"
CASE 2
    LET Taname$="Ping-Pong"
CASE 3
    LET Taname$="Patel"
CASE 4
    LET Taname$="Bjorn"
CASE 5
    LET Taname$="Zsa-Zsa"
END SELECT
PRINT Taname$;" is assigned to Section ";sec
```

In general, if you have to pick a "random string" you can do so by using this combination of an expression to pick a random number and a SELECT CASE statement that uses that number as the selection variable and assigns strings accordingly in each of the various cases. Here, we used this method to pick a random string from among the various TA names.

To say this another way, you can get a TRUE BASIC program to pick a random string out of N possible strings, by first picking a random number from 1 to N and then using this number as the CASE selector in a CASE SELECT statement. There would be one case for each string.

By the way, if you remember your syntax for SELECT CASE statements, you should know that on the SELECT CASE line you can supply any valid expression. You don't have to place a variable here. So we can combine the LET and SELECT CASE which follows on the next line into one statement such as:

```
SELECT CASE INT(RND * 5) + 1
```

8.4.3 Program: Random Numbers and Conditional Loops

Let's say you want to write the following wimpy game. (It has to be a wimpy game since we can only cover small programs in the time allotted for lecture.) Or actually, let us say that this game is part of some other much larger adventure game.

You have just entered a room. In it is a 4 foot green elf. He refuses to let you out of the room until you guess his age, IQ, and shoe size. He decides to give you a break and tell you the possible ranges that these numbers can fall into. However, in case that you might stumble upon this room again, he tells you that he is a magical elf and that all his vital stats will change by the next time you reach this room. In fact it is even worse, his shoe size changes every time you guess as to what it is. (In other words, the numbers are randomized each time you enter the room and his shoe size is randomized each time you try to guess it.) Let's say his age is between 100 and 150, his IQ between 1 and 99 and his shoe size from 1 to 10. Any information that you gain now will be of no use the next time you enter this room. Also, the elf creature refuses to even tell you if you are getting close to the right values or not. You will lose five points each time you make a guess. When you entered the room let's say you started with 1000 points. Write a program to imitate this portion of the game. It should tell you how many points you have when you leave the room.

Here is the program. It uses loops and random numbers.

```
RANDOMIZE

LET Score = 1000
LET Lose = 5

LET Age = INT (RND * 51) + 100
LET Iq = INT(RND * 99) + 1

PRINT "Hi there, I am a little green elf."
PRINT "I am between 100 and 150 years old."
PRINT "My IQ is between 1 and 99."
PRINT "My shoe size is from 1 to 10."
PRINT "You can't leave this room until you answer these questions correctly."

  DO
    INPUT PROMPT "How old am I?":Guess
    LET Score = Score - Lose
  LOOP UNTIL Guess=Age

  DO
    INPUT PROMPT "What is my IQ?":Guess
    LET Score = Score - Lose
  LOOP WHILE NOT(Guess=Iq)

  DO
    LET Shoesize = INT(RND * 10) + 1
    INPUT PROMPT "What is my shoesize?":Guess
    LET Score = Score - Lose
  LOOP UNTIL Guess=Shoesize

PRINT "You get out of the room with a score of";Score
END
```

NOTES:

- This code represents one time through the room.

- Since this program uses random numbers, you have to have the RANDOMIZE statement at the beginning.

- The first couple of LET statements initialize the original number of points and the number of points the player will lose for each guess made.

- Next we assign the values to age and IQ for this time through the room. These numbers are assigned as random numbers in a certain range. These two values never change in one time through a room, so essentially, they are initialized here.

- We now print out the instructions. You can switch this around with either of the initialization sections if you wanted.

- This initialization of the points, the randomization of the IQ and age and the prints could have been done in a different order. All that is necessary is that these few sections are somewhere *before* the following loops.

- First is the loop to allow you to guess the elf's age. Guess has the current guess you have made. Each time through the loop, you can make one guess and 5 is subtracted from the Score. The loop keeps executing until the guess is equal to the age. That is, it keeps going if you haven't guessed it yet.

- Next there is a loop that allows the user to guess the IQ. Notice that I have changed the loop condition a little. I just did this to remind you that things can be done in many ways. Here, you should realize that LOOP WHILE NOT(Guess=Iq) is exactly the same as LOOP UNTIL Guess = Iq. I can use either way.

- The last loop is for guessing the shoesize. Again I used an UNTIL. I ask for guess and modify the score as I did in the previous two loops. The important thing here to notice however, is that in this loop I calculated the random number for shoesize. Thus, each time through this loop (maybe many times), the shoesize will get a new number. (Though, because of the nature of random numbers, sometimes the number may be the same as the previous time through the loop.) Note the difference between having this statement in the loop and having it previously in the program like where the age and IQ random nums were picked.

- Lastly, the program prints out the final SCORE left when all questions have been answered correctly.

- You should clearly understand why I choose the equations I did to get the random numbers in the ranges I wanted. If not, go reread the section on how to write these random number generating equations.

Here is something to note about this program. I have used three loops. However, they are one after another. This should be really easy to follow. Once a loop is finished, you need not worry about it any more. When I talked about loops, I talked about nested loops. Nested loops are when you have a loop inside of a loop. You can nest UNTILs and WHILE loops (though I had no need to do so here). If I had wanted to force the person to travel through this room three times, I could put a FOR loop around the whole program (leaving the SCORE and LOSS initialization before this new FOR loop).

For instance:

```
FOR I = 1 to 3
<same statements as I have above>
NEXT I
```

So far you learned about mathematical functions. Some of these were: ABS, SQR, INT and RND. You also learned about RANDOMIZE and how to pick random numbers in a certain range. I have also written a little program here to show how random numbers might be used. In fact, random numbers can be used for all sorts of purposes and you will have to be creative when you try to use them in your own programs.

8.5 Summary

The main point of this chapter is that large programs can be broken down into small pieces. In some ways, we have been doing this all along, especially when we attempted to think about each program as having an INPUT, Calculation and PRINT section. Sometimes, these small sections of the program can be used in a number of places within the current program. Other times, you may want to use the same segments in totally different programs. Some subprograms are used so often that they have been supplied by the TRUE BASIC software writers. These are called built-in functions. Operations for generating squareroots and getting the current time are available. This chapter has concentrated on these built-in functions. It was also mentioned that TRUE BASIC provides the capability to allow you to write your own functions — these are called "internal" and "external" functions. As you know, a function passes back one value when it is given a number of arguments to work with. It turns out that TRUE BASIC also allows you to write up a different type of subprogram — called a subroutine. These segments of code can also be called many times by a program, but rather than returning some value as a result, subroutines just execute a set segment of statements. In this chapter, the simplest type of subprogram has been explained — that is, built-in functions. If you ever want to learn more versatile programming techniques, you'll want to learn about internal and external functions along with subroutines.

This ends another exciting chapter. Until next time . . .

Have fun,

-Jt

8.6 Problems

Errors

None of the following programs will run if you try to execute them. With what error will the computer complain when you try to run each of these programs? Point out the line, what is wrong with it and how you might fix it.

1.

```
INPUT PROMPT "Give me an integer:":SomeNum
SQR(ABS(SomeNum))
PRINT "The square root of the absolute value is ";SomeNum
END
```

2.

```
INPUT PROMPT "What is some number?":Num1
INPUT PROMPT "What is another number?":Num2
INPUT PROMPT "What is a third number?":Num3
INPUT PROMPT "What is the last number?":Num4
PRINT "The biggest of the four numbers is ";MAX(Num1,Num2,Num3,Num4)
END
```

3.

```
REM Program to print five variations of random numbers
RANDOMIZE
FOR I=1 to 5
 LET Mynumber = 100/INT(RND)
 PRINT Mynumber
NEXT I
END
```

4.

```
DATA "One","Two","Three","Done"
READ Num$
DO WHILE Num$<>"Done"
  PRINT INT(Num$),Round(Num$,3),Max(Num$,10)
  READ Num$
LOOP
END
```

Tracing

1.

```
FOR J=10 to 50 STEP 10
  LET Result1 = Max(J,J/10)
  LET Result2 = ROUND( ((J/2)/10) + .1)
  LET Result3 = SQR(J^2) + Result1 + Result2
  PRINT Result3
NEXT J
END
```

2.

Let us say that the computer picked the following numbers for the first 8 times RND was called:

```
.433672    .31209  .19956  .94356    .22801    .78201    .36243 .437743
```

```
RANDOMIZE
FOR Play = 1 to 3
  LET Die1 = INT(RND*6)+1
  LET Die2 = INT(RND*6)+1
  PRINT "You rolled a ";Die1+Die2
NEXT Play
END
```

3.

```
LET K=MIN(Max(4,14),Max(7,12))
LET J=ABS(10-ROUND(20.21,1)/2)
LET I=SQR(ROUND(6.12534)+ABS(INT(-2.15)))
PRINT I,J,K
END
```

Programs

1. Write a program that generates pairs of random numbers between 1 and 10 and tells the "closeness" of the two numbers and the squareroot of this "closeness". It should print out a table consisting of the above information for ten sets of numbers. The "closeness" of the two numbers should always be positive. An example of the beginning of such a table is:

NUMBER 1	NUMBER 2	CLOSENESS	SQUAREROOT
5	1	4	2
1	10	9	3
2	4	2	1.41

At the end of the table the program should print out the message "There was a perfect square." if it was ever true that one of the squareroots was an exact integer. (Hint: To see if a number —like X — is an exact integer, see if the INT(X) is equal to X itself. If so, there are no digits after the decimal place. Use a variable like PRINTMESSAGE$ to keep track of whether or not the message should be printed.)

2. Write a program that picks 1000 random numbers between 1 and 10. Note, the numbers should not be restricted to integers. For instance, the number 6.15382 could be picked. [If you write a proper equation, it should potentially be able to pick 1 but never be able to pick exactly 10!] The purpose of the program is to count up how many times the INT of the number is the same as the ROUND of the number. Display this count when the program ends. (Needless to say — do not print out every random number picked! You might want to test this program on much less than 1000 numbers to see if it is working — in this case, you may want to print out the random numbers as you are debugging the program.)

3. A four-sided tetrahedron has a different color on each of its four sides. Write a program that helps simulate a guessing game that involves tossing this shape. The computer should randomly pick one of the four colors. This will represent the color that is facing down when you toss the tetrahedron. The player should be given a chance to guess the color. It the player gets it right on the first try, they should be awarded three points. If they guess wrong, they get another try. If they guess on the second try, they get 1 point. Otherwise the computer wins two points. Write a program that simulates playing this guessing game one time and announces how many points the winner gets. Once you have this working, change the program to play the game ten times. At the end, it should tell how many points the player got and how many the computer got.

4. Write a program to print out a table comparing some values. In particular, for values v in the set $\{10, 10.2, 10.4, 10.6, 10.8, 11\}$ and for values x in the set $\{1,2,3,4\}$ print out v, x and the two values $\sqrt{x^v}$ and $\sqrt{v^x}$. Also, print out the larger of these last two values. You will want the output to be in tabular form — with an appropriate header line on the top. As one last chore, count up and print how many times it turned out that $\sqrt{x^v}$ was larger than $\sqrt{v^x}$.

5. You all probably know the guessing game where someone picks a number between 1 and a 100 and you have to figure out the number with as few guesses as possible — usually you are told a clue like "lower" or "higher". Write a program to play a variation of this game. It is as follows. Two random numbers are picked by the computer. These numbers are considered to be coordinates on a playing field. The numbers can be anywhere from 0 to 10 (which means numbers like 6.234 are allowed). The goal of the game is to guess pairs of coordinates, trying to focus in on this point on the field. For each pair of coordinates guessed, the computer will announce how far away from the random point the guess is. (See the equation in this chapter to calculate this distance.) The goal is to come within .5 units of the real point with as few guesses as possible. The player wins when a guess is within this distance. The computer should tell how many guesses it took to win. (A guess is considered to be a *pair* of coordinates.) Make the game automatically stop after 7 guesses have been made. If a person takes 7 guesses and still has not gotten close enough to the random point then the program should tell the player some appropriate message like "Don't become a mathematician."

[By the way you might want to note that there are simple mathematical methods to insure that such a random point can always be found with three guesses. The idea being that three circles can only intersect at one commmon point. Each guess you make is the center of a circle. Thus after three guesses you must be able to figure out the original random point.]

6. Write a program to allow two people to play blackjack. You can concentrate on a simplified version of the game — let aces always count as 1 point, don't worry about splitting etc. (If you have the motivation, you can attempt a more realistic version of the game.) The program should allow each person to play one hand and print out who came closest to 21 without going over — or print out tie if they both ended up the same distance away from 21. The easiest way to write this program to let one person play all the way to the end, before trying to handle the second person. For each person let them keep getting cards until they say they don't want any more — or they go over 21. Let the computer randomly pick the cards. All that is necessary is to pick card value from 1 to 13. (Don't pick a number from 1 to 10 because then, you won't get as many tens as you would in a real game of blackjack.) A decision making statement can be used to map the large numbers to the value that should be used for blackjack. That is, for numbers bigger than 10, they should only be counted as only ten points. [For those of you who don't know how to play blackjack, here is a simplified explanation: Cards are dealt to player's one at a time. The player keeps track of his score as the cards are being dealt. This player wants to come as close to a total of 21 without going over 21. The player adds on the value of each card to his score — realizing that Jack, Queen and Kings are worth 10 points. At any time, the player can stop and say he wants no more cards.]

7. Write a program to convert fluid ounces into gallons, quarts, pints, cups and ounces. Ask the user to supply the number of ounces. Round off the number they supply and then do the conversion. The program should print out the answer but not bother to print any value that is zero. Example: The user types in 329.7 ounces. The program should print out "330 ounces is the same as 2 gallons, 2 quarts, 1 cup and 2 ounces." (Notice it didn't print out "0 pints".) For those who need to know: 8 ounces in a cup, two cups in a pint, 2 pints in a quart and 4 quarts in a gallon.

8. In preparation for designing a new car you hope to market in Alaska you want to gather some statistics on the heights of the people who live there so that you can make sure the car has appropriate leg room in the front seat. While information on the average will be useful, you would also like to know the range of heights. Therefore, write a program that reads in the names and heights (in inches) of people and prints out the average height. To get a grasp on the range, print the name and height of the tallest individual. Then do the same for the shortest. Figure out the tallest and shortest person by using the MAX and MIN functions. For now, instead of getting data on all the people in Alaska, build data on ten people into your program. (Hint: have two variables to hold on to the name and height of the tallest person so far. Also have two more variables for the shortest person so far.)

9. A perfect square is the best rectangular shape to use if you want to enclose a set amount of area with the least amount of material around the perimeter. For example, if you want to build a closet with 25 square feet of space, it would make sense to build a square region with 5 foot long walls, rather than build a closet 25 feet long and 1 foot deep. You are rancher. You own a certain amount of sheep. You want to build a fence around your land to safely protect your animals. You decide that for each sheep you should have 200 square yards of land. Each yard of fencing will cost $25. Write a program that asks how many sheep there are and prints out how many yards of fencing the rancher must use to enclose a square field of the proper size to care for all his/her sheep. Finally, print out how much it will cost to build this fence. (Example: A rancher with 18 sheep needs 3600 square yards of land. Therefore, a square field with 60 yard sides can be used — 60 x 60 = 3600 — and the rancher would need 240 yards of fencing in all, costing $1500.)

Chapter 9

Arrays

9.1 A Note On INPUT and OUTPUT Files

[Forenote: Ah ha, there is something we haven't taught about and we aren't going to worry about for this semester. But I want to mention it just so that you know it is available if you were to do some programming in the future.

INPUT FILES: With most computer languages, there is a way to INPUT values off of a file rather than typing them in when the program runs. This file can often be created by a word processor (or other such editor). It is nice to use an input file if you are going to run the program many times using most of the same input over and over again. Then you (or someone else) can just enter the data once by using a word processor and you can run the program many times using that same data. Most computer programs use input files. In fact, input files work **very** well with the subject we are going to talk about today—ARRAYS. A lot of the program examples in the following chapter that use arrays would make more sense and seem more feasible if you didn't have to supply the data for the arrays every time you ran the program. So when considering these programs, think about how nice the programs would be if you were also using INPUT files.

We will be able to get some of the same benefits as using INPUT files by using READ and DATA statements.

By the way, there are OUTPUT files too. You can have a program print all information to a file rather than to the screen (or possibly have it do both). An OUTPUT file can be easily printed. Or you can just keep it around on the computer to look at in the future.]

9.2 Reason For Arrays

So far, most of our programs have used a very small amount of variables. (A dozen or so?) In fact, it would be quite complicated to try to work on a program that had hundreds of different variables! Well doesn't it strike you as being strange that a computer may have millions of bytes with which to hold variable values? Doesn't that seem as being a waste of space? After all, if your program had a hundred different variables, it would only need a couple hundred bytes in order to hold the values of those variables.

While you are thinking about that, why don't you also think about how you would write the following programs.

Let's say you had a list of scores on a test. You want to figure out who passed and failed the test but you want the grading to be based on a curve. Let's say you wanted people who were 20 points below the average grade to fail the exam. Well this means you first have to figure out what the average was. Then you have to print out who passed and failed. To figure out the average, you would have to read in all the scores, total them and divide by the number of scores. This means you must read, (or input) all the data.

That is, you pass through it once. However, if you were using variables like Score and Nam$, each new person will have wiped out the record of the previous person. Thus, after the average was calculated, you would then have to ask for all the names and grades again and calculate who passed and failed. If you think about the structure of the program, you would have to have one loop to figure out the average. Then after that you would have another loop to figure out who passed and failed. In each loop, you would have to get the values for Nam$ and Score for each person in the list. If you were using regular input statements, you would end up asking the user every question twice. A user isn't gonna like this. It would be nice if the computer could store all the names and scores in its RAM so that you need not get the information again from the user. How can you write a program to do this kind of problem?

Or, let's say you had a file that had a list of Beatles songs and their copyright dates. You want to write a program that allows a user to type in the name of a song and the computer will come back with the copyright date. At the beginning of the program, it should be able to read in the names of songs and dates until all info is entered, at which point someone could type in the name of songs that they needed the copyright date to. Wouldn't be nice if the program could just store all the names and copyrights in RAM and then look through that information when necessary?

9.3   What Is An Array?

An array (at least a one dimensional array) is a list of information that can be referenced under one name. In order to refer to or change one item in that list, you must specify both the name of the list and the location or position of the particular item in that list that you want. This number that is used to specify which item in the list is called an index. (Or alternatively, you can call it a subscript.) Elements of an array act as any other variables. They can be arrays of numbers or arrays of strings. Since they act as variables do, they are stored in RAM and can be changed or used just like other variables can. Where can we use variables (and thus elements of an array)? Well we have seen them used in INPUT and PRINT statements. We have seen them used on both the left hand and right hand side of assignment statements. We have also seen them used in the expressions in IF statements, SELECT statements and DO-LOOPs.

When using arrays, it is important to specify how big the list is going to be. Thus some place towards the beginning of the program, you must use a dimension or DIM statement.

9.4   The DIM statement

Syntax

> DIM *arrayname*(*size*),*arrayname2*(*size2*) ...
>
> That is, it starts out with the word DIM. A space follows this and then a list of array names with a number in parentheses. Each array on this list is separated by a comma. The name of an array must follow the same rules as names for other variables.

Meaning

> Set up room for the array or list. The number in parentheses tells how many items will be in the list. The first element of the array will have an index of 1. The last one has an index of *size* (whatever number you supplied).

Examples

> DIM X(15)
>
> DIM Nam$(22)
>
> DIM X(10),Y(55),Z(15),Apple$(100)

There is a more advanced form of the DIM statement.

Advanced Syntax

> DIM *arrayname*(*lower* **TO** *higher*) ,...

Meaning

> Set up an array that has higher-lower+1 elements in it. The first element of the array has an index of LOWER, the last one has an index of HIGHER.

Examples

> DIM X(10 TO 20)
>
> DIM Year(1987 TO 2001)
>
> DIM Name$(101 TO 120)

As I have said, if your program is going to use arrays, then you must have a DIM statement some place towards the beginning of the program. In fact, the array should be dimensioned BEFORE you try to use the array. DIM statements should be towards the beginning of the program, a lot like RANDOMIZE and so on.

It is an error if you try to use an array and haven't dimensioned it!

9.5 Using An Array

Great! And now that you have set up space for an array, how do you use it in the program? Simple, you can use it just like any other variable. That is, you can use it in the same kind of places. However, there is one thing that you have to make sure you do. Every time you use your array variable, you must also give the index of that variable in parentheses. Observe:

> DIM X(10),Y(22)
>
> $\vdots$
>
> LET X(2)=2
>
> $\vdots$
>
> LET Y(I)=X(J)+27
>
> $\vdots$
>
> PRINT X(5)
>
> $\vdots$

Notice that everywhere we use X or Y in the program, we also follow with a set of parentheses with a numeric value enclosed. That is, you can supply a number, a variable (such as I or J) or even an equation inside of these parentheses.

How is the number (or index) supplied in the parentheses used? Well, it tells what item in the list you are talking about. First evaluate the contents of the parentheses. Once you have gotten a value, use this value as the location in the list of the item you want.

What should you do when you are tracing programs that use arrays? Well in the past you would write down the names of all variables and then list and cross out the values that each variable takes. For an array, you should have a box for each element of the array and erase or change the contents of each box when necessary. Watch:

```
DIM Stuff(5)
LET Stuff(5)=3
LET Stuff(3)=22
LET Stuff(2)=0
LET Stuff(4)=19
LET Stuff(1)=45
```

At this point if you were tracing the program, the stuff array would look like

```
STUFF
----------
|   45   |
----------
|    0   |
----------
|   22   |
----------
|   19   |
----------
|    3   |
----------
```

If the next line said **LET Stuff(2+1)=4** then stuff would look like:

```
STUFF
----------
|   45   |
----------
|    0   |
----------
|    4   |
----------
|   19   |
----------
|    3   |
----------
```

Now what if the next line said
LET Stuff(1) = (Stuff(4) + Stuff(5)) /11
The trick to tracing an assignment statement that has array elements on the right side is to first look up the values of those array elements and place them into the equation. Thus you get:
LET Stuff(1)=(19 + 3) /11
The right hand side now obviously evaluates to 2. Thus Stuff(1) gets the value 2 and the array looks as follows.

```
          STUFF
        ----------
        |   2   |
        ----------
        |   0   |
        ----------
        |   4   |
        ----------
        |  19   |
        ----------
        |   3   |
        ----------
```

9.6 Possible Errors When Using Arrays

There are plenty of errors you can make when you are using arrays.

1. The first error that is possible when you are using an array is to forget to dimension it. Thus if you had the following program:

```
LET X = 23
LET Y = 14
LET A(X) = Y
END
```

The program would die at the the third line. This is because the interpreter sees the parentheses after the A and realizes you want to use an array called A but you never DIMensioned it. TRUE BASIC will complain about this. (At other times, such as in PRINT statements or the right-hand side of LET statements, if a program has parentheses after something that looks like a variable name, TRUE BASIC can't even tell if you are trying to use an array or making a function call. You must DIM your array or have your function DEFined before this so it can figure out what you mean. "DEF" is a TRUE BASIC statement that allows you to make your own functions.)

2. The most common error when using arrays is "SUBSCRIPT OUT OF BOUNDS". If an array had 7 elements in it, it doesn't make sense to have the computer use or change the 91st element of the array. It is just total craziness to the computer. Thus the computer would complain about the following code in which the array is out of bounds at line 2.

```
DIM X(7)
LET X(91)=2
```

And the following code would complain at line 4.

```
DIM X(7)
LET J=45
LET K=2
LET X(J*K+1)=2
```

And so would the following eventually complain at line 5.

```
DIM X(7)
LET Kount=1
LET K=1
DO WHILE Kount<=7
    PRINT X(K)
    LET K=K+1
LOOP
END
```

See how the loop goes on forever? Kount always stays equal to 1 so the loop never ends. Meanwhile K gets bigger and bigger until eventually it is equal to 8. Line 5 now blows up since the index is out of bounds for the array size. The programmer probably wanted the line DO WHILE $K <= 7$. When he/she sees the error "SUBSCRIPT OUT OF BOUNDS" it might not be clear to her/im to look at this line as the cause of the error. This is a typical example of the type of cascading error that can occur in array programs if you aren't careful. You make a simple error like typing "Kount" instead of "K" and the error message you receive tells you about something completely different.

3. Another error is that at some point you changed the name (accidently or on purpose) of your array from when you dimensioned it. Like:

DIM Kim(25)

$\vdots$

LET Kimm(2)=3

Or:

DIM Nam$(23)

$\vdots$

LET Nam(2)=TOM

NOTE: that a string array is a totally different variable than a numeric array even if their names are similar. Thus nam$(2) is a string while nam(2) would be a member of another array that had numbers in it.

4. Another common error is forgetting to use parentheses around your index.

DIM Age(20)

LET Age1=25

LET Age2=4

$\vdots$

FOR I=1 TO 20

PRINT Age(I)

NEXT I

The program churns through BUT it doesn't do what you want. This would print out all zeros. The computer thinks that age1 and age2 are new variables(regular variables like x and y) that you have just named. It doesn't think you are talking about the Age array. You **must** have the parentheses around your index.

5. Forgetting your index altogether is another problem. Let's say you wanted to set all the elements of an array to the same value, let's say five. You might try:

DIM A(10)

LET A=5

and expect this to set all the elements of A to 5. However what really happens is that TRUE BASIC complains at the second line. It now knows that A is an array (from the DIM statement) and expects you to use it as such by using parentheses and an index whenever you supply the name. If it doesn't see these extensions to the variable name, it thinks you are trying to use a regular variable with the same name as the array.

So make sure you are clear on the differences between

X, X\$, X\$(1),X1\$,X1

Which are regular variables? Which are arrays? Which are strings? Which are numbers? Are any of them equivalent?

6. Finally, the last interesting problem has to do with using loops and arrays. We will see in a moment that loops and arrays were made to work together. Typically you will use a FOR loop. For instance if you wanted to print everything in an array, you could use the following set up:

DIM Things(10)

FOR I=1 TO 10

PRINT Things(I)

NEXT I

Note how we use the loop counting variable as the index into the array. Cute eh? Many times a loop will be set up in this manner. That leads to the following potential error. Look closely:

DIM Things(10)

FOR I=1 TO 10

PRINT Things(J)

NEXT I

See in line 3 the index used is J? Where the heck did J come from? Seems stupid when magnified like this here but many people make this very error. In general, for most (not all) programs you write with arrays and loops, the loop counter will also be used as an index into the array. A program won't die if you make this error, it just won't do what you want. (What I am saying here is that if a program looks like this, it is probably a STUPID program but there is no real syntax error here. This is a lot like having a program with no PRINTs. I am just warning about this because this is the type of situation that might crop up when you write your own programs.)

9.7 Loops And Arrays

When using arrays, there are often a number of chores you may want to do with your programs. Most of the time, you want to perform similar operations on all (or some) of the elements of the array. And what type of structure do you know that will perform the same (or similar) operations over and over? A loop! If you know the size of the array, you may use a FOR loop. Other times, you may have set up a large amount of space for an array, but you don't know what portion of the array you really plan to use. For instance, you may have a file that has a list of names in it. You may read in these names and place them into an array. You don't know exactly how many names are in that file but there exists a sentinel at the end. To handle this problem, you could set up the array to be a large size, maybe 100 elements and then use up whatever portion of the array you need. You could then use a while loop to read in the names.

Keep in mind that your program now has a limitation. That is, it can't work for a file that has more than 100 names in it. In fact, the program could very well bomb if the file has more than 100 names. So when working with programs like this you want to make sure of two things. 1) Make sure you pick a practical array size. Set up enough space for whatever situations may arise but don't take up too much space since a computer can only deal with so much space at one time. 2) Make sure the users of the program know the limitations of your program.

Let's look at some of the possible chores you might have to do to an array.

9.7.1   Initializing

Like any other variable, elements of an array should be (or may have to be) initialized. Initializing means to give a variable an original value. This initializing can be built into the program by assignment statements or you may read or input the initial values from a user (or a file). It depends on the particular program you are working on.

For the following discussion assume you have an array

DIM Z(30)

How can you initialize all the elements in the array to the same value? In this case let's say that value is 5.

Easy:

```
FOR J=1 TO 30
   LET Z(J)=5
NEXT J
```

In other words, for all values of J from 1 to 30, give the jth element of the array the value 5.

You remember how easy it is to trace FOR loops, don't you? Give J the value 1. So LET Z(J)= 5 really means LET Z(1)=5. That is, the first item in the list gets the value 5. Now loop around, increment J making it 2. So plug in the J value in the body of the loop and you get LET Z(2)=5 — ah, the second item in the list becomes the value 5. And so on. The list gets intialized to all 5's.

Notice how the index into the array is the same as the loop counter; in this case j. Notice how the expression on the right hand side of the equation is a constant; in this case five.

Or how could you initialize so that the elements of the array represent the sequence 1,4,9,16 .... That is, the value for the 1st value is 1 squared or 1. The value of the second element is 2 squared or 4. The value of the third is 3 squared and so on. That is, the value of the ith element is i squared.

```
FOR I=1 TO 30
   LET Z(I)=I^2
NEXT I
```

Notice how I is used for three purposes here. First of all, it is the loop counter. Secondly, it is used as the index. Thirdly, it is used in the equation on the right hand side in order to calculate the values.

Or how about setting the array to values of the fibonacci sequence. That is, 1,1,2,3,5,8,13....

```
LET Z(1)=1
LET Z(2)=1
FOR K=3 TO 30
    LET Z(K)=Z(K-1)+Z(K-2)
NEXT K
```

Let's look a little deeper into this. In the fibonacci sequence, each element of the sequence is equal to the sum of the previous two. This is true except for the first two numbers in the sequence. (After all, think about it, there are not two values before them, so the definition doesn't make sense for these elements.)

So what I have done here is to just assign the first two values of the sequence (the array) by using direct assignment statements. I supplied both the index and the values in lines 1 and 2. Then I use a loop to fill in all the rest of the elements. K is used in this loop for three uses. 1) as usual it is used as the loop counter so the program knows how many times to loop around. 2) It is used as an index on the left hand side of the equation so the program knows which element of the array I am trying to give a value to. 3) Finally it is used in order to calculate the indices of the previous two numbers in the sequence. By doing this, I can get the values of the previous two numbers and sum them up.

If you still don't get this, try some values for K. Say K is 3, then the assignment statement in the loop becomes $Z(3) = Z(3-1) + Z(3-2) = Z(2) + Z(1)$. If you look up the values of these previous two items in the list — which were given a value before the loop started you get $Z(3) = 1 + 1 = 2$. Which reads: "the third number in the fibonacci series is 2". Now say K is 23, then the assignment statement in the loop becomes: LET $Z(23) = Z(22) + Z(21)$. Which says that the 23rd number in the fibonacci series is the sum of the 22nd number and the 21st number. This is correct.

It would be a good idea to understand this in detail. It seems straightforward but can you reproduce this on your own? Can you do the sequence 1,5,2,10,4,20,8,40.... where each element is twice the value of the element two places ahead in the sequence.

Finally, it is also possible to initialize an array based on values in other arrays. For instance, let's say that at some point in a program, two arrays have already been set up and used. They have some values in them as follows:

A	B
--	--
15	10
9	7
12	13
12	0
17	25

There are two arrays. They are named A and B and both have five elements. How can you initialize an array C to have the sum of the array A and B elements. You want it to end up like:

C
--
25
16
25
12
42

The following loop will do it for you:

```
FOR Q=1 TO 5
    LET C(Q) = A(Q) + B(Q)
NEXT Q
```

Notice that Q has four uses here. It is the loop counter again (as I and K were in previous examples). It is the index for the C array on the left hand side of the equation. We need this so we know where in the array to place the result. It also acts as the index for both the A array and the B array. We need this so we can find the numbers that are added.

9.7.2   Inputting Arrays

Often we want to get the initial values for an array by inputting them. That is, we can get them from a user (or from a file). As usual, there are two possibilities. Either we know exactly how much input there is, or there is a sentinel acting as the last element.

Let's try an example were we know exactly how much input there will be. Let's get the input from the keyboard and, of course, use a counted loop. Look at the following example:

```
DIM X(5)
PRINT "GIVE ME FIVE NUMBERS"
FOR A=1 TO 5
    INPUT PROMPT " A NUMBER PLEASE ":X(A)
NEXT A

                  .
                  .
                  .
```

Notes:

1. We put a PRINT statement before the loop to tell the user how many numbers we are going to be asking for.

2. We use a FOR loop that goes around 5 times.

3. The variable in the input statement is an element of the array. This shows that arrays can be used in input statements.

4. A acts as an index into the array in this input statement.

5. This program can be easily changed to work for an array that had 500 elements.

How About Using A Sentinel

Let's input the following list of names and place it into an array:

```
Tom
Ted
Tim
Tod
 .
 .
 .
TTT
```

Notice that this list ends with the sentinel "TTT". We will say that there are no more than 100 names in this file.

```
DIM Nam$(100)
LET Kount=1
INPUT Nam$(Kount)

DO WHILE Nam$(Kount)<>"TTT"
    LET Kount=Kount+1
    INPUT Nam$(Kount)
LOOP
LET Kount=Kount-1
```

You should look at this very, very carefully. There is a lot of subtle stuff going on here.

1. The array is DIMensioned to 100 since it is known there are no more than 100 names.

2. There is a variable called Kount that will keep count of how many records (names) are being inputed. Start this variable at 1 since Kount acts as an index into the array and it is needed in the next line.

3. Read in the first element of the array (the first name in the file) *before* the loop. This is the priming done for the loop.

4. The loop will end when the last name read in (it will be the kount element of the array) is equal to "TTT".

5. In the loop the Kount of names is incremented by 1. This new number is used as an index so that it is known where to place the next name in the array.

6. Next read in the next name into the Kount position of the array.

7. After the loop adjust Kount by subtracting one. You don't want "TTT" to be counted as one of the names. In general, you don't want the sentinel to be counted as data. Since the Kount-th element of the array is "TTT", subtract one from Kount to get the proper number of names. From now on in the program, it is possible to use FOR loops, since we know the exact number of names that are stored in the array. Kount is this number.

Associated Arrays

Often input has more than one piece of information for each record of data. For instance, the following data has three fields per record.

```
"BANANA","YELLOW",101
"ORANGE","ORANGE",62
"LIME","GREEN",19
"LAST"," ",0
```

Notice that each line has the name of a fruit, its color and how many calories it has. There is a sentinel at the end.

We can use code similar to what I have just shown, in order to read in the information in this file:

```
DIM Fruit$(100),Color$(100),Cal(100)
LET Kount=1
INPUT Fruit$(Kount),Color$(Kount),Cal(Kount)

DO WHILE Fruit$(Kount)<>"LAST"
   LET Kount=Kount+1
   INPUT Fruit$(Kount),Color$(Kount),Cal(Kount)
LOOP

LET Kount=Kount-1
```

Notice the similar structure to what we did above. All that has changed here is we now have three arrays which are read in on the input statements and we've changed the DIM statement, DO loop and sentinel. The structure is exactly the same. Note that Kount is used in the same way as before.

When a number of arrays all hold separate pieces of information for some record, they are called **associated arrays**. (Another name for this is "parallel arrays".) Here I have three arrays, Fruit$, Color$ and Cal that hold the information for my pieces of fruit. Fruit$(3), Color$(3) and Cal(3) give me the information on my third piece of fruit.

9.7.3 READ/DATA To Fill Arrays

Often in programs that use arrays, you want the values of the arrays to be initialized with certain data. We have seen how we can do this by using assignment statements. We have also seen that it is possible to have the user supply the original values to the array through the use of input statements. It turns out that many times we would prefer to have the programmer, rather than the user, assign the original values. The programmer could do this by using assignment (LET) statements, but this may be a real pain. An easier way is by using READ/DATA statements. In this way, the programmer (or a helper) can supply the original values in the code of the program and thus the program need not ask the user. Also, the data on the DATA statement lines can easily be changed if that becomes necessary for further runs of the program.

Consider the previous program that used associated arrays. We can also redo that program by using READ and DATA. Watch:

```
DIM Fruit$(100),Color$(100),Cal(100)
LET Kount=1
READ Fruit$(Kount),Color$(Kount),Cal(Kount)

DO WHILE Fruit$(Kount)<>"LAST"
   LET Kount=Kount+1
   READ Fruit$(Kount),Color$(Kount),Cal(Kount)
LOOP

LET Kount=Kount-1

REM Put the rest of the program here......

DATA "BANANA","YELLOW",101
DATA "ORANGE","ORANGE",62
DATA "LIME","GREEN",19
DATA "LAST"," ",0

END
```

Notice that very few changes were made here. We changed INPUT into READ and added all the data at the end with DATA statements. It will turn out that in many of your own programs that use arrays, you will want to use READ/DATA statements to supply much of the data to fill the arrays. You can then use INPUT PROMPT statements to only ask users for pertinent data that only they can supply. (You probably will want to use some sentinel loop to load up the arrays with their initial values.)

9.7.4 Printing Out

A common operation to perform on arrays is to print out all or part of their contents. For instance, if an array called Book$ has 15 elements in it, you could print them out as follows:

```
FOR I=1 TO 15
  PRINT Book$(I)
NEXT I
```

Or if you had read those books in by using a sentinel loop and had kept a Kount, you could do:

```
FOR I=1 TO Kount
  PRINT Book$(I)
NEXT I
```

Often you want to label what you are printing out like:

```
FOR I=1 TO Kount
  PRINT "BOOK NUMBER ";I;" IS "; Book$(I)
NEXT I
```

Finally, you might want to only print out certain elements of the array. For instance, let's say you had an array of numbers called Numm and you only wanted to print out those that were greater than 50. You could do:

```
FOR Index=1 TO Amount
  IF Numm(Index) > 50 THEN PRINT Numm(Index)
NEXT Index
```

I have changed the name of the loop counter — naming it Index, and turned Kount into Amount here, but you shouldn't be confused by that.

9.7.5 Modifying

Another operation you might want to do to an array is change the contents of some or all of the elements of the array. In fact, a program may spend a considerable amount of time modifying its arrays.

Let's look at five simple examples:

- The simplest example would be that you want to change one particular element in the list. For instance, if you want to add on five to the 37th element in the list you could do so by using an equation that referred to that element on both sides of the equal sign. On the righthand side, the array reference would be used to look up the 37th value in the list. Then, five would be added to this. On the lefthand side of the equation, an array reference would be placed here to let the computer know we want to place the answer right back into the array — in the 37th place. Like this:

```
LET X(37) = X(37) + 5
```

- Possibly, we may want to perform some modification on all elements in an array. Here you'd use a loop. Let's double the value of each element of an array called DOLLARS that has 25 elements.

```
FOR I=1 TO 25
  LET Dollars(I)=Dollars(I)*2
NEXT I
```

- Sometimes, you want to perform some test on each element and decide to change it if it passes this test. In such a case, you use a loop which contains an assignment statement inside of an IF. Let's set every element of an array called LINES that is over 66 to 0.

⋮

```
FOR J=1 TO Kount
  IF Lines(J) > 66 THEN LET Lines(J)=0
NEXT J
```

⋮

- Sometimes information provided by the user tells you which array element should change. The variable supplied by an INPUT PROMPT acts as the index. Here is an example in which the elements of the array are acting as accumulators — keeping the sum of various input. Let's have an array called SALES that keeps track of the total sales that various salespeople have made. A main loop will keep asking which salesperson and how much in sales that person has made. The loop stops when the user specifies a 0 for the salesperson.

⋮

```
INPUT PROMPT "WHICH SALESPERSON?":Sp
DO WHILE Sp<>0
  INPUT PROMPT "HOW MUCH DID THIS SALESPERSON MAKE?":Amount
  LET Sales(Sp)=Sales(Sp)+Amount
  INPUT PROMPT "WHICH SALESPERSON":Sp
LOOP
```

⋮

- Also each element of the array can act as separate counter. Let's say you own a book store and you want to keep track of how many of each book was sold. Assuming that each book has a number (that is used as an index into an array) and the array has been initialized to all zeroes, then a cash register program might consist of a loop that partially looks as follows:

```
INPUT PROMPT "Which book is being sold?":Booknum
DO WHILE Booknum<>0
  LET Sold(Booknum) = Sold(Booknum) + 1
  ...do other stuff like notify person of cost...
  INPUT PROMPT "Which book is being sold?":Booknum
LOOP
```

(After this loop finished, Sold would tell how many of each book was sold.)

9.7.6 "Tallying" Arrays

Another common task you may perform on arrays is a "tally" or other computation based on all (or some) elements of the array.

- For instance, using the above book store data, how can you find out how many total books were sold? Assuming you knew the number of the last book in the store (Maxbooknum) then how about writing:

```
LET Kount = 0
FOR Book = 1 TO Maxbooknum
    LET Kount = Kount + Sold(Book)
NEXT Book
PRINT Kount  ;" BOOKS WERE SOLD"
```

Notice how Book is used as an index and in this way, each number in the Sold array is added on to the Kount. This is how the total count is calculated.

- Or how about if you had a array with 240 students' test scores in it and you wanted to take the average of all students who got over 75 on the exam. Then try:

```
LET Total=0
LET Num_Over_75=0
FOR I=1 TO 240
  IF Score(I) > 75 THEN
    LET Num_Over_75 = Num_Over_75 + 1
    LET Total = Total + Score(I)
  END IF
NEXT I
LET Special_Average=Total/Num_Over_75
PRINT "THE AVERAGE SCORE FOR STUDENTS WHO GOT OVER 75 WAS:"
PRINT Special_Average
```

⋮

Here, Total is keeping track of the sum of all the test scores over 75. Num_Over_75 is keeping track of how many students got over 75 on the exam. The FOR loop looks through all 240 students. In the body of this loop is a simple IF statement. It checks to see if the test score of the current (Ith) student is over 75. If so, then both the accumulator and counter are adjusted.

9.7.7 Typical Programs

A typical program using arrays initializes the arrays, then modifies or uses the values and finally prints out some or all of the values in the array. For each one of these tasks, a separate loop is used.

9.8   Reasons For Using Arrays

Why would you use an array? First of all, you would want to use an array when you must go through a series of data several times. For instance, use an array if you must go through some data once to figure out a value such as an average and then again later in order to use that value for some or all the values of the array (to give a grade). You would want to use an array when you want to keep running totals (or other calculations) on a number of items at the same time. (For instance, the total amount of sales for a lot of salespeople.) Finally, you want to use arrays when you want to do sorting or searching on a large amount of records. (We will learn about searching in a future lecture.) Actually, there are a number of reasons you would want to use an array; with more experience, you will get a better feel for when they are necessary or handy.

9.9   Programs

9.9.1   The IQ Problem

Let's say that you have a data which has a number of records like:

```
DATA "Rose",131
DATA "Rich",123
DATA "Ryan",151
    .
    .
    .
DATA "ZZZZ",0
```

Each line has a name and the person's IQ. You want to write a program that figures out the average IQ of these people and then prints out all people who are 20% above the average IQ and all people who are 20% below the average.

The structure of this program is simple. It has four parts. Input all the data. Calculate the average. Print the 20% above average people. Print the 20% below average people.

Well, we know how to input the data, including getting a count of the number of items. We discussed that before. And we saw how to sum up all items in an array. Getting the average from this sum is easy if you also know the count. Printing only certain values from an array is an easy task ,too.

Putting it all together here is a program that will do this task:

```
    DIM Nam$(100),Iq(100)

! read in data
    LET Kount=1
    READ Nam$(Kount),Iq(Kount)
    DO WHILE Nam$(Kount)<>"ZZZZ"
      LET Kount=Kount+1
      READ Nam$(Kount),Iq(Kount)
    LOOP
    LET Kount=Kount-1

! calculate average
    LET Total=0
    FOR I=1 TO Kount
      LET Total=Total+Iq(I)
    NEXT I
    LET Aver=Total/Kount

! print out names of people 20% over average
    PRINT "PEOPLE 20% ABOVE AVERAGE"
    LET Breakoff=Aver+Aver*.20
    FOR I=1 TO Kount
      IF Iq(I)>Breakoff THEN PRINT Nam$(I)
    NEXT I

! print out names of people 20% below average
    PRINT "PEOPLE 20% BELOW AVERAGE"
    LET Breakoff=Aver-Aver*.20
    FOR I=1 TO Kount
      IF Iq(I)<Breakoff THEN PRINT Nam$(I)
    NEXT I

    END
```

NOTES:

1. The main program consists of setting up some arrays and then four loops.

2. The first loop is my typical loop for reading in associated arrays from data that has a sentinel at the end.

3. The second loop figures out the average by using a loop to total up all the items in the array. That is, a total of the IQs is found. Then it divides by Kount to get the average. See that Kount from the input routine comes in handy. It is possible to combine the first two routines into one. That is, I could figure out the total as I was reading in the input.

   By adding:

   LET Total=0

   before the first loop and

   LET Total=Total + Iq(Kount)

after the READ statement in the body of the loop and

LET Aver = Total / Kount

after that first loop.

This would make the second loop unnecessary. Sometimes, it is better to use more lines and separate the individual functions of the program. It is up to personal programming taste.

4. The other two loops are similar. Before a loop that goes through the whole array, I print out a line on the screen to notify the user what the following list of names is. Why do I print this header before the loop? Well, I certainly don't want it in the loop. I only want it to print once. Then I figure out the "interesting" number and use this number in an IF statement in the loop to decide what names to print out.

9.9.2   The Temperature Problem

Let's try another program!

Let's assume that for two months, the meteorology department has been keeping data on the daily high temperatures. The data looks as follows.

```
DATA "10/1/86",59
DATA "10/2/86",67
....
DATA "LAST",0
```

Now, they want you to write a program that will figure out the highest daily high for those two months and then print out how much lower than this high each daily high was. For instance, let's say it finds out that the highest high was 87 degrees. It should print

```
On 10/1/86 the daily high was 28 degrees below the high for this period.
On 10/2/86 the daily high was 20 degrees below the high for this period.
 .
 .
 .
```

This is even easier than the previous program. All we have to do is three steps. Read in the data. Find the maximum value. And finally, print out a statement for each day — that is, for each value in the array.

Reading in and printing out are the same as has been discussed already. Getting the maximum is something new. We can have some variable called Maxx, which is the largest daily high so far. We can start this at zero and then go through each value in the daily high array. Every time we find a value that is bigger than the current value of Maxx, we set Maxx to this new higher value. (Of course, we use an IF to compare the value from the array with Maxx.) By the end of the loop, Maxx must have the largest value that was in the array.

Well, let's write the program:

```
DIM Dat$(100),Degrees(100)

LET Kount=1
READ Dat$(1),Degrees(1)
DO WHILE Dat$(Kount)<>"LAST"
  LET Kount=Kount+1
  READ Dat$(Kount),Degrees(Kount)
LOOP
LET Kount=Kount-1

! Find maximum high.
  LET Maxx=0
  FOR I=1 TO Kount
    IF Maxx < Degrees(I) THEN LET Maxx=Degrees(I)
  NEXT I

! Print out stuff.
  FOR I=1 TO Kount
    LET Diff=Maxx-Degrees(I)
    PRINT "On ";Dat$(I);" the daily high was ";
    PRINT Diff;" degrees below the high for this period."
  NEXT I
  END
```

Stuff to realize:

1. You should understand the first loop. It reads in the data.

2. Kount ends up with the total number of days.

3. In the code starting at LET Maxx=0, we figure out the maximum high. What we do is set the maximum to be zero. Then in the loop, I look at each daily high (in the array); if it is greater than what my Maxx variable currently says is the largest high, then I reset Maxx to be this larger number.

4. The last loop is where I print out the results. Notice how I have to loop through all the days again. I print out the date and the difference between that date's high and the maximum high. That day's high is in the array — Degrees(I) and Maxx, of course, is the high for the period.

9.9.3   A Counting Problem

Let us try one more. Using the data from above, let us keep a record of how many times the high was each particular number. For instance, how many times was the high 60 degrees? The way to do this is to use an array (let us call it Temp), and every time a particular temperature shows up, add one to the appropriate location in the array. We will be cautious and say that any temperature from -20 to 120 can show up in this period. We won't print out results for any temperature that never showed up. We want the output to look as follows:

```
In this period the following results were obtained:
A high of 30 was reached on 1 day(s).
A high of 58 was reached on 3 day(s).
A high of 59 was reached on 5 day(s).
```

⋮

Here is the program:

```
    DIM Temp(-20 TO 120)

! Initialize.
    FOR I=-20 TO 120
      LET Temp(I)=0
    NEXT I

! Read in data and adjust TEMP count using day's high.
    READ Dat$,High
    DO WHILE Dat$<>"LAST"
      LET Temp(High)=Temp(High)+1
      READ Dat$,Degree
    LOOP

! Print out stuff.
    PRINT "In this period the following results were obtained:"
    FOR I=-20 TO 120
      IF Temp(I)>0 THEN
        PRINT "A high of ";I: " was reached on ";Temp(I);" day(s)."
      END IF
    NEXT I

    END
```

First, notice that we don't even save the date and the high temperatures in an array. We just use normal (non-array) variables to hold on to the current date and daily high – that is what Dat$ and High are for. These values disappear the next time around in the loop, when we process the data for another day. The temperatures are the indices of the Temp array — not the values!!!!! The value of this array is a counter telling us how many times we have come across that daily high in the data so far. This is something new that we did not see in the previous programs. The values in the arrays are acting as counters. Each element in the array is counting up something different. For instance, if Temp(25) has the value 7, this means "on seven different dates, the high temperature was 25" and Temp(44) = Temp(44)+1 means "add one to the number of times the daily high of 44 has shown up."

A big thing to notice here is that we don't use a FOR-LOOP counter as an index into the array. Rather we use the **value we read in as DATA** as the index. This is totally different from what we have seen prior to this. Think about it carefully and see why.

By the way, in all three of these example programs the program just runs right through once it is started. These are all examples of programs that run without asking for any values (through INPUT PROMPT statements) from the user.

That should be enough for now. In the next chapter we will be learning a bit more about arrays and I will show you some other programs.

Have fun,

-Jt

9.10 Problems

Errors

What errors occur when you try to run the following programs? Where exactly should the error be fixed? What can be done to fix the program?

1.

```
FOR I=1 to 5
  READ A,B
  LET Summ(I) = A + B
NEXT I
FOR J=5 to 1 STEP -1
  PRINT Summ(J)
NEXT J
DATA 3,7,12,45,12,56,98,12,55,39,745,1,77,12
END
```

2.

```
DIM Name$(5),Age(5)
READ Name$(1)
LET I=1
DO WHILE Name$(I)<>"DONE"
  LET I=I+1
  READ Name$(I)
LOOP
DATA "Nancy","Kitrina","Julianna","Gonca","Angela","DONE"
END
```

3.

```
RANDOMIZE
DIM LotteryNums(200)
RANDOMIZE
FOR Day = 1 to 100
  PRINT "We are picking a lottery number for Day ";day
```

```
      LET N = INT(RND * 1000) + 1
      PRINT "It is ";N
      LET LotteryNums(N) = LotteryNums(N) + 1
   NEXT Day
   FOR I=1 to 200
      PRINT "Number ";I;" showed up ";LotteryNums(I);" times."
   NEXT I
   END
```

4.

```
   DIM Food(100)
    FOR F=1 to 5
      READ Food(F)
    NEXT F
   DATA "Coffee","Shrimp","Ice Cream","Hot Dogs","Filet Mignon"
   END
```

5.

```
   DIM Value1(200),Value2(200)
   FOR K=1 to 200
    INPUT PROMPT "Give me a number ":Value1(K)
    INPUT PROMPT "Enter the other value: ":Value2(K)
   NEXT K
   LET Most = MAX(Value1,Value2)
   PRINT "The highest number was ";Most
   END
```

Tracing

1.

The input to this program is:

5, 19, 23, 14, 64, 12, 46, 33, 21, 52

```
DIM Stuff(10),Rest(10)
FOR I = 1 TO 10 STEP 2
   INPUT PROMPT "How much stuff did you get?":Stuff(I)
   INPUT PROMPT "How much is left?";Rest(I)
NEXT I
LET TheAnswer = 25
FOR K = 2 TO 10 STEP 2
   LET TheAnswer = TheAnswer + Min(Stuff(K-1),Rest(K-1))
NEXT K
PRINT "The Answer is ";TheAnswer
END
```

2.

```
DIM Complaints(3)
FOR I = 1 to 3
  LET Complaints(I) = 0
NEXT I
READ Mailing$
DO WHILE Mailing$ <> "LAST"
  SELECT CASE Mailing$
    CASE "Too many commercials"
         LET Complaints(1) = Complaints(1) + 1000
    CASE "Bad Show"
         LET Complaints(2) = Complaints(2) + 1000
    CASE ELSE
         LET Complaints(3) = Complaints(3) + 1
  END SELECT
  READ Mailing$
LOOP
PRINT "Estimate: "
PRINT Complaints(1);" people thought there were too many commercials."
PRINT Complaints(2);" people thought it was a bad show."
PRINT "There were ";Complaints(3);" other complaints."
DATA "Too many commercials",  "Too many commercials", "Lousy Cast"
DATA  "Too many commercials", "Bad Show",  "Bad Show"
DATA  "Not enough violence", "Trite", "Bad Show"
DATA   "Bad Show", "Too many commercials",  "Too many commercials"
DATA "LAST"
END
```

3.

```
DIM Track(10)
FOR I=1 to 10
 LET Track(I) = 0
NEXT I
FOR J = 10 TO 1 Step - 2
  LET Track(J) = Track(J) + 1
NEXT J
FOR K = 5 TO 10 Step 3
  LET Track(K) = Track(K) + 10
NEXT K
FOR L = 5 TO Track(2)
  LET Track(L) = Track(L) + 100
NEXT L
FOR M = 1 to 10
 PRINT Track(M)
NEXT M
END
```

Programs

1. You drive a space taxi and you want to keep track of how much money you have made in a day and the number of lightyears you have traveled. Build DATA into the program on the names of destinations, the mileage to that location and the cost. There should be at least six possible destinations. (Assume all trips are round trips. The passenger leaves from Earth to that destination and then comes back. Thus all distances are from Earth to the destination and back.) As each passenger enters the taxi they should be shown a numbered menu consisting of the names of the possible destinations. They should pick one of the numbers from that menu. When the day is over, 0 should be entered as the menu choice. As each passenger is handled, the total distance traveled and money made should be updated. At the end of the day these totals should be printed.

2. A study needs to be done on the typical heights of buildings in a major city. Write a program that builds a histogram of the heights of the buildings. No building is over 200 feet tall. Every building is at least 10 feet tall. You should keep totals on categories broken down for every ten feet. (Thus, 10-19, 20-29, 30-39 and so on.) Keep asking for heights of another building and adjusting the totals. Have some sentinel value to indicate there are no more buildings. Before the program ends print out a table showing the ranges and how many buildings fell into each category. Use arrays! (Hint: a good way to get the subscript is to divide the height by 10 and truncate. Thus a building that is 153 feet tall will fall into category 15.)

3. Write a program that analyzes how much money has made from toll booths on a major highway. The program should have READ and DATA with some appropriate sentinel value to mark that there are no more toll booths. Each booth should have a name and two money amounts. The first amount tells how much was collected from cars at that booth. The second tells how much was made from trucks. Calculate the total made from cars at all the booths. Calculate the total made from trucks. Figure out and print the average amount made on cars and the average amount made on trucks. Print the overall amount of money made from cars and trucks combined at all the booths on the highway. Finally, print out the names of all booths that made more than the average on trucks but less than the average on cars.

4. You've gone to get your car inspected and have become quite bored as you wait on line. You decide to keep some statistics on the cars that are being inspected. Write a program that uses these statistics to calculate some values. This program should have a collection of data of the form:

```
DATA "Honda",3,"passed"
DATA "Chevrolet",7,"failed"
```

The first item is the make of the car, the second is the number of minutes it took to inspect that car and finally the last value tells if the car passed or failed inspection. There should be some sentinel value at the end of the data. (Pick it yourself.) There will be no more than 100 cars. (Have at least 10 lines of data.)

Your program should calculate and print the average amount of time it took to inspect a car. For the cars that took two or more minutes over the average to be inspected — print out the percentage of *these* cars that passed inspection. Also print out the percentage of the big-three Japanese makes (Honda, Toyota and Nissan) which passed inspection.

5. Write a program that will analyze the birthdays of a number of your friends. In particular, the program should keep asking for names of friends, the month they were born and the day of that month. You will eventually enter some value to indicate that you have no more friends. For each possible day of a month, the program should print out how many times there was someone with a birthdate on that day. The month itself is not important — if someone was born on Jan. 17 and someone else was born on Sep. 17, then two people were born on day 17. Only print out information on days for which more than 0 people had a birthdate with that day in it. Here is a concrete example: if your friend Tim has a birthday on August 14th and your friend Sue has a birthday of February 14th, the program should later print "2 people where born on day 14 of some month". One other thing: the program should count up and print how many times more than one person were born on the same day of the month. (Ie, a statement should be printed like "There were 3 different month days where more than one person had that number in their birthdate.") When you run this program, enter data on at least 15 people you know.

6. Write a program that will print out a table of baseball scores. In particular, the program should use data of the following form:

```
DATA "Boston","Cleveland",7,3
```

These lines will represent the scores in a baseball games. The first string will be the home team, the next piece of data will be the visiting team. The first number is the number of runs the home team got and the second, the number of runs the visitors got. Let there be 13 lines of data. You can make up any data you want — you do not have to use the names of real baseball teams.

The program should count up the number of times the home team won and the number of times the home team lost. Choose the smaller of these two numbers and print up a table of the scores of all games that fit into this smaller category. The table should have a proper title and header line. Also for the games printed in this table, total up the number of runs that the home team, and separately the visitors scored. Print these totals after the table is printed.

Example: If the home team won 10 times but lost 3 times, you want to print out a table containing the scores from the games in which the home team lost. (The number of losses, 3, is less than the number of wins, 10, so print out this smaller table containing the 3 losses.) The title would be something like "Home Team Losses" and after the table is printed you might have a line like "Total Runs — Home Team:7 Visitors: 16".

7. Write a program that gets names of countries and the colors in their flag. You can assume that the flag of the country has up to three colors — so have three arrays for colors (maybe Color1$, Color2$ and Color3$). If a country's flag doesn't have three colors — just type in something line "NO MORE" or " " for the rest. You should use READ/DATA to fill in the arrays. Say there are 8 countries. Once the arrays have their information, the program should ask the user to supply a color and the program should tell how many countries have that color in their flag. (That is, the program should print out a number — not the name of the countries.) The program should keep doing this for colors the user supplies until the user enters "CLEAR" for the color.

8. Write a program that reads in the information on the names of parks, their total acreage and how many miles of hiking trails they contain. Use READ/DATA and a sentinel to mark the end of the data. This program should produce two pieces of output. First, print the name of the park with the most miles of hiking trails. Secondly, print the name of the park closest in size to the average acreage. (Hint: to get this second item, you will have to calculate the average and have two other variables — one to hold the name of the closest sized park so far and the other to contain how far away from the average size it was. As you work your way through all the parks calculating how far each park's size is from the average – you only need to worry about the absolute value of this difference. Each time, you find a park closer to the average, you adjust these two variables. You will want to initialize the "how far away" variable to some large number before you start.)

9. Write a program that allows a meteorologist to analyze the snow storms during a particular winter. The user should enter three items on each storm: the date, the duration (in hours) and the amount of snow that fell (in inches.) The program should print out the dates of the severest storms. A storm is considered "severe" if it dropped more than 30% more snow per hour than the average storm that winter. That is, a 20 inch storm during a ten hour period is *less* severe than a storm that lasts one hour but drops four inches. (Hint: You must calculate and use the figure for "amount of snow per hour" for each storm — which is not part of the input — to do this problem.)

Chapter 10

Arrays And Linear Search

10.1　What Is A Linear Search

Today we will learn about searching through a collection of data in the computer's memory. Generally, to do this type of operation you need to use arrays in your program. In particular, we will be learning about one type of search called linear search.

In this type of search, the program starts at the beginning of the collection of data and slowly works its way through it one item at a time. It stops searching when it has found what it is looking for or when it gets to the last item of data.

In BASIC, this data can be either a list of strings or a list of numbers. And how do we create a list using BASIC? We use arrays.

A linear search is similar in structure whether you are looking for numbers or looking for strings. The only thing that would change is the actual variable names you use. For the following discussion, let's say that we are searching for a number.

In fact, we will say that the program has already read in all the data and placed it into an array called Values. We will say that a variable called Kount tells how many items are in the array. Finally we will say that the particular number we are looking for is stored in a variable called Goal. We want to find out if this number (Goal) is one of the items in the Values array.

Now let's try to explore how we can find out if Goal is one of the numbers in the array Values that has Kount numbers in it. Let's ask a typical novice how he/she would do it. See if you can follow the following discussion and the BASIC code that is eventually arrived at:

10.2　The Process of Writing a Linear Search

TEACH Ok you in the front row, how would you go about writing this portion of a program that we call a linear search?

SADEYES (Sitting in the front row just waking up from a vivid daydream...) What?

TEACH I said, how would you write this linear search using GOAL, KOUNT and VALUES?

SADEYES I, like, would get one of those people who works in the computer room, you know, those student consultant people, to write it for me.

TEACH Ok, that's a start. But we all know that some of those people who work in the computer room don't know what the heck they are doing. Plus, they don't really care about your grade, nor do they care if your learn anything or not. You on the other hand might want to learn something and you

245

most likely do care about your grade. So let's assume that this time you gotta think totally on your own.

SADEYES This is gonna be a little difficult, I haven't done thought in years.

TEACH Ok. So let's see if you got the question correct before we go on. What are we trying to do?

SADEYES A linear search???

TEACH Right, and what is a linear search?

SADEYES It is when you search for some stuff linearly.

TEACH Right. Which means?

SADEYES When you look through a list of stuff and try to find one particular item by starting at the top of the list and looking at each item in succession until you find the item you want.

TEACH So what happens if you don't find the item you want?

SADEYES I dunno.

TEACH Ok. Well it turns out that a linear search might not always find the item it is looking for. Sometimes the item just isn't there. We have to make sure that the linear search can handle this possibility. Ok, now let's see if you understand the variables that I have assigned. First of all, what is the name for this list of stuff? What is the name of the array that has this list...

SADEYES VALUES?

TEACH Right. For this example I said VALUES was a list, or an array of numbers. And what number are we looking for?

SADEYES The one that is in the variable GOAL?

TEACH You are definitely smarter than you look...... Ok, what else do we know about the array VALUES?

SADEYES That it holds numbers....

TEACH True, we have established that. But how many numbers does it hold?

SADEYES 100 or less?

TEACH Nice try, but that is from examples I used in previous lectures. I didn't mention an actual number for how many items are in VALUES, rather I used a variable. What variable tells me how many numbers are in the array VALUES?

SADEYES Oh right, it's that KOUNT variable.

TEACH Ok, so now it seems you do understand what the variables KOUNT, VALUES and GOAL mean...

SADEYES If you say so......

TEACH Ok, just stay with me.......Ok, now what kind of BASIC structure should we use in order to do this problem?

SADEYES A Subprogram?

TEACH Well, often you can make the linear search be one of the subparts of a big program. A linear search doesn't have to be in a subpart though. Someday you may learn about subparts you can write on your own — for instance, subroutines, but let us ignore them for now. Let's think in English. How would you search through this array? At any time, how do you know if you found what you are looking for?

SADEYES You just look at it?

TEACH At what?

SADEYES You look to see if GOAL is the same as VALUES?

TEACH Ok, what do you mean by the term VALUES? Do you mean every item of the array values or just one item?

SADEYES I mean a particular value.

TEACH Which one?

SADEYES The current one you are looking at...

TEACH How do you single out one item of an array?

SADEYES You use an index......

TEACH Ok, so let's take a specific example. What could you do to check if the first item of the array VALUES was equal to goal?

SADEYES You could say something like "If values(1) is equal to GOAL then so and so"

TEACH And how can we check if the second item in the VALUES array was equal to GOAL?

SADEYES IF Values(2) = Goal ......

TEACH In general, how can we check to see if the nth value in the array is equal to goal?

SADEYES IF Values(N) = Goal ....

TEACH Ok, so you suggest we use some type of condition to check if the current value we are looking at is equal to the number that the variable GOAL holds?

SADEYES Is that what I said?

TEACH Yep. Ok, now back to a question I asked a while ago, what kind of BASIC structure can you use to do this for you? That is, what can you use to make the job of doing these comparisons over and over again? What kind of structure does things over and over again?

SADEYES A loop?

TEACH Ok, what type of loop do you suggest...

SADEYES A FOR loop. Something like For x = 1 to KOUNT ...

TEACH That is a good try. You can write a type of linear search by using a for loop......you are suggesting something like....

```
FOR X=1 TO Kount
  IF Values(X) = Goal THEN ....
NEXT X
```

That is good, but we can make a better loop. Consider the following question. How many times will this loop go around if KOUNT is 1000?

SADEYES 1000 times.

TEACH How many times will the loop go around if the GOAL is in the 55th place in the array?

SADEYES 55 times?

TEACH No, look at the FOR loop carefully. How many times does it go around no matter what?

SADEYES Oh, KOUNT times.....so 1000.

TEACH So if the GOAL isn't in the array then the loop goes around 1000 times. If the GOAL is in the 55th place then the loop goes around 1000 times. If the GOAL is in the first place then the loop goes around 1000 times. In general, once you find what you want, the loop is gonna finish up anyway. What a waste of time. Furthermore, we are using an IF statement inside of a loop, but we know a way of placing a condition so that it is part of the loop — that is, by using a conditional rather than a counted loop. You following me?

SADEYES I guess so, because you seem to be making me very dizzy.

TEACH Well, loops can do that to a person. But if you had to guess as to what I am talking about, what do you think it is?

SADEYES Uhhhhhh, how about using a WHILE loop?

TEACH Or as my friend Michele says, how about an UNTIL loop?

SADEYES Same thing.

TEACH Yeah, now you are sounding a lot like me. But let's use an Until loop and make her happy. Ok so go to it?

SADEYES Is Michele a student consultant?

TEACH Yeah. Well, actually she used to be. Then she became a TA.

SADEYES So let her do it....

TEACH She has tried many times, I am not sure she knows how. But for now let's let you do it.

SADEYES How about something like

```
DO UNTIL Values(I)=Goal
   ..something...
LOOP
```

TEACH Ok, we are getting close now, but what is I?

SADEYES The index.

TEACH True, but normally we get an index because it is also the counting variable in a FOR loop. Here we don't have a FOR loop and thus the variable I has no value. What should you do before an until loop?

SADEYES Initialize.....

TEACH So go ahead...

SADEYES Set I to one so you start looking at the beginning of the list..

```
LET I=1
DO UNTIL Values(I) = Goal
   ....
LOOP
```

TEACH Ok, now what should be done in the loop?

SADEYES Whatever you want to do when you find what you are looking for?

TEACH Is that what you want to do **in** the loop? If you are still in the loop then it means what?

SADEYES That you found what you want........no wait a second, if you are IN the loop? Oh, if you are IN the loop, it means you haven't found what you want.....

TEACH So what should you do if you don't find it? Look at it this way: In the condition of the loop, you look at VALUES(I). But what is I? We know we have set it to 1 before the loop. But what other values should I take? What should you do to I in the loop?

SADEYES You should change it I guess.....you should add one to it, (increment???) so that the next time through the loop it looks at the next item in the list.

TEACH Hmmmmmm, you don't sound much like a 110er anymore, you must be a fictional character. So how can you increment it?

SADEYES LET I=I+1 : so we get something like

```
LET I=1
DO UNTIL Values(I)=Goal
  LET I=I+1
LOOP
```

TEACH Very good. Now let's say you wanted to print something like "I found it" if you do find it. Where should you place a print statement? Before the loop? In the loop? After the loop?

SADEYES Not before the loop, that is stupid. When you are in the loop that means you haven't found it. Besides if we placed it in the loop, it might print out "I found it" a thousand times and I would have to use the STOP command in TRUE BASIC. It must belong after the loop?

TEACH Right. So our linear search now looks like:

```
LET I=1
DO UNTIL Values(I)=Goal
  LET I=I+1
LOOP

PRINT "I found it"
```

SADEYES Well, why didn't you just show me that in the first place, that is all easy to understand....

TEACH So, here we have a perfectly good linear search eh?

SADEYES It's good enough for me....but knowing you teacher types.... you're gonna mess with it some more....

TEACH Maybe. Let me ask some questions first? How many times does it go into the loop if the **GOAL** is in the first position?

SADEYES .....none because the condition on the until is TRUE right away.

TEACH I guess you know your loops. And how many times does it go into the loop if GOAL is the third item in VALUES?

SADEYES Must be 2 times.....

TEACH Now the good question is how many times does it go around in the loop IF the goal isn't there at all?

SADEYES 1000 times.

TEACH So it goes around 1000 times....you mean if KOUNT is 1000 I guess....

SADEYES Right, assuming that KOUNT is 1000...

TEACH Well, how does this UNTIL loop know anything about KOUNT....

SADEYES Uhhhmmmm, I guess it doesn't.

TEACH So now what would the loop do?

SADEYES It must be one of those infinite types....

TEACH Well, in theory it is. But it turns out that in all of history no loop has ever really gone on for an infinite amount of time... somehow they usually end. Someone uses the STOP command, the computer crashes.... an error message is generated... Here we are dealing with arrays and we are using I as an index. I keeps getting bigger...... What is gonna happen?

SADEYES Oh, the loop is gonna get "Subscript Out Of Bounds" when the index gets too big...

TEACH Right. How can we stop it from happening?

SADEYES I don't know......

TEACH Well, in English, when do we want the loop to stop?

SADEYES When we find what we are looking for.

TEACH And if we don't find it when should the loop stop?

SADEYES When we get to the end of the array?

TEACH So the loop should stop if either of two conditions is met. That is, if you find what you are looking for or you reach the end of the array. How can you combine two conditions into one?

SADEYES Use an AND or OR.

TEACH Right, We can use an AND or OR in the condition in our UNTIL clause and we can now check to see if we have reached the end of the loop. How will we know?

SADEYES I guess when the index gets too big.

TEACH Give me an expression that can check to see if the index represents the last item we have in the array....

SADEYES I = KOUNT

TEACH Good. So stick that in the code we have so far

SADEYES Should I use an AND or an OR?

TEACH You figure it out.

SADEYES

```
LET I=1
DO UNTIL Values(I)=Goal OR I=Kount
  LET I=I+1
LOOP

PRINT "I found it"
```

TEACH Why did you use an OR?

SADEYES Because I want the loop to stop if one or the other condition is true. I would use an AND if I wanted the loop to stop when both conditions were true at the same time.

TEACH Very good. One small problem now. The loop now ends when the last item of the array is reached and the goal might not be found. What happens after the loop ends?

SADEYES It prints "I found it". That isn't good...it prints "I found it" even if it didn't.

TEACH This is true. What kind of statement can you use after the loop to make a decision on whether you should print "I found it" or not?

SADEYES An IF statement?

TEACH An IF-THEN statement would be good.... something like IF condition THEN PRINT "I found it". What condition would have to be **true** in order for you to find it? Keep in mind that at this time, you have an array VALUES, an index I, a KOUNT and a GOAL.

SADEYES I am not sure....

TEACH Well, the loop either ended because it found the goal at the current index in the array or it ran out of room and is at the last location. In either case, the item at the current location would have to be the same as GOAL in order for goal to be in the array.....that is, in order for the linear search to find what it is looking for....so what can you say....

SADEYES How about

```
IF Values(I)=Goal THEN PRINT "I found it"
```

TEACH How did you know that?

SADEYES I have no idea.....

TEACH So what does the whole linear search look like now?

SADEYES THE LINEAR SEARCH IS:

```
LET I=1
DO UNTIL Values(I)=Goal OR I=Kount
  LET I=I+1
LOOP
IF Values(I) = Goal THEN PRINT "I found it"
```

TEACH Good, now keep in mind that this is a special linear search. In your own programs you would fill in your own index name (for I), use the size of your own array (for KOUNT), and most likely have different variable names for your array and goal (for VALUES and GOAL). Also after you found what you want, you might want to do something else rather than just print out the message "I found it". You have to realize that if you do find it, then I means something special. It is the location in the array of the goal. Thus if I ends up as 5, then the GOAL is the fifth item in the array. This is the information you may need in further parts of your program. For instance, you may use this index to refer to something else in an associated array. Let us say you read in some data. Each record in this data has two numbers. The second number is stored in an array called Numm2. How can we do a linear search to find out if the number 24 was ever the first number on a line and if so, what was the second number on that line of the data?

SADEYES How about

```
LET Goal=24
LET I=1
DO UNTIL Values(I)=Goal OR I=Kount
  LET I=I+1
LOOP
IF Values(I) = Goal then
   PRINT "The second number on the line was ";Numm2(i)
  ELSE
   PRINT Goal; " wasn't there"
END IF
```

TEACH How did you know that?

SADEYES Because I bought Jt's Conversations on TRUE BASIC at the bookstore and read Chapter 10 prior to coming to class....

TEACH It figures.......

10.3 Programs: Associated Arrays And Linear Search

10.3.1 Beatles And Copyrights

Let's say you have the following data:

```
DATA "Maxwell's Silver Hammer",1969
DATA "TaxMan",1966
DATA "The Fool on the Hill",1967
DATA "I'm Down",1965
DATA "Tomorrow Never Knows",1966
DATA "Your Mother Should Know",1967
DATA "You're Going to Lose That Girl",1965
DATA "A Day In The Life",1967
DATA "Do You Want To Know A Secret",1963
DATA "From Me To You",1963
DATA "Hold Me Tight",1963
DATA "I Want To Hold Your Hand",1963
DATA "Nowhere Man",1965
DATA "Help",1964
DATA "With a Little Help From my Friends",1967
DATA "Girl",1965
DATA "You Like Me Too Much",1965
DATA "P.S. I Love You",1962
           .
           .
           .
DATA "EOF",0
```

You want to write a program that allows a user to keep entering Beatles songs until the user types "STOP" as the name of the song. For each song name entered, the program should print out the copywrite date of that song. How can you do it?

Well it really isn't that hard. The main program should read in two associated arrays out of the data (an input file would be great for this problem) and then have a main loop that keeps asking for song titles, does a linear search for that song title and if it finds the title, uses the index that it was found at as an index into the array of copywrites in order to find the date.

We use the typical sentinel loop to read data into an array. Then the second part of the program is a typical sentinel loop that processes the user's data — stopping when they type in the sentinel "STOP". For processing, we just do a linear search and and print out the value in the associated array. All three of these elements have been discussed in detail in previous sections of this book. All we have to do is use them here with the proper variables.

Let's go for it ...

```
DIM Song$(500),Cdate(500)

! Read in the data into associated arrays
  LET Kount=1
  READ Song$(1),Cdate(1)
  DO UNTIL Song$(Kount)="EOF"
    LET Kount=Kount+1
    READ Song$(Kount),Cdate(Kount)
  LOOP
  LET Kount=Kount-1

! Typical sentinel loop that stops when person enters STOP for song name
  INPUT PROMPT "Name of Beatles song (STOP when done)":Query$
  DO UNTIL Query$="STOP"
    ! linear search for song and print date
    LET I=1
    DO UNTIL Song$(I)=Query$ OR I=Kount
      LET I=I+1
    LOOP
    IF Song$(I) = Query$ THEN
      PRINT Query$; " was copywritten in ",Cdate(I)
    ELSE
      PRINT Query$; " not found"
    END IF

    ! Get the song name for the next time around --- or STOP
    INPUT PROMPT "Name of Beatles song (STOP when done)";Query$
  LOOP
  END
```

Some things:

1. Notice, that I set up space for up to 500 songs.

2. Notice KOUNT will have the actual number of songs read from the data.

3. If you think about this program, I have a loop inside of a loop. I use a loop to do the linear search. Meanwhile this loop is inside of the main loop of the program.

4. I is initialized prior to the linear search. If we had initialized I at the beginning of the program, it wouldn't work. I must be set back to 1 right before starting a linear search for any of the songs.

5. The linear search was created by using the appropriate variables in this program. Notice how the structure is the same as what was discussed in this chapter.

6. This is a linear search of a string.

7. The user of this program would have to type in the song name exactly the same as it appears in the data. All caps must be the same, any spaces and so on. (This wouldn't be good for a really useful program.)

8. Essentially, this program is just a combination of two things. a) Read in some associated arrays using some data that has a sentinel. b) Do a linear search.

9. Note that this program uses READ/DATA to load the arrays but also has some INPUT PROMPT statements to ask the user of the program some questions.

10.3.2 Salesperson Problem

Let's write a program that causes the contents of the array to be changed many times. Let's write a program that reads in some data of some salespeople's names. We will say that there are less than 100 names in this list and there is the sentinel "EOF" at the end.

We will say that a secretary uses the program by supplying the names of salespeople and the amount of sales they made. The secretary keeps entering data like this while the program is running. In fact, information for a particular salesperson may be entered many times. For instance, there may be a receipt that says Jen sold $1500 worth of merchandise. Then later, another receipt pops up that says he sold another $457 worth. The program should calculate that he has earned $1957 so far. There is no order to the names being typed in. To signal that s/he is done, the secretary will type "LAST" for the salesperson's name. The program should then print the total sales that each salesperson made.

To do this program, you would have to first get all the names into an array. You would also need an associated array to keep track of the sales. Whenever a record is read off of the sales record data, a search will have to be done for the salesperson's name. Once it is found, that index is used for the sales array. Cake, right?

```
DIM Nam$(100),Sales(100)

! Read salesmen names from DATA statements
  LET  Kount=1
  READ Nam$(1)
  DO UNTIL Nam$(Kount)="EOF"
   LET Kount=Kount+1
   READ Nam$(Kount)
  LOOP
  LET Kount=Kount-1

! Initialize.....really not necessary in this basic.
  FOR I=1 TO 100
    LET Sales(I)=0
  NEXT I

! Main loop. Secretary should keep supplying information.
  INPUT Persona$,Amount
  DO UNTIL Persona$="LAST"
   !linear Search
    LET I=1
    DO UNTIL Nam$(I)=Persona$ OR I=Kount
      LET I=I+1
    LOOP
          !If salesperson is found, then add on to his/her sales total
          ! in associated array.
    IF Nam$(I) = Persona$ THEN
      LET Sales(I)=Sales(I) + Amount
    ELSE
      PRINT Persona$; " not found"
    END IF

   !Get info for next time around loop.
    INPUT Persona$,Amount
  LOOP
DATA "Jen", "Jimmy", "Jerry"
  .
  .
DATA "EOF"
END
```

Yo people, we have reached the last chapter.
Have Fun,
-Jt

10.4 Problems

Tracing

1.

```
DIM Flower$(5),Value(5)
FOR I = 1 TO 5
  READ Flower$(I)
  LET Value(I) = 1
NEXT I
DATA "Rose","Daisy","Sunflower","Violet","Aster"
FOR K = 1 TO 9
  READ Name$
  LET Place=1
  DO UNTIL Name$=Flower$(Place) OR Place=5
    LET Place = Place + 1
  LOOP
  IF Name$=Flower$(Place) THEN LET Value(Place) = Value(Place)*2
NEXT K
FOR J = 1 TO 5
PRINT Value(J)
NEXT J
DATA "Rose", "Lily", "Daisy", "Rose", "Aster","Rose","Daisy","Violet","Rose"
END
```

Programs

1. Write a program to help a person look up information on various government agencies. The data should be of the form:

```
DATA "CIA",75000,"secret",110000000
DATA "EPA",225000,"open",230117000
```

The first item is the name of a government agency. The second is the number of employees in this agency, third indicates whether information on this agency is secret or available to anyone and fourth is the amount of money budgeted to this agency this year. There is no set number of agencies, but there will never be over 100. You can use any sentinel you want to mark the end of the data. (Your program should include semi-realistic-looking information on at least 6 agencies.)

The program should load this data into arrays and then allow the user to get information on the various agencies. It will do this until the user says they are done seeking information. The user should indicate what agency they are interested in and then whether they want to see the information on the employee count or the budget. The proper amount is then displayed on the screen. The one catch is that the user can not see information on the secret organizations unless they enter some appropriate password first. (You can pick any password you want — build this into the program — this is likely to be in some IF statement.)

Demonstrate this program on at least three agencies. Look up both types of information. Give an example where the user can see secret information and another when they are turned away for failure to enter the correct password. Also show an example of how your program handles the case when they enter an agency that the program does not know about.

2. This program's purpose is to analyze NJ indoor shopping malls. There is two types of data statements. The first part of the data should be a list of common store names such as:

```
DATA "The Gap","Waldenbooks","The Disney Store","EMS","Victoria's Secret"
```

There should be ten store names. The rest of the data should be of the form:

```
DATA "The Gap", "Willowbrook"
DATA "EMS", "Princeton MarketFair"
DATA "Victoria's Secret", "Bridgewater Commons"
```

That is, there are a number of lines with store names and a mall in which that store can be found. The stores used should be constrained to the list of ten stores you included in the previous data. You should include plenty of data — enough so you mention some stores a number of times, in different malls. Be careful when you enter the store names so that you type them in exactly the same in all places you use them — punctuation, spacing and capitalization should be consistent. There is no set amount of this second type of data — there should be some sentinel at the end of this data (pick it yourself).

Simply stated, this program should list the number of times that each store was in a mall. That is, it prints out lines like:

```
The Gap was in 7 malls.
Waldenbooks was in 4 malls.
```

3. Pizzeria AlkaSeltza is a new wave pizza place. There are 20 different items you can place on your pizza. This list of toppings is quite varied. To be fair to the customers, each item is priced separately according to how much the item costs the restaurant. Write a program to help this pizzeria calculate the price of a pizza. There should be data of the form:

```
DATA "Lox",250
DATA "Doritos",85
```

To figure out the price to charge the customer for pizza the first question the program should ask is whether they want a small, medium or large pizza. The prices for these are: $5.50, $6.50 and $8.00. Then the program should ask what toppings to place on the pizza. The customer can ask for as many toppings as they want. They should get charged the appropriate amount for each one. If they ask for the same item more than once — they pay the appropriate extra charge for each time they request it. If they ask for an item that doesn't exist — they are told this. The final price should be printed when the customers indicate that they want no further toppings.

Special Chapter 4

In the last three chapters we have learned about built-in functions, arrays and linear search. The following program attempts to use some of these concepts.

As you may realize, the United States does not do as well in the Olympics as uhhhhh — let us just say, as well as we'd like. Because of this, a special secret organization has been created called the Official Olympic Organization or the OOO (— Sam Kenison is their spokesperson —).

Anyway, this organization, being up on all the latest technology, has decided to write software for a Cray Y/MP supercomputer to help them simulate what goes on during the Olympics. This was a good move on their part.

On the other hand, they didn't make too many good moves. For instance, they decided to use TRUE BASIC to write this software. Not exactly the langauge of choice for advanced computer applications. And secondly, this program is not going to tell them too much. It certainly gives them no clues on how to fix America's athletics problem. Nevertheless, money is to be spent on this program and we are to write it.

The main idea is that this program should pick the winners for different events throughout the Olympics. It does this by randomly picking the countries which get the Gold, Silver and Bronze medals for each event. There will be 125 countries involved in the Olympics – each with the same chance of winning. The medal count will be kept for each country. In the end, a table should be printed containing the name of each country, the amount of gold, silver and bronze medals they received, and their overall medal count. As a final piece of information, the name of the country with the most of each type of medal should be printed out.

The way they want to be able to use the program is that it should give a choice of simulating another event OR looking up the current medal counts of any country. They'll be able to perform either of these operations as many times as they want until eventually they declare that the Olympics are over and the final results should be printed.

As a final, small elaboration, they want 3% of all athletes to fail their drug tests. In which case the country does not get the medal and (in their version of the Olympics) no new country is picked to receive that medal.

How can we write this program?

The first thing to realize is that we most definitely want to use arrays. We have many, many counters that we must keep track of. For instance, "How many gold medals has the USA won so far?" and "How many silver medals has Bulgaria won?" In fact, we have to keep at least three counters for each of the 125 countries. It might strike you that we could use a fourth array — in order to hold the overall medal count. But, we can probably do without this array. We can always add up the values in the other three arrays if we need the overall medal count for a country. However, there is one last array we do want. It should store the names of all the countries. Since we are going to store large lists of information, array make sense.

Let us use three arrays. Like

```
DIM Country$(125), Gold(125), Silver(125), Bronze(125)
```

So as we go along whenever we see Country$(17) we know we are talking about the name of the 17th country. Bronze(42) will mean the number of bronze medals the 42nd country received. More likely, we will use items like Gold(J) which means the number of gold medals the j-th country got so far.

Also, because this is a simulation program, we are going to be picking winners randomly. So we need the following towards the beginning of the code:

```
RANDOMIZE
```

For a moment let us look into how random numbers will be used. We will get more detailed later. For instance, how can we pick the gold medal winner? Well, there are 125 countries. Randomly we want to pick one of those. Well, this is easy enough. We know how to pick one number out of 125. Something like this would suffice:

```
LET GoldWinner = INT(RND*125) + 1
```

Now, realize that GoldWinner is a number. It might end up as 89 for instance. This will mean that the 89th country won the gold. Well, once we know that what do we do? Probably we want to print the country's name and update the number of gold medals they have gotten by incrementing the proper counter. How do we do this? We use the arrays that hold the name and medal count. That is, we use this number, GoldWinner, as an index into the array. For instance, to print the country's name you could do:

```
PRINT "The winner of the gold medal is: ";Country$(GoldWinner)
```

And to update the counter for gold medals, use the Gold array:

```
LET Gold(GoldWinner) = Gold(GoldWinner) + 1
```

If you have a hard time with this last line, consider the following. Let us say the 117th country wins the gold medal. This means that GoldWinner=117. If you plug this number into the equation you get:

```
LET Gold(117) = Gold(117) + 1
```

Reading this in English it says: "The new number of gold medals for country number 117 is equal to the old number of gold medals for this country, plus one." So, for instance, let us say the 117th country had 45 gold medals all ready. Then in the gold array, in the 117th place in the list would be the number 45. Plugging this number into the equation above you get:

```
LET Gold(117) = 45 + 1
```

Which means, the number 46 should be placed into the array in the 117th location. So the country now has 46 gold medals.

Ok, so now that we see the program will use arrays and random numbers, what should the overall structure be? This isn't too hard. What we really need is three parts. The first part of the program should be an initialization section, then the main "processing" section and finally a print section.

First, what should we do for the intialization section? Well, besides having our DIM and RANDOMIZE statements, we are going to want to place some initial values into our arrays.

What do we want to initialize the counter arrays to? Well, this is simple, they should all start out as zero. And what do we want in the name array? We want to place the various country's names into this array. How can we get these into the array? We can use READ and type in the names into DATA statements. Do we have to use our usual sentinel READ/DATA loop? No – because here we know exactly how many countries there are. We do not have to look for a sentinel. So, we can use a simple FOR loop. We can use four FOR loops, one to initialize each array, or we can collapse all these FOR loops into one bigger loop. That is, we can work through all four arrays at the same time. "Initialize the first element in the gold counter array to zero; read in the first country's name, etc." So we end up with:

```
FOR I=1 to 125
  READ Country$(I)
  LET Gold(I) = 0
  LET Silver(I) = 0
  LET Bronze(I) = 0
NEXT I

DATA "USA","England","Australia","USSR","Cuba" ....
DATA ...
```

Now, let us remember that the second part of the program is going to adjust the various medal counts as new events are simulated. We won't write the code for this yet. But we should realize that when this second section of the code is completed the medal count arrays will be full of numbers indicating how many of each medal the various countries won. In the last part of the program, we want to print out the results from the Olympics by making a table.

We can make a column for the various items. One column for country name, one for the number of gold medals, then silver medals, then bronze and finally the total count of medals for that country. We want to print out some header on the table. Easy:

```
PRINT "Country","Gold","Silver","Bronze","Total"
PRINT "-------","----","------","------","-----"
```

Then we have to work through the arrays and print out the medal counts for each country. How can we work through the array? Well, again, we just use a simple FOR loop, printing out the proper element in the three medal count arrays. But wait a second, we also want to print the total. So, before we print out the next line in the table, we should figure out the total amount of medals that country got — this isn't in an array, we have to calculate it. Simple, we just pick a variable to hold on to this total for a moment. Let us call it Tot. Notice, this is a regular variable. No need to use an array here. We are just going to figure out the total for this country, print it — and then we can forget about it. We don't have to save it into a list. We have been spending a lot of time on arrays — but certainly, you remember how regular variables work, right? One last thing — do we want the header lines in this loop? Of course not! We don't want the header to print many times. We only want it to print once — before we start printing out the info for each country. So we place the header lines before the loop. Now we know enough to write the loop. Here it is:

```
FOR I=1 to 125
   LET Tot= Gold(I) + Silver(I) + Bronze(I)
   PRINT Gold(I),Silver(I),Bronze(I),Tot
NEXT I
```

After this table, we probably want to print a couple of blank lines and then print out which countries got the most gold, silver and bronze medals. How can we do this? Well, the printing is easy. If we knew that country number 88 got the most gold medals we can print:

```
PRINT Country$(88);" got the most gold medals."
```

Notice, we use 88 as an index into the array that holds the countries' names. Of course, we probably won't use a constant. Instead we would have some type of variable. Let this variable tell us the number of the country that got the most gold medals. Call it CountryMaxGold. So we would print:

```
PRINT Country$(CountryMaxGold);" is the country that won the most gold medals."
```

Now before we can print this statement, we have to determine the value for the number CountryMax-Gold. How do we do this? Well, there is only one procedure to do this. We must go through the whole list of gold medals and find the largest number in that list. How do you go through the whole list? Start at the first value and work your way to the end. Ah ha. Use a FOR loop to go through all 125 values. Update CountryMaxGold each time you come to a number bigger than anyone you have seen before. Before this loop, you should intiialize the variable to some number. Heck, let us initialize it to 1 — we will start out assuming that the first country has the most gold medals. This is probably wrong, but it will quickly change to something else when we spot a country that has more medals than the first country. So the loop would look like:

```
LET CountryMaxGold = 1
FOR I = 1 to 125
    If this country (the Ith) has more gold than the country we think
      has the most so far --- then let this country now be the country
      we think has the most.
NEXT I
```

That is a lengthy way to say what we want in English, but there is a simpler way in BASIC. Here it one such way:

```
LET CountryMaxGold=1
FOR I=1 to 125
    IF Max(Gold(CountryMaxGold),Gold(I)) = Gold(I) THEN LET CountryMaxGold=I
NEXT I
```

Essentially the IF statement says "Check to see what the maximum of this country's gold medal count and the country we thought had the most is. If the maximum of these two numbers is this country's gold medal count, then we had better reset our variable CountryMaxGold to this country's number." This is because, obviously, the current country has more gold medals and so this should be our guess as to the country with the most. For instance, let us say that I=79 and at the moment CountryMaxGold=47 (which means so far the 47th country had the most gold medals). Looking up Gold(47) we see the count is 117. Now we look up Gold(79) and see the count of 123. 123 is larger than 117. 123 is equal to the count of the current country Gold(79) (that is Gold(I)). So the IF statement is true and we do the THEN part. This means we should do LET CountryMaxGold=I, which in this case means set CountryMaxGold to 79. In English we have just set the country with the most gold medals to the current (79th) country. This made sense since this country has 123 gold medals and the previous best was country number 47, which only had 117 gold medals. You can see that by following this procedure through all 125 countries, in the end CountryMaxGold must have the number of the country that had the most gold medals.

You can see that we can do this same procedure for silver and bronze medals too. We just have to write a new loop using the proper variables for these medals. We can see that the program's last section may have four different loops. One to print the table, then one to figure out which country has the most gold, and then one for the silver and one for the bronze. Turns out, these four loops can easily be collapsed into one loop. The final version of this program collapses these four loops into one.

Now for the middle section of the program. Here we want to have a sentinel loop that processes requests from the people using the program. They either want to do a simulation for an event, look up the medal count for a country or quit the Olympics and have the final results printed. An INPUT statement to ask this question could be:

```
INPUT PROMPT "Simulate an event (SIM), Look up stats (LOOK) or Declare events over (OVER)":Do$
```

This is easy enough to place into a sentinel loop. Something like the following would work:

```
INPUT PROMPT "Simulate an event (SIM), Look up stats (LOOK) or Declare events over (OVER)":Do$
DO WHILE Do$<>"OVER"

    handle the request

INPUT PROMPT "Simulate an event (SIM), Look up stats (LOOK) or Declare events over (OVER)":Do$
LOOP
```

You should certainly understand this section of code since we have used this same pattern over and over again. Now all we have to do is handle the user's request. This is simple — there are two possible requests, either SIM or LOOK. Well, at first you might think IF statement but then you realize there is a third possibility. Maybe the person types in an error! So let us use a SELECT CASE with the selection variable being the request variable Do$

In the loop we'd have the following SELECT statement:

```
SELECT CASE Do$
  CASE "SIM''
      simuluate one event
  CASE "LOOK"
      look up the stats on one country
  CASE ELSE
      handle bad input
END SELECT
```

The CASE ELSE which handles the bad data is simple — so we need not discuss it here.

Only two cases left to do. Let us handle the case for the simulation first. What do we have to do? First pick the gold medal winner for the event. Then pick the silver winner and finally the bronze winner. This is simple enough. We have already discussed how to do this with random numbers. Next, we want to print out the winning country's name and update the number of medals that country got. But we saw how to do that very early on in this discussion.

Ah, but we forgot one thing. The drug testing has to be done. Again, we want to randomly decide when a country loses a medal because someone failed to pass a drug test. Well, 3% of the time this should happen. We could try something like:

```
LET Drugtest = INT(RND*100) + 1
IF DrugTest <= 3 THEN PRINT "You fail the drug test"
```

However, this turns out to be a waste of effort. Here we generate a number from 1 to 100 and then if the test comes out to be 1, 2 or 3 – it means failure. Well, why should we have to generate a number from 1 to 100? Why can't we just use a simple random number that is generated by RND instead of mapping it into another range? In fact we can. In particular, RND picks a number between 0 and 1. So we can do something like the following instead:

```
LET Drugtest = RND
IF Drugtest < .03 THEN PRINT "You fail the drug test"
```

So, at least for this example, we can accomplish pretty much the same thing whether or not we map the random number onto the range 1 to 100 or keep it in its original range of 0 to 1. In fact, this doesn't even take two lines to do. In the IF condition we can just have a call to the function RND and forget about using a Drugtest variable at all. So we get something along the lines of:

```
IF RND < .03 THEN PRINT "You fail the drug test"
```

The random number RND is forgotten immediately after it is used. So we can include a number of lines like this. If we have one for each medal then each one will use a different random number. Something like:

```
IF RND < .03 THEN PRINT "The country that won the gold loses its medal."
IF RND < .03 THEN PRINT "The country that won the silver loses its medal."
```

Here the two RNDs are different numbers. This is because RND is a function call — not a variable! So in the first line, let us say RND is called and comes back with the number .825536. Well, this is bigger than .03 so the first IF is false and the print statement doesn't happen. Now the program would go on to the second line and see RND again. This means call this funciton one more time. So the program would. Maybe this time the random number picked would be .016559 which is smaller than .03 and this time the IF is true and the statement "The country that won the silver loses the medal." would be printed.

Putting these ideas together, we now can see what to do to handle each medal for each simulation. For instance, the following code could handle the gold medal for the event.

```
LET GoldWinner = INT(RND*125) + 1
IF RND > .03 THEN
    PRINT Country$(GoldWinner) " won the gold."
    LET Gold(GoldWinner) = Gold(GoldWinner) + 1
ELSE
    PRINT Country$(GoldWinner) "disqualified for the gold."
END IF
```

We pick the country that wins the gold medal. We then generate a random number. If the number is big enough the drug test is passed. So, the gold winner is printed and the gold medal count for that country is adjusted. Otherwise the number being too small causes this country to lose the gold medal due to failing the drug test.

Simple eh? The same thing can be done for the silver and bronze medals so the code isn't shown here. Look at the final version of the program to see the complete code for the simulation part.

Finally, there is only one more case to worry about. What if the user of the software enters the LOOK request? What should happen? Well, this means they want to print out the medal count for a particular country. We'd like them to be able to type in the country's name. So we should start off with an INPUT PROMPT like:

```
INPUT PROMPT "What country do you want information on?":Which$
```

Now we have the country's name and we just print out the medal count from the arrays. Wait a second! We need an index. We don't have one. We have the name for the country, not a number. What can we do? Well, what did we learn in the last chapter? We learned about linear search. We can use this to look through the list of country names and find the country they typed in. By doing this we can pinpoint exactly what location in the array the country is at. We can then use this location as in index into the associated arrays for the medal counts, Gold, Silver and Bronze, and thus print out these numbers.

Just your usual linear search. We need to know three things. 1) How big is the array? Easy, it has 125 elements. 2) What array are we looking through? Simple! The array name is Country$. 3) What are we looking for? Well, the variable Which$ has the country name we are searching for in it. So we have the three things we need and we just write the typical linear search with these three items.

```
LET I = 1
DO UNTIL I=125 OR Which$ = Country$(I)
  LET I=I+1
LOOP

IF Which$=Country$(I) THEN
    PRINT Which$
    PRINT "Gold medals:";Gold(I)
    PRINT "Silver medals:";Silver(I)
    PRINT "Bronze medals:";Bronze(I)
  ELSE
    PRINT Which$;" is not in these Olympics."
END IF
```

Notice that in the IF statement following the loop we either print out the country's name and its medal counts from the associated arrays (notice that I is our index) or we print out a message saying we couldn't find that country's name in our list. And that is all there is to it.

We now have discussed all the parts we need to build a complete program. On the following pages is all the code placed together into one complete program.

```
REM The Olympics Simulation Program
REM Jt --- July 1990 --- New Program for Fall 90
RANDOMIZE
DIM Country$(125), Gold(125), Silver(125), Bronze(125)

! Read in country names and set counters to zero.
FOR I=1 to 125
  READ Country$(I)
  LET Gold(I) = 0
  LET Silver(I) = 0
  LET Bronze(I) = 0
NEXT I

DATA "USA","England","Australia","USSR","Cuba" ....
DATA ...

! Simulate the Olympics one event at a time until Olympics are over.
!     Be able to check on a country's progress at any time.
INPUT PROMPT "Simulate an event (SIM), Look up stats (LOOK) or Declare events over (OVER)":Do$
DO WHILE Do$ <> "OVER"
  SELECT CASE Do$

  CASE "SIM"                                      ! Simulate an event
    LET GoldWinner = INT(RND*125) + 1
    LET SilverWinner = INT(RND*125) + 1
    LET BronzeWinner = INT(RND*125) + 1

    IF RND > .03 THEN
        PRINT Country$(GoldWinner) " won the gold."
        LET Gold(GoldWinner) = Gold(GoldWinner) + 1
      ELSE
        PRINT Country$(GoldWinner) "disqualified for the gold."
    END IF

    IF RND > .03 THEN
        PRINT Country$(SilverWinner) " won the silver."
        LET Silver(SilverWinner) = Silver(SilverWinner) + 1
      ELSE
        PRINT Country$(SilverWinner) "disqualified for the silver."
    END IF

    IF RND > .03 THEN
        PRINT Country$(BronzeWinner) " won the silver."
        LET Bronze(BronzeWinner) = Bronze(BronzeWinner) + 1
      ELSE
        PRINT Country$(BronzeWinner) "disqualified for the bronze."
    END IF
```

```
    CASE "LOOK"                              ! Look up status of a country's medal counts.
      INPUT PROMPT "What country do you want information on?":Which$

      LET I = 1
      DO UNTIL I=125 OR Which$ = Country$(I)
        LET I=I+1
      LOOP
      IF Which$=Country$(I) THEN
          PRINT Which$
          PRINT "Gold medals:";Gold(I)
          PRINT "Silver medals:";Silver(I)
          PRINT "Bronze medals:";Bronze(I)
        ELSE
          PRINT Which$;" is not in these Olympics."
      END IF


    CASE ELSE                               ! Handle Bad input
      PRINT "You entered a bad command.  Please enter either SIM, LOOK or OVER."
    END SELECT

  INPUT PROMPT "Simulate an event (SIM), Look up stats (LOOK) or Declare events over (OVER)":Do$
  LOOP

  ! Print out table of results. Calculate total medal count for each country.
  ! Determine who won the most of each type of medal.

  LET CountryMaxGold=1
  LET CountryMaxSilver=1
  LET CountryMaxBronze=1

  PRINT "Country","Gold","Silver","Bronze","Total"
  PRINT "-------","----","------","------","-----"
  FOR I=1 to 125
     LET Tot= Gold(I) + Silver(I) + Bronze(I)
     PRINT Gold(I),Silver(I),Bronze(I),Tot

     IF Max(Gold(CountryMaxGold),Gold(I)) = Gold(I) THEN LET CountryMaxGold=I
     IF Max(Silver(CountryMaxSilver),Silver(I)) = Silver(I) THEN LET CountryMaxSilver=I
     IF Max(Bronze(CountryMaxBronze),Bronze(I)) = Bronze(I) THEN LET CountryMaxBronze=I
  NEXT I

  PRINT
  PRINT
  PRINT Country$(CountryMaxGold);" is the country that won the most gold medals."
  PRINT Country$(CountryMaxSilver);" is the country that won the most silver medals."
  PRINT Country$(CountryMaxBronze);" is the country that won the most bronze medals."
  END
```

Have fun,
-Jt

Answer Key

This section contains the answers to the problems contained in this book. If you don't understand the correct answer ask one of your instructor to explain it to you.

Chapter 2

Syntax Errors

1. Missing END statement.

2. Should be INPUT PROMPT.

3. The INPUT PROMPT statements should have colons (:) not semicolons (;) before the final variable.

4. Can't have spaces in variable names (ie. two word variable names).

   Better variables would be Payment_Source etc.

   Also, since the input is likely to be text, string variable names would be a wise choice. So the best variable names would be something like: Payment_Source$ etc.

5. Mismatch between type of variable and data. Here there are numeric variables but the data is strings.

6. Print statement uses colons (:) to separate items. Should use commas (,) or semicolons (;).

7. Not enough DATA. There are three READs but only two pieces of DATA.

Rewrites

1.

```
PRINT "Enter three words."
INPUT PROMPT "What is the first word?":Word1$
INPUT PROMPT "What is the second word?":Word2$
INPUT PROMPT "What is the third word?":Word3$
INPUT PROMPT "What is the fourth word?":Word4$
PRINT "The four words, placed on one line, separated by spaces but shuffled are:"
PRINT Word2$;
PRINT " ";Word4$;
PRINT " ";Word3$;
PRINT " ";Word1$
END
```

Notice the semicolons at the end of the PRINT lines!

2. Here are two ways — you can think up others.

```
READ Food_1$,Protien_1
READ Food_2$,Protien_2
READ Food_3$,Protien_3
DATA "Chocolate",23
DATA "Cookies",45
DATA "Jello",5
...
END
```

OR

```
READ Food_1$,Protien_1,Food_2$,Protien_2,Food_3$,Protien_3
DATA "Chocolate",23,"Cookies",45, "Jello",5
...
END
```

3.

```
INPUT PROMPT "Who is driving car number 1?":Driver1$
READ Car1$
INPUT PROMPT "Who is driving car number 2?":Driver2$
READ Car2$
INPUT PROMPT "Who is driving car number 3?":Driver3$
READ Car3$
DATA "Porsche","Ferrari","March"
END
```

Tracing

1.

```
Give me a color:Red
Give me another color:Green
Give me some third color:Blue
Blue was entered after Green which came after Red
```

2.

```
What is the cost?17
23 55
77
```

3.

```
Country        Population      Area
USA            260            1014

Sweden         23             53

Japan          225            72
```

Chapter 3

Syntax Errors

1. LET statement is wrong. A variable must be on the lefthand side. Here there is an equation there!

2. LET statement is wrong due to mismatched parentheses. There are two left parentheses and one right parenthesis. Thus the equation is wrong.

3. The assignment statements are missing the keyword LET

Tracing

1.

```
30      20      50
30      20      50
100
```

2.

```
What is the power?3
38
```

3.

```
40      80      40
```

Chapter 4

Syntax Errors

1. This IF statement is ill-formed. The keyword THEN should be at the end of the first line. The keyword ELSE should be on a line by itself.

2. The IF statement does not have a valid condition after the keyword IF. A condition must consist of two "equations" separated by a relation operator. Here the condition consists of one variable and nothing else.

3. A single-line IF statement can not have an END IF at the end of it. Use END IF only for multi-line IF statements.

4. This is just garbage. You can't tack an IF statement on the end of a LET statement. IF statements and LET statements are totally separate statements in BASIC. You could rewrite this statement by making the LET statement be the clause after a THEN in an IF statement.

5. The third IF statement (the second mulit-line IF) is missing a END IF to mark its ending. This END IF should appear right before the fourth IF statement on a line by itself.

6. And IF statement can't have two ELSE clauses. The ELSE clause must be the very last clause. You might be able to fix this statement by thinking up an appropriate condition and turning the first ELSE here into an ELSEIF clause.

7. The line ELSEIF Aisle = 5 OR 6 is wrong. First of all, there should be a THEN at the end of that line. But even worse, you can't have a condition like "Aisle = 5 OR 6". This is not a legal way to use OR. An OR connects two conditions. Here "Aisle = 5" is a legal condition but on the other side of the OR all we find is "6". This by itself is not a legal condition. You can fix this line by making it be

   ELSEIF Aisle = 5 OR Aisle = 6 THEN

Tracing

1.

```
?7
More than a dozen.
Quality is Good
```

2.

   (a)

```
A long night
Not too long
```

   (b)

```
Quick Reading
Not too long
```

   (c)

```
A long night
Give me a week
```

   (d)

```
Not too long
```

3.

   (a)

```
A long night
```

   (b)

```
Quick Reading
```

   (c)

```
A long night
```

   (d)

```
Not too long
```

Chapter 5

Syntax Errors

1. CASEs which us a relational operation must have the keyword IS in them.

2. The SELECT CASE line is wrong. This line must end in an "equation". Here it is ending in some type of convoluted IF statement. Don't confuse If and SELECT like this.

3. Can't use an OR inside of a CASE.

4. There is no END SELECT for the first SELECT statement. (The one inside of the THEN clause.)

5. Technically there is no syntax error here. But when you try to run this program it will bomb immediately. There is no CASE to handle the situation when Insults is equal to 15. Since, there is no CASE ELSE to capture situations which are not caught by the other CASEs, the program will bomb. Put in a CASE ELSE on all your SELECT statements just to keep this from happening.

Tracing

1.

   7

2.

   (a)

   200

   (b)

   100

   (c)

   400

3.

   The Answer is 0

4.

   This program

5.

   There are too many satellites.
   But at least there are more American than Russian satellites.

Chapter 6

Syntax Errors

1. Should be NEXT I. The variable on the next should match up with the variable on the FOR.

2. Badly formed statement. You can't just attach a FOR statement anywhere in the program. If you want a FOR/NEXT loop, the FOR line has to be on a line by itself.

3. The FOR statement doesn't have a matching NEXT. Here, NEXT Counter should appear on a line right before the ELSE.

4. The FOR line is badly form. The syntax requires that a variable appear right after the keyword FOR and then an equal sign. Here we can see the variable is an I (see the NEXT statement) so this statement should be FOR I = 20 TO 100

5. The loops overlap. You have to end the FOR Smaller loop with a NEXT Smaller before you end the FOR Bigger loop. The last unended loop must be completed first. So switch the NEXT statements around here.

6. Can't use the keyword IS inside of a FOR statement. IS can only be used on CASE lines. Here the IS should be replaced by an equal sign (=).

Tracing

1.

```
The answer is 50
The answer is 15
The answer is 40
The answer is 16
The answer is 37
```

2.

    120

3.

    20

4.

    60

5.

    6000

Chapter 7

Syntax Errors

1. The DO line must have a WHILE or UNTIL on it besides having the condition.

2. The UNTIL line should begin with the keyword LOOP.

3. DO loops don't end with the keyword NEXT. They must end with LOOP instead.

4. It shouldn't be DO IF. Instead it is DO WHILE.

5. The loops are overlapping. The DO should end with a LOOP before the FOR loop ends with its NEXT. (Always end the "inner" or last unended loop, first.)

Tracing

1.

```
Using 3 we are now up to 7
Using 1 we are now up to 15
Using 6 we are now up to 36
The answer is 16
```

2.

    20

3.

    7

Chapter 8

Syntax Errors

1. You can't just put a built-in function on a line by itself. You must place it wherever an equation can go — for instance, in a LET statement. So the line SQR(ABS ...) is wrong.

2. The built-in function MAX only has two arguments. You can't give it four arguments as we have attempted here.

3. INT(RND) is always zero. (Try it out and see why!) Thus, we are always dividing by zero in this program. A computer bombs when an attempt is made to divide by zero.

4. The arguments to INT, ROUND and MAX must be integers. Here the variable Num$ is a string. So there is a type mismatch.

Tracing

1.

```
21
41
62
82
103
```

2.

```
You rolled a 5
You rolled a 8
You rolled a 7
```

3.

```
3     .1      12
```

Chapter 9

Syntax Errors

1. Missing DIM statement. Here Summ is an array but we never set up room for it by using a DIM.

2. Array out of bounds. There are six pieces of DATA (including the sentinel) but only room for five in the array.

3. Array will go out of bounds. N can get as large as 1000. It is used as an index into the array. But the array is only 200 big.

4. Type mismatch between variable in READ and its DATA. Food is a numeric array (there is no dollar sign) but the DATA consists of strings.

5. Once a variable is set up to be an array, you always must specify a subscript whenever you use that variable. Here, when Value1 and Value2 are given to the built-in function MAX, no subscript is specified to tell us which item in those arrays we want to use. There should be a set of parentheses and a number specifying which item after each of these variables.

Tracing

1.

```
How much stuff did you get?5
How much is left?19
How much stuff did you get?23
How much is left?14
How much stuff did you get?64
How much is left?12
How much stuff did you get?46
How much is left?33
How much stuff did you get?21
How much is left?52
The Answer is 110
```

2.

```
Estimate:
5000 people thought there were too many commercials.
4000 people thought it was a bad show.
There were  3 other complaints.
```

3.

```
0
1
0
1
10
1
0
11
0
1
```

Chapter 10

Tracing

1.

```
16
4
1
2
2
```

Afterword

YOU MIGHT WANT TO READ THIS!!!!!! IT JUST MIGHT BE THE ONLY IMPORTANT PART OF THE WHOLE BOOK.

The following was written with my students at Rutgers in mind. Yet, it is highly possible that other readers of this book may find this inspirational.

Ok people. That is the end of the course 110:Introduction to Computers and Applications for the Fall 94 and Spring 95 semesters. We have had a few laughs but for many of you, the course involved a certain amount of frustration sitting in front of a Macintosh Plus microcomputer's tiny high-resolution screen fiddling with a mouse that was tethered nearby. I just want to say a few words before I let you escape from my literary grasp once and for all. Clearly, the following is solely my own opinion and certainly not the policy or even a viewpoint of the administration of Rutgers University. Furthermore, it may not be applicable to all who read this. Nevertheless.....

What do I expect that you should have gotten out of this course? Well, first of all, many of the students in this course had already been exposed to computers prior to this semester. Then there were others who never touched a computer before. Clearly, some people were presented with many more new ideas than other people to whom the course was merely a review of their knowledge. (Yes, this is not "fair", but that is college for you.....) So what you got out of this course is a very personal thing. Ok now, what do I expect that you should have gotten out of this course? Look, the world of computers is strange. There are many many different types of computers, application software packages and languages. Even things that seem to have the same name can be very different. Take all the different BASICs that exist in the computer world. So, I don't really care if you remember the TRUE BASIC language or how to use Microsoft WORKS, MacPaint, or the Chooser desk accessory. Heck, some of you will only remember how to insert a disk and steer a mouse. I am realistic about this. It is just a simple fact that if you don't continue to use what you have learned in this course, a good deal of it will fade from your mind. So, if I am right, then why should so many people at Rutgers be taking this course if it is going to fade from their memories. I can think of a few things you should leave this course with...

First of all, know that you have seen one particular computer used for many different tasks. You should realize that a computer, if used appropriately, can be an extremely useful tool. This doesn't mean that you should run to a computer whenever you have a certain "job" to do. Often a calculator or a typewriter will serve you well. However, now that you have seen what a computer can do there may be times later on in college or your professional career after school when you will come across a problem and realize a computer would be a really good tool to aid you to solve that problem. This can mean anything from using a word processor (which I strongly recommend) to using spreadsheets, computer mail, database management software or writing a program on your own. Now that you have seen some of the uses that a computer is good for, you should realize that for certain tasks a lot of time and energy can be saved by utilizing a computer. With this in mind, the second thing you should get out of this course is some confidence about your ability to use a computer. Sure, you may not all feel like experts at this point. On the other hand, you should realize that many of the chores that you perform on a computer are not very involved. Sure they may be tedious and require a lot of patience, but a person of average intelligence can quickly acquire the skill to use a computer in order to complete various tasks. You should feel that if a situation arose where you really need to use a particular computer, you could eventually learn most of what is necessary to use its application software or even maybe write a small program (though this is usually not necessary). Finally, though you might not realize it, you should have acquired a general sense as to what programming is about, what a spreadsheet is, what an electronic mail system can do, how to do graphics and so on. Some day you may end up on a computer system that has commands or software totally different than what you have used. Nevertheless, you will find that it will be relatively easy to pick up these new commands and utilize these new programs. On the surface another computer system may seem totally different, but you will find that most things that another computer can do will be equivalent to what you learned on the Mac. You have the general ideas inside of you; you will find the details a lot easier to pick up the next time around. In short, what you should get out of this course is a general feeling of how to use a computer and insight into what tasks a computer is good for. You should no longer be afraid or timid about using a computer (in case you once were...) and should be somewhat confident that if the need arose, you too can use a computer.

Ok, ok so that was a really long paragraph on what you should have gotten out of this course...... Or maybe it was about the things that you *might consider* that you have gotten out of the course. And what if you didn't get anything at all out of this course?

Well I have a complex opinion of this. In fact, my opinion has much more to do with what I really think anyone gets out of college. I have always wondered if college is really worth it. Sure potential employers love the fact that you are a college grad and thus simply by graduating you have improved your life somewhat. But how much does the average student learn in school and how much does the average student forget? And how often does the average student get by without even trying to learn the material.... In a way, society has just accepted that college is a good thing, without really checking up on it and really seeing what people get out of it. Oh sure, there are some people, maybe even a number of people, who truly get a lot out of it. And most of us pick up some general ideas that stick with us the rest of our lives. There is no doubt that almost everyone is intellectually changed from what they learn in college. But what about all the details? How many of us feel like we are missing out because we forget all the details from a course we had last semester? And such is college....

Here is what I suggest. Don't put too much emphasis on the grades. Don't be too discouraged if your grades aren't as good as you would like. Your life will progress no matter what your grades are. Don't worry about that too much. Rather, concentrate more on the effort you make. Do the best you can. Feel good about the fact that you are really making an effort. If a particular professor doesn't recognize your effort or penalizes you because you don't think in the same way that the professor tried to teach the subject (you can't parrot what was preached to you), then don't feel too bad. Learn to think on your own. Be open to ideas but be yourself. Always make an effort and do the best you can and you'll end up feeling good about yourself no matter what "grade" you get. I was always a person who never had to work for my grades. I didn't take notes, missed a lot of my classes, if I did my HW it was at the last minute, never went to the library and so on. Fortunately, I was still able to get good grades. A lot of my friends however, couldn't get the good grades. They were seemingly as intelligent as me (I never felt "better" than them) and they worked much harder than me. I always felt bad that they couldn't get the grades; but I always respected them. They were making a much greater effort than I was. I really don't think much of a person who gets good grades because everything comes easy to him or at the other end of the spectrum a person who cheats for the grades. That is garbage. To me, I will always feel much better about a person who tries his or her hardest; even if they end up with a C. Perseverance, patience, some honor, drive, ambition ....that is how a person should be. Get real ok? (Sorry if this sounds like I am preaching here...) Anyway, if you did good in this course — good for you. If you didn't do as good gradewise but you tried, then don't feel too bad. I guess in a way I am proud of you people. No matter what your grade however, don't let it effect you as to possibly using a computer again later in life.... You got a grade now for using the computer; later you no longer get a grade.......it is just another tool to get you through life. You can use it as well as the next person...

And as for college and the rest of your classes? Well try your best. Really concentrate on those subjects that interest you. There is a lot to learn in life and it can be a lot of fun to learn. And lastly, remember there is more to college than just grades. Probably the thing you will remember most about college is the social life you had here. The things you learn from this socializing will mold you at least as much as anything you will learn in class. Maybe no one emphasizes it, but dealing with other people is probably one of the most important skills you can acquire in life. Friends, family, lovers......learn to get along with them. This is more important than learning some particular subject or having a career. Learn to be happy. Learn to feel good about yourself. Learn to care about others...... Learn to deal with life's upsets.....Learn. Not just in class. Have fun everyone. Be happy. I have enjoyed teaching you. Oh, by the way, I recommend that you give a big, passionate, juicy kiss to your boyfriend or girlfriend as soon as possible — and for that matter, as often as possible.

Have fun ......

-Jt